D0016121

PEOPLE, POWER, AND PROFITS

ALSO BY JOSEPH E. STIGLITZ

The Euro: How a Common Currency Threatens the Future of Europe

Rewriting the Rules of the American Economy:
An Agenda for Growth and Shared Prosperity

The Great Divide: Unequal Societies and What We Can Do about Them

Creating a Learning Society: A New Approach to Growth,
Development, and Social Progress
(with Bruce C. Greenwald)

The Price of Inequality: How Today's Divided Society Endangers Our Future

Freefall: America, Free Markets, and the Sinking of the World Economy

The Three Trillion Dollar War: The True Cost of the Iraq Conflict
(with Linda J. Bilmes)

Making Globalization Work

Fair Trade for All: How Trade Can Promote Development
(with Andrew Charlton)

The Roaring Nineties: A New History of the World's Most Prosperous Decade

Globalization and Its Discontents

JOSEPH E. STIGLITZ

PEOPLE, POWER, AND PROFITS

PROGRESSIVE CAPITALISM
FOR AN AGE OF DISCONTENT

W. W. NORTON & COMPANY
Independent Publishers Since 1923
New York | London

Copyright © 2019 by Joseph E. Stiglitz

All rights reserved
Printed in the United States of America
First Edition

For information about permission to reproduce selections from this book, write to
Permissions, W. W. Norton & Company, Inc., 500 Fifth Avenue, New York, NY 10110

For information about special discounts for bulk purchases, please contact
W. W. Norton Special Sales at specialsales@wwnorton.com or 800-233-4830

Manufacturing by LSC Communications Harrisonburg
Book design by Chris Welch
Production manager: Lauren Abbate

ISBN: 978-1-324-00421-9

W. W. Norton & Company, Inc., 500 Fifth Avenue, New York, N.Y. 10110
www.wwnorton.com

W. W. Norton & Company Ltd., 15 Carlisle Street, London W1D 3BS

1 2 3 4 5 6 7 8 9 0

To my grandchildren.

And to my dear friends Tony Atkinson
and Jim Mirrlees, who left this world all too soon.

CONTENTS

PREFACE

I grew up in the golden age of capitalism, in Gary, Indiana, on the southern shore of Lake Michigan. It was only afterward that I found out that was the golden age. At the time, it didn't seem so golden—I saw massive racial discrimination and segregation, great inequality, labor strife, and episodic recessions. One couldn't help but see the effects, both on my schoolmates and on the façade of the city.

The city traced the history of industrialization and deindustrialization in America, having been founded in 1906 as the site of the largest integrated steel mill in the world, and named after the founding chairman of US Steel, Elbert H. Gary. It was a company town through and through. When I went back for my fifty-fifth high school reunion in 2015, before Trump had become the fixture in the landscape that he is today, the tensions were palpable, and for good reason. The city had followed the country's trajectory toward deindustrialization. The population was only half of what it was when I was growing up. The city was burned out. It had become a filming location for Hollywood movies set in war zones, or after the apocalypse. Some of my classmates became teachers, a few, doctors and lawyers, and many, secretaries. But the most poignant stories at the reunion were from classmates who described how, when they graduated, they had hoped to get a job in the mills but the country was in another episodic downturn and instead they went into the military, setting their life trajectory into a career in policing. Reading the roster of those of my classmates who had passed away, and seeing the physical condition of many of those who remained, was a reminder of the inequalities in life expectancy and health in the country. An argument broke out between two classmates, a former policeman virulently criticizing the government, and a former schoolteacher pointing out that the Social Security and disability payments the former policeman depended on came from that same government.

When I left Gary in 1960 to study at Amherst College in Massachusetts, who could have predicted the course history would take and what it would do to my city and my classmates? The city had shaped me: the gnawing memories of inequality and suffering induced me to switch from my passion for theoretical physics to economics. I wanted to understand why our economic system failed for so many, and what could be done about it. But even as I studied the subject—coming to better understand why markets often don't work well—the problems were growing worse. Inequality was increasing, beyond anything that had been imaginable in my youth. Years later, in 1993, as I entered the administration of President Bill Clinton at first as a member, and then chair, of the Council of Economic Advisers (CEA), these issues were just beginning to come into focus; sometime in the mid-1970s or early 1980, inequality took a nasty turn upward, so that by 1993, it was far greater than it had been any time in my life.

My study of economics had taught me that the ideology of many conservatives was wrong; their almost religious belief in the power of markets—so great that we could largely simply rely on unfettered markets for running the economy—had no basis in theory or evidence. The challenge was not just to persuade others of this, but to devise programs and policies that would reverse the dangerous increases in inequality and the potential for instability from the financial liberalization begun under Ronald Reagan in the 1980s. Troublingly, faith in the power of markets had spread by the 1990s to the point where financial liberalization was being pushed by some of my own colleagues in the administration, and eventually by Clinton himself.[1]

My concern with increasing inequality grew while I served on Clinton's CEA, but since 2000 the problem has reached ever more alarming heights as inequality grew, and grew, and grew. Not since before the Great Depression have the country's richest citizens captured such a large proportion of the nation's income.[2]

Twenty-five years after entering the Clinton administration I find myself reflecting: How did we get here, where are we going, and what can we do to change course? I approach these questions as an economist, and not surprisingly, I see at least part of the answer lying in our economic failures—the failure to handle well the transition from a manufacturing economy to a service-sector economy, to tame the financial sector, to properly manage globalization and its consequences, and most importantly, to respond to the growing inequality, as we seemed to be evolving into an economy and democracy of the 1 percent, for the 1 percent and by the 1 percent.[3] Both experience and studies have made it clear to me that economics and politics cannot be separated, and especially not in America's money-driven politics. So while most of this book focuses on the economics of our current situation, I would be remiss if I did not say something about our politics.

Many elements of this diagnosis are by now familiar, including excessive financialization, mismanaged globalization, and increasing market power. I show how they are interrelated, how, together, they explain both why growth has been so anemic and why the fruits of what little growth we've had have been so unequally shared.

This book, though, is not just about diagnosis; it is also about prescription: what we can do, the way forward. To answer such questions, I have to explain the true source of the wealth of nations, distinguishing wealth creation from wealth extraction. The latter is any process whereby one individual takes wealth from others through one form of exploitation or another. The true source of "the wealth of a nation" lies in the former, in the creativity and productivity of the nation's people and their productive interactions with each other. It rests on the advances in science, which teach us how we can discover the hidden truths of nature and use them to advance technology. Further, it rests on advances in understanding of social organization, discovered through reasoned discourse, leading to institutions such as those broadly referred to as the "rule of law, systems of checks and balance, and due process." I present the outlines of a progressive agenda that represents the antithesis to the agenda of Trump and his supporters. It is, in a sense, a twenty-first-century blend of Teddy Roosevelt and FDR. The central argument is that following these reforms will lead to a faster-growing economy, with shared prosperity, in which the kind of life to which most Americans aspire is not a pipe dream but an attainable reality. In short, if we truly understand the sources of the wealth of the nation, we can achieve a more dynamic economy with greater shared prosperity. This will require government to take a different, probably larger, role than it does today: we cannot shy away from the need for collective action in our complex twenty-first-century world. I show too that there is a set of eminently affordable policies that can make a middle-class life—the life which seemed within our grasp in the middle of the last century but now seems increasingly to be out of reach—once again the norm rather than the exception.

Reaganomics, Trumponomics, and the Attack on Democracy

As we reflect upon our current situation, it is natural to think back some forty years to when the Right again seemed triumphant. Then too, it seemed a global movement: Ronald Reagan in the US, Margaret Thatcher in the UK. Keynesian economics, which emphasized how government could maintain full employment through managing *demand* (through monetary and fiscal policy) was replaced with *supply-side economics*, emphasizing how deregulation and tax cuts would free up the economy and incentivize it, increasing the supply of goods and services and thereby the incomes of individuals.

Deja vu: Voodoo economics

Supply-side economics did not work for Reagan and it won't work for Trump. Republicans tell themselves and the American people that the Trump tax cut will energize the economy, so much so that the tax losses will be less than the skeptics claim. That's the supply-side argument, and we ought to know by now that it does not work. Reagan's tax cut in 1981 opened up an era of enormous fiscal deficits, slower growth, and greater inequality. Trump, in his 2017 tax bill, is giving us an even bigger dose of policies grounded not in science but in self-serving superstition than that provided by Reagan. President George H. W. Bush himself called Reagan's supply-side economics *voodoo economics*. Trump's is voodoo economics on steroids.

SOME OF TRUMP'S supporters admit that his policies are far from perfect, but they defend him by saying: at least he is paying attention to those who have long been ignored, at least he has given them the dignity and respect of being heard. I would put it differently: he has been shrewd enough to detect the disgruntlement, to fan the flames of discontent and exploit it ruthlessly. That he is willing to make the people of Middle America worse off, taking away health care from thirteen million Americans, this, in a country already reeling from declining life expectancies, shows that he holds them not in respect but in contempt; and so too for the giving of tax breaks to the rich while actually increasing taxes on the majority of those in the middle.[4]

For those who lived through Ronald Reagan, there are striking similarities. Like Trump, Reagan exploited fear and bigotry: his
was the welfare queen who robbed hard-earning Americans of their
money. The "dog-whistle," of course, was that they were African
American. He too showed no empathy for the poor. Reclassifying
mustard and ketchup as the two vegetables required for nutritious
school lunches would be funny if it weren't so sad. He too was a
hypocrite, combining free-market rhetoric with strong protectionist
policies. His hypocrisy entailed euphemisms like "voluntary export
restraints": Japan was given the choice of either curtailing its exports
or having its exports curtailed for it. It's no accident that Trump's
Trade Representative, Robert Lighthizer, got his training as Deputy
US Trade Representative under Reagan, forty years earlier.

There are other points of similarity between Reagan and Trump:
one is a naked willingness to serve corporate interests, in some cases,
the same interests. Reagan engineered a giveaway of natural resources,
a fire sale allowing the big oil companies to take out the country's
abundance of oil at a fraction of its value. Trump came to power by
promising to "drain the swamp" and thus give voice to those who
believed that Washington's power brokers had long ignored them. But
never has the swamp been muddier than since he took office.

AND YET, for all these similarities, there are some deep differences that
have led to a rift with some of the elders of the Republican Party.
Reagan had, of course, surrounded himself with some party hacks,
as to be expected; but he also had a number of distinguished public
servants, like George Shultz, in key positions of power (Shultz served
for Reagan, at different times, as secretary of state and secretary of
treasury.)[5] These were people for whom reason and truth mattered,
who saw climate change, for instance, as an existential threat, and who

believed in America's position as a global leader. They, like members of all administrations before and after, would be embarrassed in being caught in an outright lie. While they might try to shade the truth, truth meant something. Not so for the current inhabitant of the White House and those who surround him.

REAGAN KEPT UP at least the façade of reason and logic. There was a theory behind his tax cuts, the supply-side economics to which we referred earlier. Forty years later, that theory had been disproved over and over again. Trump and the twenty-first-century Republicans didn't need a theory: they did it because they could.

It is this disdain for truth, for science, for knowledge, and for democracy that sets the Trump administration and similar leaders elsewhere apart from Reagan and other conservative movements of the past. Indeed, as I explain, Trump is in many ways more a revolutionary than a conservative. We may understand the forces that make his distorted ideas resonate with so many Americans, but that doesn't make them any more attractive, or any less dangerous.

THE 2017 TRUMP TAX "REFORM" illustrates how far the country has shifted from previous traditions and norms. Tax reform typically entails simplifying, eliminating loopholes, making sure that no one gets away without paying their fair share, and ensuring that taxes are adequate to pay the country's bills. Even Reagan, in his 1986 tax reform, made an appeal to tax simplification. The 2017 tax bill, by contrast, added a whole new set of complexities, and left most of the gaping loopholes intact, including one by which those working in private equity funds manage to pay a maximum 20 percent tax rate rather than the rate, almost twice as high, paid by other working Americans.[6]

It repealed the minimum tax designed to ensure that individuals and corporations not make *excessive* use of loopholes, and pay at least a minimum percentage of their income in taxes.

This time, there was no pretense that the deficit would fall; the only question was by how much it would increase. By late 2018, estimates were that the government would have to borrow a record amount of more than $1 trillion in the next year.[7] Even as a percentage of GDP, it was a record for the country at a time when it was neither in war nor in recession. With the economy approaching full employment, the deficits were clearly counterproductive, as the Federal Reserve would have to increase interest rates, discouraging investment and growth; and yet only one Republican (Senator Rand Paul of Kentucky) made more than a peep in objecting. Outside the American political system, however, the criticism came from all corners. Even the International Monetary Fund, always loathe to criticize the US, a country whose voice has long been dominant in that body, weighed in on the country's fiscal irresponsibility.[8] Political observers were stunned at the magnitude of the hypocrisy—when the economy really needed a stimulus, a fiscal boost, in the aftermath of the 2008 crisis, Republicans had said that the country couldn't afford it, that it would lead to intolerable deficits.

The Trump tax bill was born out of the deepest political cynicism. Even the pittances this Republican-devised plan threw to ordinary citizens, small reductions in taxes for the next few years, were temporary. The party strategy seemed predicated on two hypotheses, which, if true, bode poorly for the country: that ordinary citizens are so shortsighted that they will focus on the small reductions in their taxes now, ignoring their temporary nature, and the fact that for a majority in the middle taxes would increase; and that what really matters in American democracy is money. Keep the rich happy and they will shower the Republican Party with contributions, and the contributions will buy the votes necessary to sustain the policies. It showed how far America had descended from the idealism upon which it was founded.

The blatant attempts at voter suppression and unbridled gerrymandering, the undercutting of democracy, also set the current administration apart. It's not that these things weren't done in the past—unfortunately, they are almost part of America's tradition—it's that they haven't been done with such ruthlessness, with such precision, and so baldly.

Perhaps most importantly, leaders of the past, of both parties, have tried to unite the country. After all, they swore to uphold the Constitution, which begins with "We the People . . ." Underlying this was a belief in the principle of the Common Good. Trump has, by contrast, set about exploiting divisions and making them larger.

The civility required to make a civilization work has been thrown aside, along with any pretense of decency either in language or action.

OF COURSE, the country and the world find themselves in a far different place than they were four decades ago. Then, we were just beginning the process of deindustrialization, and had Reagan and his successors undertaken the right policies, perhaps the devastation we see in America's industrial hinterland wouldn't be what we see today. We were also in the early days of the Big Divide, the huge divisions between the country's 1 percent and the rest. We had been taught that, once a country reaches a certain stage of development, inequality shrinks—and America had exemplified that theory.[9] In the years after World War II, every part of our society had prospered, but the incomes of those at the bottom grew faster than those at the top. We had created the greatest middle-class society the world had ever seen. By the election of 2016, by contrast, inequality had reached levels not seen since the Gilded Age at the end of the nineteenth century.

A LOOK AT where the country is today and where it was four decades ago makes it clear that as dysfunctional and ineffective as Reagan's policies may have been in his day, Trumponomics is even more poorly suited for today's world. We couldn't then have gone back to the seemingly idyllic days of the Eisenhower administration; even then, we were moving from an industrial economy to a service-sector economy. Today, forty years on, such aspirations seem totally untethered to any sense of reality.

America's changing demographics, though, have put those looking to this "glorious" past—a past from whose prosperity large fractions, including women and people of color, were excluded—in a democratic dilemma. It's not only that a majority of Americans will soon be people of color, or that a twenty-first-century world and economy can't be reconciled with a male-dominated society. It's also that our urban centers, whether in the North or the South, in which a majority of Americans live, have learned the value of diversity. Those living in these places of growth and dynamism have learned too of the value of cooperation and seen the role that government can, and must, play if there is to be shared prosperity. They've shredded the shibboleths of the past, sometimes almost overnight. But if this is so, the only way in a democratic society for the minority—whether it's large corporations trying to exploit consumers, banks trying to exploit borrowers, or those mired in the past trying to recreate a bygone world—to maintain their economic and political dominance is by suppressing democracy, in one way or another.

It doesn't have to be this way—it doesn't have to be that America is a rich country with so, so many poor people, with so many people struggling to get by. While there are forces—among them, changes in technology and globalization—that are increasing inequality, the markedly different patterns across countries demonstrate that policies matter. Inequality is a choice. It is not inevitable. But unless we change our current course, inequality is likely to become greater and our growth is likely to remain mired at its current low levels—itself something of a puzzle, given that we are supposed to be the most innovative economy in the most innovative era in the history of the world.

Trump doesn't have a plan to help the country; he has a plan to continue the robbery of the majority by those at the top. This book shows that the Trump agenda and that of the Republican Party is likely to worsen all the problems confronting our society—increasing the economic, political, and social divide, shortening further life expectancies, worsening the country's finances, and leading the country to a new era of ever slower growth.

Trump can't be blamed for many of our country's problems, but he has helped crystallize them: the divides were there for any demagogue to exploit. If Trump hadn't entered the scene, in a few years' time, some other demagogue would have. As we look around the world, there is an ample supply—Le Pen in France, Morawiecki in Poland, Orbán in Hungary, Erdogan in Turkey, Duterte in the Philippines, and Bolsonaro in Brazil. While these demagogues are all different, they share a disdain for democracy (Orbán talked proudly of the virtues of *illiberal* democracies), with its rule of law, free media, and independent judiciary. They all believe in "strongmen"—in themselves—a cult of the personality that has gone out of fashion in most of the rest of the world. And they all seek to blame their problems on outsiders; they are all nativist nationalists championing the innate virtues of their people. This generation of autocrats and would-be autocrats seems to widely share a crudeness, in some cases open bigotry and misogyny.

Most of the problems I've discussed plague other advanced countries; but as we shall see, America has led the way, with more inequality, worse health, and a greater divide than elsewhere. Trump serves as an important reminder to others of what can happen if these sores are left to fester for too long.

BUT, AS THE OLD saw goes, you can't beat something with nothing. So too in economics: one can only beat a bad plan by showing that there is an alternative. Even if we hadn't fallen into the current morass, there was a need for an alternative vision to the one the country, and much of the world, had embraced for the past three decades. This view of society put the economy at the center; and it viewed the economy through the lens of "free" markets. It pretended to be based on advances in our understanding of markets, but the truth was just the opposite: advances in economics over the past seventy years had identified the limits of free markets. Of course, anyone with open eyes could have seen this for themselves: episodic unemployment, sometimes massive, as in the Great Depression and pollution so bad in some places that air was unbreathable were just the two most obvious "proofs" that markets on their own don't necessarily work well.

My objective here is first and foremost to advance our understanding about the real sources of the wealth of the nation, and of how as we strengthen the economy we can be sure that its fruits will be equitably shared.

I present here an alternative agenda to those put forward by Reagan on the one hand and Trump on the other, an agenda based on the insights of modern economics, one which I believe will lead us to shared prosperity. In doing so, I will clarify why neoliberalism, the ideas based on unfettered markets, failed; and why Trumponomics, the peculiar combination of low taxes for the rich and financial and environmental deregulation with nativism and protectionism—a highly regulated globalization regime—will also fail.

Before embarking on the journey, it might be useful to summarize the modern understanding of economics upon which much of this agenda depends.[10]

First, markets on their own will fail to achieve shared and sustainable prosperity. Markets play an invaluable role in any well-functioning economy and yet they often fail to produce fair and efficient outcomes, producing too much of some things (pollution) and too little of others (basic research). And as the 2008 financial crisis showed, markets on their own are not stable. More than 80 years ago, John Maynard Keynes explained why market economies often have persistent unemployment and taught us how government could maintain the economy at or near full employment.

If there are large discrepancies between the social returns of an activity—the benefit to society—and the private returns to the same activity—the benefit to an individual or company—markets alone will not do the job. Climate change represents the example *par excellence*: the global social costs of carbon emissions are enormous—excessive emissions of greenhouse gases present an existential threat to the planet—and far exceed the costs borne by any firm, or even any country. Either through regulations or charging a price for carbon emissions, carbon emissions have to be curbed.

Nor do markets work well when information is imperfect and some key markets are absent (for instance, for insuring important risks, like that of unemployment); or when competition is limited. But these market "imperfections" are pervasive, and of course, especially important in certain areas, like finance. And so too, markets won't produce enough of what are called "public goods," like fire protection or national defense—goods whose use is easily shared by the entire population and hard to charge for in any way other than taxes. To achieve a better functioning economy and society, with citizens who feel more prosperous and secure, government needs to spend money, such as in providing better unemployment insurance and financing basic research; and regulate, to keep people from harming others. Capitalist economies have thus always involved a blend of private markets and government—the question is not markets *or* government, but how to combine the two to best advantage. When applied to the subject of this book, there is a need for government action to achieve an efficient and stable economy with rapid growth, and to ensure that the fruits of that growth are shared fairly.

Secondly, we need to recognize that the wealth of a nation rests on two pillars. Nations grow wealthier—achieving higher standards of living—by becoming more productive, and the most important source of increases in productivity is the result of increases in knowledge. Advances in technology rest on scientific foundations provided by government-funded basic research. And nations grow wealthier as a result of good overall organization of society, which allows people to interact, to trade and to invest with security. The design of good societal organization is the product of decades of reasoning and deliberation, empirical observations on what has worked and not. It has led to views about the importance of democracies with the rule of law, due process, checks and balances, and a host of institutions involved in discovering, assessing, and telling the truth.

Third, one must not confuse the wealth of a nation with the wealth of particular individuals in that country. Some people and companies succeed with new products that consumers want. That is the good way to become wealthy. Others succeed by using their market power to exploit consumers or their workers. This is nothing more than a redistribution of income; it does not increase the nation's overall wealth. The technical term in economics is "rent"—rent-seeking is associated with attempting to get a large share of the nation's economic pie, in contrast with wealth creation, which strives to increase the size of the pie. Policymakers should zero in on any market in which there are excessive rents because they are a sign that the economy could perform more efficiently: the exploitation inherent in excessive rents actually weakens the economy. A successful fight against rent-seeking results in redirecting resources into wealth creation.

Fourth, a less divided society, an economy with more equality, performs better. Particularly invidious are inequalities based on race, gender, and ethnicity. This is a marked shift from the view that was previously dominant in economics, which held that there was a trade-off, that one could only have more equality by sacrificing growth and efficiency. The benefits of reducing inequality are especially large when inequality reaches the extremes that it has in America and when it is created in the ways that it is, for instance, through exploitation of market power or discrimination. Thus, the goal of increased income equality does not come with a bill attached.

We also need to abandon the mistaken faith in trickle-down economics, the notion that if the economy grows, everyone will benefit. This notion underpinned the supply-side economics policies of Republican presidents from Ronald Reagan on. The record is clear that the benefits of growth simply do not trickle down. Look at the broad swath of the population in America and elsewhere in the advanced world living in anger and despair after decades of the near stagnation in their incomes produced by supply-side policies, even as GDP has increased. Markets on their own won't necessarily help these people, but there are government programs that can make a difference.

Fifth, government programs to achieve shared prosperity need to focus both on the distribution of market income—what is sometimes called pre-distribution—and redistribution, incomes that individuals enjoy after taxes and transfers. Markets don't exist in a vacuum; they have to be structured, and the way we structure them affects both the distribution of market income and growth and efficiency. Thus, laws that allow abuses of corporate monopoly power or that enable CEOs to take for themselves large fractions of corporate income lead to more inequality and less growth. Achieving a fairer society requires equality of opportunity, but that in turn requires greater equality of incomes and wealth. There will always be some transmission of advantage across generations, so that excessive inequalities of income and wealth in one generation translate into high levels of inequalities in the next. Education is part of the solution, but only part. In the United States there is greater inequality in educational opportunity than in many other countries, and providing better education for all could reduce inequality and increase economic performance. Compounding the effects of inequalities in educational opportunity, today's excessively low inheritance taxes mean that the United States is creating an inherited plutocracy.

Sixth, because the rules of the game and so many other aspects of our economy and society depend on the government, what the government does is vital; politics and economics cannot be separated. But economic inequality inevitably gets translated into political power, and those with political power use it to gain advantage for themselves. If we don't reform the rules of our politics, we make a mockery of our democracy, as we evolve into a world more characterized by one dollar one vote than one person one vote. If we, as a society, are to have an effective system of checks and balances checking the potential abuses of the very wealthy, we have to create an economy with greater equality of wealth and income.

Seventh, the economic system toward which we have veered since the early 1970s—American-style capitalism—is shaping our individual and national identities in unfortunate ways. What is emerging is in conflict with our higher values—the greed, selfishness, moral turpitude, willingness to exploit others, and dishonesty that the Great Recession exposed in the financial sector are evidenced elsewhere, and not just in the United States. Norms, what we view as acceptable behavior or not, have been changing in ways that undermine social cohesion, trust, and even economic performance.

Eighth, while Trump and nativists elsewhere in the world seek to blame others—migrants and bad trade agreements—for our plight, and especially that of those suffering from deindustrialization, the fault lies within ourselves: we could have managed the process of technological change and globalization better, so that as individuals lost jobs, most got new jobs elsewhere. Going forward, we will have to do better, and I'll describe how that can be done. Most importantly, though, isolationism is not an option. We live in a highly interconnected world and thus have to manage our international relations—both economic and political—better than we have in the past.

Ninth, there is a comprehensive economic agenda that would restore growth and shared prosperity. It combines taking down impediments to growth and equality, such as those posed by corporations with excessive market power, and restoring balance, for instance, giving more bargaining power to workers. It entails providing more support for basic research and more encouragement to the private sector to engage in wealth creation rather than rent-seeking.

The economy, of course, is a means to an end, not an end in itself. And the middle-class life that seemed a birthright of Americans in the years after World War II seems to be slipping out of the reach of a large swath of the country. We are a far richer country now than we were then. We can afford to ensure that this life is attainable for the vast majority of our citizens. This book shows how this can be done.

Finally, this is a time for major changes. Incrementalism—minor tweaks to our political and economic system—are inadequate to the tasks at hand. What are needed are dramatic changes of the kind called for by this book. But none of these economic changes will be achievable without a strong democracy to offset the political power of concentrated wealth. Before economic reform there will have to be political reform.

PART I
LOSING THE WAY

A house divided against itself cannot stand.

—MARK 3:25; ABRAHAM LINCOLN

CHAPTER I

Introduction

That things are not going well in the US and in many other advanced countries is a mild understatement. There is widespread discontent in the land.

It wasn't supposed to be this way, according to the dominant thinking in American economics and political science in the last quarter century. After the fall of the Berlin Wall on November 9, 1989, Francis Fukuyama declared *The End of History*, as democracy and capitalism at last had triumphed. A new era of global prosperity, with faster-than-ever growth, was thought to be at hand, and America was supposed to be in the lead.[1]

By 2018, those soaring ideas seem finally to have crashed to Earth. The 2008 financial crisis showed that capitalism wasn't all that it was supposed to be—it seemed neither efficient nor stable. Then came a rash of statistics showing that the main beneficiaries of the growth of the last quarter century were those at the very top. And finally, anti-establishment votes on both sides of the Atlantic—Brexit in the United Kingdom and the election of Donald Trump in the United States—raised questions about the wisdom of democratic electorates.

Our pundits have provided an easy explanation, correct as far as it goes. The elites had ignored the plight of too many Americans as they pushed for globalization and liberalization, including of financial markets, promising that all would benefit from these "reforms." But the promised benefits never materialized for most citizens. Globalization hastened deindustrialization, leaving behind a majority of citizens, especially the less educated, and of these, especially the men. Financial market liberalization led to the 2008 financial crisis, the worst economic downturn since the Great Depression that began in 1929. Yet while tens of millions around the world lost their jobs and millions in America lost their homes, none of the major finance executives who brought the global economy to the brink of ruin were held accountable. None served time; rather, they were rewarded with mega-bonuses. The bankers were rescued, but not those they had preyed upon. Even if economic policies successfully avoided another Great Depression, it is not a surprise that there have been political consequences of this unbalanced rescue.[2]

Hillary Clinton's referring to those in the deindustrialized parts of the country supporting her opponent as the "deplorables" may have been a fatal political error (saying that was itself deplorable): to them, her words reflected the cavalier attitude of the elites. A series of books, including J. D. Vance's *Hillbilly Elegy: A Memoir of a Family and Culture in Crisis*[3] and Arlie Hochschild's *Strangers in Their Own Land: Anger and Mourning on the American Right*[4] documented the feelings of those who had experienced deindustrialization and the many others who shared their discontent, showing how distant they were from the country's elites.[5]

One of Bill Clinton's 1992 campaign slogans was, "It's the economy, stupid." That's an oversimplification, and these studies suggest why: people want respect, they want to feel that they are being listened to.[6] Indeed, after more than a third of a century of lectures by Republicans that government can't solve any problems, people don't expect government to solve theirs. But they do want their government to "stand up" for them—whatever that means. And when it does stand up for them, they don't want the government to castigate them as "those who have been left behind." That's demeaning. They've made hard choices in an unfair world. They want some of the inequities to be addressed. However, in the 2008 crisis, one created by elite-driven policies of financial market liberalization, government seemed to stand up just for the elites. That, at least, was a narrative that came to be believed, and as I will make clear, there is more than a grain of truth in it.[7]

While President Clinton's slogan may have oversimplified things by suggesting that economics was *everything*, it may not have oversimplified by much. Our economy hasn't been working for large parts of the country. Meanwhile, it has been enormously rewarding for those at the very top. Indeed, it is this deepening divide that is at the root of the country's current predicament, and that of many other advanced countries.

OF COURSE, it is not just economics that has been failing but also our politics. Our economic divide has led to a political divide, and the political divide has reinforced the economic divide. Those with money and power have used their power in politics to write the rules of the economic and political game in ways that reinforce their advantage.

The United States has a very small elite, controlling an increasing share of the economy, and a large and increasing bottom, with almost no resources[8]—forty percent of Americans can't cover a four-hundred-dollar calamity, whether it's a child getting sick or a car breaking down.[9] The three richest Americans, Jeff Bezos (Amazon), Bill Gates (Microsoft) and Warren Buffet (Berkshire Hathaway), are worth more than the bottom half of the US population combined, testimony to how much wealth there is at the top and how little there is at the bottom.[10]

Buffett, the legendary billionaire investor, got it right when he said, "There is a class warfare, all right, but it's my class, the rich class, that's making war, and we're winning."[11] He said it not belligerently; he said it because he thought it was an accurate description of the state of America. And he made clear he thought it was wrong, even un-American.

Our country began with a representative democracy, where the Founding Fathers worried about the possibility of the majority oppressing the minority. Thus, they put safeguards in the Constitution, including limits on what the government could do.[12] Over the more than two hundred subsequent years, however, things have evolved. Today the US has a political minority that, if not oppressing the majority, is at least dominating it, thwarting the majority from doing what would be in the interests of the country as a whole. A vast majority of the electorate would like to see better gun control, a higher minimum wage, more stringent financial regulation and better access to health care and to a college education, without burdensome debt. A majority of Americans voted for Al Gore over George Bush, for Hillary Clinton over Donald Trump. A majority of Americans has repeatedly voted for Democrats for the House of Representatives, yet partially because of gerrymandering, the Republicans have nonetheless typically retained control—in 2018, at last, with enough of a lopsided vote, the Democrats regained control. An overwhelming majority of Americans voted for Democratic senators,[13] and yet, because states with few people like Wyoming have the same two senators that our most populous states, New York and California, have, the Republicans have maintained control over the Senate, so important because of the role it plays in approval of Supreme Court justices. Regrettably, the Court has ceased being a fair arbiter and interpreter of the Constitution, and become just another battlefield in which politics plays out. Our Constitutional safeguards haven't been working for the majority, as a minority has come to dominate.

The consequences of this misshapen economy and polity go well beyond economics: They are affecting not just our politics, but the nature of our society and identity. An unbalanced, selfish, myopic economy and polity leads to unbalanced, selfish, and shortsighted individuals, reinforcing the weaknesses in our economic and political system.[14] The 2008 financial crisis and its aftermath exposed many of our bankers as suffering from what could only be called moral turpitude, as they displayed high levels of dishonesty and a willingness to take advantage of the vulnerable. These lapses are all the more stunning in a country whose political discourse for decades now has been so obsessed with "values."

TO UNDERSTAND HOW we can restore shared growth, we need to begin by understanding the true sources of our nation's—or any nation's—wealth. The true sources of wealth are the productivity, creativity, and vitality of our people; the advances of science and technology that have been so marked over the past two and a half centuries; and the advances in economic, political, and social organization that have occurred over the same period, including the rule of law, competitive, well-regulated markets, and democratic institutions with checks, balances, and a broad range of "truth-telling" institutions. These advances have provided the basis of the enormous increases in standards of living that have occurred over the past two centuries.

The next chapter describes, however, two disturbing changes that have emerged over the past four decades, which we have already noted: growth has slowed, and incomes of large parts of the population have stagnated or even declined. A large divide has opened up between the very top and the rest.

Describing the trajectory that our economy and society have taken is not enough. We have to understand better the power of the ideas and interests that have taken us so far off course for the past four decades, why they had such a hold over so many, and why they are so fundamentally wrong. Leaving the economic and political agenda to be set by the corporate interests has led to more concentration of economic and political power, and it will continue to do so. Understanding why our economic and political systems have failed us is the prologue to showing that another world is possible.

This is the hopeful note: there are easy reforms—easy economically, though not politically—that could lead to greater shared prosperity. As we'll see, we can create an economy more consonant with what I believe are widely shared basic values—not the greed and improbity so evidenced by our bankers, but the higher values so often expressed by our political, economic, and religious leaders. Such an economy will shape us—make us more like the individuals and society to which we aspire. And in doing so, it will enable us to create a more humane economy, one capable of delivering for the vast majority of our citizens the "middle-class" life to which they aspire, but which has increasingly become out of reach.

The Wealth of Nations

Adam Smith's famous book of 1776, *The Wealth of Nations,* is a good place to start for understanding how nations prosper. It is usually thought of as the beginning of modern economics. Smith rightly criticized mercantilism, the economic school of thought that dominated Europe during the Renaissance and the early industrial period. Mercantilists advocated exporting goods in order to get gold, believing that this would make their economies richer and their nations more politically powerful. Today, we might chuckle at these foolish policies: having more gold sitting in a vault doesn't provide higher standards of living. Yet similar misperceptions are prevalent today—especially among those who argue that exports must exceed imports, and pursue misguided policies aimed at achieving this.

The true wealth of a nation is measured by its capacity to deliver, in a sustainable way, high standards of living for all of its citizens. This in turn has to do with sustained productivity increases, based partly on investments in plants and equipment, but most importantly, in *knowledge*, and in running our economy at full employment, ensuring that the resources we have are not wasted or simply sitting idly by. It most definitely does not have to do with just the accumulation of financial wealth or gold. Indeed, I will show that the focus on financial wealth has been counterproductive—its growth has come at the expense of the real wealth of the country, helping to explain the slowdown of growth in this era of financialization.

Smith, writing at the dawn of the industrial revolution, could not have fully appreciated what gives rise to the real wealth of nations today. Much of Great Britain's wealth at the time and in the subsequent century derived from its exploitation of its colonies. Smith, however, focused neither on exports nor the exploitation of colonies, but on the role of industry and commerce. He talked about the advantages that larger markets gave for specialization.[15] This was good as far as it went, but he did not address the basis of the wealth of a nation in a modern economy: He did not talk about research and development, or even advances in knowledge as a result of experience, what economists call "learning by doing."[16] The reason was simple: advances in technology and learning played little role in the eighteenth-century economy.

For centuries before Smith wrote, standards of living had been stagnant.[17] Slightly after Smith, the economist Thomas Robert Malthus described how an increasing population would ensure that wages were kept at a subsistence level. If wages ever rose above the subsistence level, the population would expand, driving the wage back down to subsistence. There simply was no prospect of increasing standards of living. Malthus turned about to be quite wrong.

The Enlightenment and its aftermath

Smith himself was part of a great intellectual movement of the late eighteenth century called the Enlightenment. Often associated with the scientific revolution, the Enlightenment was built on developments over the preceding centuries, beginning with the Protestant Reformation. Before the sixteenth-century Reformation, initially led by Martin Luther, truth was revealed, ordained by authorities. The Reformation questioned the authority of the Church, and in a thirty-year war that begin around 1618, Europeans fought over alternative paradigms.

This questioning of authority forced society to ask and answer: How do we know the truth? How can we learn about the world around us? And how can and should we organize our society?

A new epistemology arose, which governed all aspects of life aside from the spiritual world: that of science, with its system of trust with verification, where each advance rested on earlier research and the progress of those who had come before.[18] Over the years universities and other research institutions arose to help us judge truth and discover the nature of our world. So many of the things that we take for granted today, from electricity, to transistors and computers, to the smartphone, lasers, and modern medicine, are the result of scientific discovery, undergirded by basic research. And it's not just these hi-tech advances: even our roads and our buildings rest on scientific advances; without them, we couldn't have skyscrapers and superhighways, we couldn't have the modern city.

THE ABSENCE OF royal or ecclesiastical authority to dictate how society should be organized meant that society itself had to figure it out. One couldn't rely on authority—either on Earth or above—to ensure that things worked out well, or as well as they could. One had to create systems of governance. Discovering the social institutions that would ensure the well-being of society was a more complicated matter than discovering the truths of nature. In general, one couldn't do controlled experiments. A close study of past experiences could be informative, however. One had to rely on reasoning and discourse—recognizing that no individual had a monopoly on our understandings of social organization. Out of this reasoning came an appreciation of the importance of the rule of law, due process, and systems of checks and balances, supported by foundational values like justice for all and individual liberty.[19]

Our system of government, with its commitment to fair treatment of all, required ascertaining the truth.[20] With systems of good governance in place, it is more likely that good and fair decisions are made. They may not be perfect, but it is more likely that they will be corrected when they are flawed.

Over time, a rich set of truth-telling, truth-discovering, and truth-verification institutions evolved, and we owe to them much of the success of our economy and our democracy.[21] Central among them is an active media. Like all institutions, it is fallible; but its investigations are part of our society's overall system of checks and balances, providing an important public good.

The advances in technology and science[22] as well as changes in social, political, and economic organization associated with the Enlightenment led to output increases that outpaced increases in population, so per capita income started to increase. Society learned how to curb population growth, and in advanced countries, increasingly, people decided to limit family size, especially as living standards rose. The Malthusian curse had been lifted. Thus began the enormous increases in standards of living over the past 250 years (illustrated in Figure 1: after centuries in which living standards had largely stagnated, they began to increase rapidly, at first in Europe, toward the end of the eighteenth and beginning of the nineteenth century, but then in other parts of the world, especially after World War II[23]) and the increase in longevity from which we have benefited so much.[24] It was a dramatic change in the fortunes of humanity. While in the past, most efforts went just to provide the basic necessities of life, now those could be obtained by just a few hours of work a week.[25]

In the nineteenth century, however, the fruits of this progress were very unequally shared.[26] Indeed, for many, life seemed to be getting even worse. As Thomas Hobbes had put it more than a century earlier,[27] "life was nasty, brutish, and short"—and for many, the industrial revolution seemed to make things, if anything, even worse. Charles Dickens's novels vividly described the suffering in mid-nineteenth century England.

In the United States, inequality reached new peaks at the end of the nineteenth century—in the Gilded Age, and in the "Roaring Twenties." Fortunately, there was a governmental response to these grave inequities: Progressive Era legislation and the New Deal curbed the

FIGURE 1: Historical Living Standards

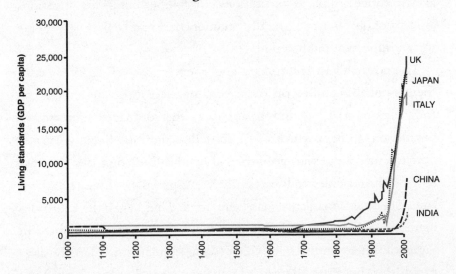

Source: INET

exploitation of market power and tried to address the failures of the market that had been exposed—including the unacceptable levels of inequality and insecurity to which it had given rise.[28] Under President Franklin D. Roosevelt, the US passed its public old age and disability program (Social Security, officially called OASDI, Old Age, Survivors, and Disability Insurance). Later in the century, President Lyndon B. Johnson provided health care for the aged and waged a war on poverty. In the UK and most of Europe, the State ensured that all had access to health care, and the US became the only major advanced country not to recognize access to medical care as a basic human right. By the middle of the last century, the advanced countries created what were then called "middle-class societies," in which the fruits of that progress were shared, at least to a reasonable degree, by a majority of citizens—and were it not for exclusionary labor market policies based on race and gender, even more would have shared in this progress. Citizens led longer and healthier lives and had access to better housing and clothes. The State provided education for their children—thus offering the promise of ever more prosperous lives going forward and greater equality of opportunity. The State also provided them a modicum of security in old age and social protection against other risks such as unemployment and disability.

Progress in the market and political institutions that evolved from the eighteenth century on was not always smooth. There were episodic economic crises, the worst being the Great Depression beginning in 1929, from which the US did not fully recover until World War II. Before the war, government provided unemployment insurance for those temporarily out of work. After the war, advanced countries also undertook an obligation to maintain their economies at full employment.

So too, movement in ensuring that the fruits of progress were evenly distributed was not always steady. As we observed earlier in this chapter, things got much worse in the last part of the nineteenth century and in the 1920s, but then improved significantly in the decades after World War II. While all groups saw their incomes grow, the income of those at the bottom grew more rapidly than of those at the top. But then, matters took a very negative turn in the late 1970s and early 1980s. Groups at the bottom started to see their incomes stagnate or even decline as others' soared. For the rich, life expectancies continued to increase, but eventually, for those with less education, they started to decline.

The Counterattack

The progress associated with the Enlightenment always had its enemies. The list now includes religious conservatives, who didn't like ideas like evolution, and some who felt uncomfortable with the tolerance and liberalism preached by the Enlightenment.* To these have been added people who found their economic interests at loggerheads with the findings of science—for instance, the owners of coal companies and their workers who face the prospect of being forced to shut down in the face of overwhelming evidence that they are a major contributor to global warming and climate change. But this coalition of the religious and social conservatives and those whose self-interest went directly against the scientific findings was not broad enough to attain political power. That power required the support of the broader business community. Its aid came with a quid pro quo, deregulation and tax cuts. In the US, the cement for this alliance is an unlikely president, Donald Trump. It has been painful to watch the silent support of a bigoted, misogynist, nativist, and protectionist

---

* I should emphasize that the association between conservatism and illiberalism is not inevitable. But it's the way things have, by and large, played out, though there are many outstanding conservatives who are beacons of tolerance.

president—so contrary to the values for which many in the business community say they stand—simply so they could get a more business-friendly environment with minimal regulations, and especially a tax cut for themselves and their corporations. Evidently, money in their pockets—greed—trumped all else.

Since launching his campaign, and especially since becoming president, Donald Trump has gone well beyond the traditional "conservative" economic agenda. In some ways, as we have noted, he is in fact revolutionary: he has vigorously attacked the central institutions of our society by which we attempt to acquire knowledge and ascertain the truth. His targets include our universities, the scientific community, and our judiciary. His most vicious attacks, of course, have been on the standard news media, which he labels as "Fake News." The irony is that for these media, fact-checking plays a central role, while Trump unabashedly lies grandly on a regular basis.[29]

These attacks are not only unprecedented in America, they are also corrosive, undermining our democracy and our economy. And while each piece of the attack is well known, it is critical to understand what motivates them and how broadly they are aimed. It is also important to recognize that what is at issue goes beyond Trump: if he had not hit such a resonant chord, his attacks on the truth-telling institutions would not have had such influence. We also see similar attacks elsewhere. If Trump had not waged this war, someone else would have.

It is especially in this context that the support of the business community for President Trump seems so cynical and disheartening, especially for those who have even faint memories of the rise of fascism in the 1930s. Historian Robert O. Paxton has drawn parallels between Trump's favors to the rich and the strategies behind the Nazis' rise in Germany.[30] Just as Trump's core support is a distinct minority, the core support of the fascists was too low to attain power democratically—they never got anything near a majority of votes. What success Trump has achieved has been based on forming a coalition with the business community, just as then: the fascists only came to power because of the support of a broad conservative coalition that included the business community.

Attacks on universities and science

The attacks on our universities have not received the same attention as those on the media, but they are equally dangerous for the future of our economy and democracy. Our universities are the wellspring from which all else comes. Silicon Valley—the center of the country's innovation economy—is what and where it is because of the advances in technology coming out of two of our great universities, Stanford and the University of California, Berkeley. MIT and Harvard have similarly spawned a great biotech center in Boston. Our country's entire reputation as the leader in innovation rests on foundations of knowledge emanating from our universities.

Our universities and science research centers have also done more than just advance knowledge: they have attracted to our shores some of our leading entrepreneurs. Many were drawn here by the opportunity to study at these great universities. Between 1995 and 2005, for example, immigrants founded 52 percent of all new Silicon Valley companies.[31] Immigrants also founded more than 40 percent of the companies on the 2017 US Fortune 500 list.[32]

And yet, Trump tried to slash government funding for basic research in his 2018 budget. [33] Further, for the first time probably *ever*, in the 2017 Republican tax bill, a tax has been imposed on some of our private not-for-profit universities—many of which have been central in the advances in knowledge that have been pivotal both in increases in standards of living and creating America's competitive advantage.

Some Republicans criticize our universities for being politically correct and intolerant of bigotry and misogyny. It's true that academics almost universally teach that climate change is real, and many cast doubts about supply-side economics. Universities also do not give equal weight to theories that the world is flat, to the phlogiston theories in chemistry, or to gold bugs in economics. There are some ideas that deservedly do not receive equal weight in higher education.[34] It would be malpractice to teach outdated ideas that have been repeatedly disproved by the scientific method.

So far, the universities have withstood the siege. But one can only imagine what will happen to America's economy and our standing in the world were Trump and the others waging this war to succeed. Our position in the vanguard of innovation would quickly recede. Already, others are taking advantage of Trump's anti-immigrant and anti-science stance: Canada and Australia, for instance, are actively trying to recruit talented students and create research institutions and laboratories to provide viable alternatives to those of Silicon Valley.

Attacks on the judiciary

In any society, there will be disputes, and when parties disagree, whether it's two individuals, two corporations, or individuals and their government, the task of our courts is to assess the truth, so far as can be ascertained. Almost by definition, the resolution of such disputes is not easy: if it were, the parties could have done it on their own and wouldn't have resorted to costly and time-consuming courts. When courts give rulings that Trump dislikes, he refers to "so-called judges." His disdain for the judiciary is mostly demonstrated by his willingness to appoint thoroughly unqualified judges—one nominee to the US District Court for the District of Columbia, Matthew Spencer Petersen, hadn't even had any trial experience. Petersen withdrew his nomination after humiliating questioning in his confirmation hearing, but he was only the most unqualified of many deeply unqualified Trump appointees.

Explaining the attacks: Self-defense

There is a pattern here. From the perspective of Trump and his supporters, the dangers of all of these truth-telling institutions is that they come to views that contradict the prejudices of Trump, those surrounding him and his party. Such attacks, and an attempt to create another reality, have long been part of fascism, from Goebbels's Big Lie onwards.[35] Rather than adapting his views to make them consonant with reality (say, about climate change), Trump would rather attack those who work to uncover the truth. That these attacks have such resonance is testimony in part to the failure of our education system. But we cannot blame what is going on solely on that. We know through advances in behavioral economics and marketing that one can manipulate perceptions and beliefs. Cigarette companies succeeded in using these methods to cast doubt on scientific findings that smoking was bad for health; and firms of all kinds succeed in persuading individuals to buy products that they might not otherwise have bought, that upon deeper reflection, they neither need nor want. If you can sell bad and even dangerous products, you can sell bad and even dangerous ideas—and there are strong economic interests to do so. These insights were picked up and used with vengeance by Steve Bannon and Fox News to change perceptions on a host of topics, from climate change to the inefficiency and inequities of government.

Selling the majority on policies that are against their own interest

That Trump and his clique have an interest in subverting the truth is no surprise. But one has to ask, with so much at stake, including our democracy and the advances in standards of living that have marked the past 250 years, why does this concerted attack on the very institutions and ideas that have done so much for our civilization seem to resonate among so many? Part of my motivation in writing this book is the hope that if there were greater understanding of the importance of these institutions, there would be more rallying around them when they are subject to such attack.

This is, however, not the only mystery concerning today's politics.

One might also ask: why is there such tolerance of such high levels of inequality in a democratic society? Of course, there are some at the top—a group whose wealth and political influence is disproportionate with its numbers—who are, to put it bluntly, simply greedy and shortsighted. They want to be at the top of the pack, no matter what the cost to society. Too many are enthralled with zero-sum thinking, which means that the only way one can get rich is to take something away from those below.

But even most of those at the top—if they truly understood their self-interest—should be supportive of more egalitarian policies, and this is even more the case for the 99 percent below who are being hurt by today's inequality. Even those in the top 10 percent who have seen a modicum of growth worry about falling down the rungs of the ladder. Even many of those in the 1 percent are hurt: In other countries, the rich are forced to live in gated communities and are constantly worried about their children being kidnapped.[36] The country's overall growth is being hurt, and that too hurts the 1 percent, much of whose wealth derives from money that trickles up from below; when there is less wealth below, there is less wealth to trickle up. One of the insights of modern economics is that countries with greater inequality (especially when inequality becomes as large as in the US, and engendered in the way that it is in the US) perform more poorly.[37] The economy is not zero sum; growth is affected by economic policy—and actions that increase inequality slow growth, especially over the long run.

In short, it is hard to find a *rational* explanation of the country's tolerance of inequality. So too, there are several other aspects of American economic policy for which it's hard to provide a good explanation, that is, if one believes that individuals are, by and large, rational and support policies which are in their own self-interest, and if one assumes that we have a functioning democracy, where policies should reflect what's in the interests of the majority. For instance, except for the owners of coal, gas, and oil companies, most of the country's interests should be in doing something about climate change.

But just as money has contaminated America's politics, it has contaminated beliefs more generally. The Koch brothers, oil and coal companies, and other vested interests have managed to hoodwink large parts of America into becoming climate skeptics, just as we noted earlier the cigarette companies, some fifty years ago, persuaded large parts of America into becoming skeptics over the findings that cigarettes were bad for one's health. The coal companies don't like the evidence concerning the role of greenhouse gases in climate change any more than the cigarette companies liked the evidence that cigarettes cause cancer and lung and heart diseases.[38] In that case, hundreds of thousands of people died earlier than they otherwise would have as a result.

So too, the rich have seemingly persuaded a large fraction of Americans that the country would be better off without an inheritance tax, even though that would lead to an inherited plutocracy—so contrary to American ideals; and even though there is but the remotest of chance that most Americans would ever be touched by the estate and inheritance tax, which effectively exempts from taxation for a married couple more than $11 million.

Science and reasoned argument has been replaced by ideology. Ideology has become a new instrument in the pursuit of capitalist greed. In some segments of the country, a culture has been created that is by and large antithetical to scientific reason. The best explanation for this I alluded to in the previous paragraph: those making money in ways that science questions—whether it is by producing cigarettes, chemicals, or coal—have an incentive to cast doubt on the entire scientific enterprise. If this continues, and if the Republicans who support these perspectives continue in power, it is hard to see how America's wealth-creation machine, resting as it does on the foundation of science, can be kept going.

The failure of our elites

While it's hard to understand why so many support the attacks on the very institutions that are at the core of our economic progress and democracy, it is actually easy to understand why large parts of the country would turn against the "establishment" and their views on globalization and financialization, and more broadly on the economy. The elites (in both parties) made promises about what the reforms of the past four decades would do—and what they promised was never delivered.

The elites had promised that lowering taxes on the rich, globalization, and financial market liberalization would lead to faster and more stable growth from which everyone would benefit. The disparity between what was promised and what happened was glaring. So, when Trump labeled it "rigged," it resonated.

No wonder that in the aftermath of the economic failures we have described—liberalization and globalization brought wealth to a few but stagnation, insecurity, and instability to the rest—there developed a skepticism of the elites and of the knowledge institutions from which they had supposedly derived their wisdom. That was a wrong conclusion: good academics had pointed out that globalization could actually lead to lower wages of unskilled workers, even adjusting for the lower prices of the goods they purchased, unless the government took strong countervailing measures. They had pointed out that financial liberalization would lead to instability. But the cheerleaders of globalization and financial market liberalization drowned them out.[39]

Whatever the reason,[40] we neglected those who suffered as the country went through the process of deindustrialization. We ignored the stagnation of wages and incomes, and the growing despair. We thought that the "cover-up"—a housing bubble that created temporary jobs in construction for some of those who had lost industrial jobs—was a real solution.

In short, our elites, in both parties, thought that focusing on GDP could be a substitute for focusing on people. In effect, they dissed large parts of the country. This disrespect was perhaps almost as painful as the economic tragedy that was befalling them.

Alternative Theories to the Sources of the Wealth of Nations

I've described the real source of the wealth of nations—resting on foundations of science and knowledge and the social institutions that we've created to help us not just live peacefully with each other but cooperate together for our common good. I've described too the threat to these foundations represented by Trump and his ilk. With an inchoate set of beliefs, untethered to any reality other than serving the economic interests of some shortsighted wealth-grabbers (rent-seekers), success required mounting a wholesale attack on our truth-telling institutions and on democracy itself.

THERE'S AN ALTERNATIVE, longer standing and more widespread theory of what gives rise to the wealth of nations, one that unfortunately has held much sway in the country for the past forty years: the view that an economy performs best if things are left entirely, or at least mostly, to unfettered markets. The advocates of these theories didn't rip principles of truth to shreds, as Trump did. Like a good magician, they concentrated more on shaping what we focus on. If globalization left many behind, if Reagan's reforms led to more people in poverty and income stagnation for large fractions of the population, the trick was to stop gathering data about poverty and stop talking about inequality. Focus on the competition that always remains within a market, rather than the power that each of the few dominant firms in the market has.

Look at a standard college economics textbook. The word *competition* is amply sprinkled through all of its chapters; the term *power* is reserved for but one or two. The term *exploitation* will likely be totally absent, a word long expunged from the conventional economist's vocabulary. In turning to the economic history of America's South, one is more likely to see a discussion of the (competitive) market for cotton, or even for slaves, than of the exploitive use of power by one group to extract the fruits of the labor of another, or that group's use of political power to ensure that it could continue to do so after the Civil War. The huge disparities in wages across genders, races, and ethnicities—a central feature of the American economy we note in the next chapter—if mentioned at all will be discussed using a mild term like *discrimination*. Only recently have epitaphs like *exploitation* and *power* been used to describe what is going on.

Too little competition—too much power in a few hands—is only one of the reasons that markets often don't work well. That they don't should be obvious: there are too many individuals with too little income to live a decent life; the US spends more per capita on health care than any other country in the world, yet life expectancy, already lower than in other advanced countries, is declining; we have an economy marked simultaneously by empty homes and homeless people. The most dramatic failures occur when there is large unemployment—with work to be done and people wanting to do it. The Great Depression of the 1930s and the Great Recession beginning in 2007 are the two most vivid instances, but since the beginning of capitalism, market economies have always been characterized by episodic periods of significant unemployment.

In each of these instances, government policies, even when they don't work perfectly, can improve matters from what they otherwise would have been. In our economic downturns, for instance, government stimulus, through monetary and fiscal policy, has lowered unemployment.[41]

Beyond ensuring full employment, is there still a role for government or should markets be left to themselves? The first step to answering this question is to recognize that markets are not an end in themselves, but a means to an end: a more prosperous society. Thus, the central question is, when do markets deliver prosperity, not just for the top 1 percent but for society as a whole? Adam Smith's invisible hand (the notion that the pursuit of self-interest leads as if by an invisible hand to the well-being of society) is perhaps the single most important idea in modern economics, and yet even Smith recognized the limited power of markets and the need for government action. Modern economic research—both theory and experience—has enhanced our understanding of government's fundamental role in a market economy. It is needed both to do what markets won't and can't do as well as make sure that markets act as they are *supposed* to.

For markets to work well on their own, a host of conditions have to be satisfied—there has to be robust competition, information has to be perfect, and actions of one individual or firm can't impose harm on others (there cannot, for example, be pollution). In practice, these conditions are never satisfied—often by a large measure—which means that in these instances markets fail to deliver. Before environmental regulations, our air was unbreathable and our water undrinkable and unswimmable—and the same is true today in China, India, and other countries where environmental regulations are too weak or too weakly enforced.

Most importantly for a dynamic, innovation economy, the private sector, on its own, will spend too little on basic research. The same is true for other areas of investments with wide public benefit (infrastructure and education, for instance). The benefits of government spending to accomplish these ends far exceed the costs. This spending has to be financed, and of course, that requires taxes.[42] (Not surprisingly, the private sector trumpets what it does: its applied research is important, but this research rests on foundations of publicly supported basic research.)

I once asked the finance minister of Sweden why his country's economy was doing so well. His answer: because they had high taxes. Of course, what he meant was that Swedes knew that a prosperous country required a high level of public expenditures, on infrastructure, education, technology, and social protection, and that the government needed revenues to sustainably finance these expenditures. Many of these public expenditures complement private expenditures. Advances in technology financed by government can help support private investment. Investors find their efforts to be more profitable when there is a highly educated labor force and good infrastructure. Central to rapid growth is an increase in knowledge, and the underlying basic research has to be supported by government.

These insights fly in the face of Reagan-style "supply-side" policies, based on the assumptions that deregulation would free up the economy, lower taxes would incentivize it, and the two together would lead to economic growth. However, after Reagan's reforms, growth actually slowed. Deregulation, especially of the financial market, brought us the downturns of 1991, 2001, and most grievously, the Great Recession of 2008. And lower taxes did not have the energizing effect that supply-siders claimed. Thomas Piketty and his coauthors have documented that lowering top tax rates has actually been accompanied by unchanged or lower growth around the world.[43] As anticipated by the critics of these tax cuts, neither Reagan's cuts for the rich nor the later cuts enacted under George W. Bush led to increased labor supply or savings[44]—and accordingly, neither led to faster growth.[45]

Evidently, there is much less than meets the eye to "supply-side" economics and its faith in the unfettered free market as the path to growth. There is much more to good economic performance than low tax rates and weak regulation.

The dangers of a return to Reaganomics

Many conservatives are almost as appalled by Trump and his attack on norms and institutions as are those on the Left. They had been, in particular, at the forefront in the fight for globalization, and to see it being defeated from within their own party is an abomination. But what these (a group often referred to as "Never Trumpers") have to offer the country is just another dose of the failed policies of the past—still lower taxes for the rich and corporations, still fewer regulations, a still smaller role of the State, a twenty-first-century version of Reaganomics.

The American economy today is characterized, to too great an extent, by underregulated, monopolistic markets, where wealth creation has been replaced by exploitation. Meanwhile, the real danger of the growth of populism* and nativism in the US is that they are worse than a distraction. Our problems do not arise from unfair trade agreements or immigrants, and what Trump has proposed in these arenas risks worsening the country's problems, including the plight of those hurt by deindustrialization. So too, no country ever set itself on a fast and sustainable growth path by simply ignoring budget constraints, as Trump seems to have done in his budget-busting tax bill of December 2017 and the expenditure increases of January 2018.

The real problems in the US, as I'll explain, are of our own making—too little investment in people, infrastructure, and technology, too much faith in the ability of markets to solve all of our problems, too little regulation where we need it, combined sometimes with

---

* While demagogues like Trump are often called (in a castigating way) populists, in this book, I've largely avoided using that term. In some cases, populists are simply honest politicians who strive to respond to popular demands, like for education or health care, and do so within the limits imposed by the economy. Often, however, anyone who criticizes elitist doctrines concerning deregulation, liberalization, and privatization is labelled populist.

too much regulation where we don't. The daily Trump show distracts us from working on these deeper and important issues.

The true risk is to our democracy

This book is mostly about economics—showing that our current situation is the predictable consequence of flawed choices in the past, and that there are alternatives that will make matters better. But a recurring theme in this book is that politics and economics are intertwined. Our economic inequalities get translated into political inequalities, reverberating back with rules exacerbating these inequalities even more. So too, our economic failures reverberate on our political system. Trump is a manifestation. Here is my deepest worry for the future:

The truly greedy and shortsighted in the 1 percent have come to understand that the globalization, financialization, and other elements of the current economic rulebook are not supported by the vast majority of Americans, and understandably so. For these, this has one deeply disturbing implication: if we let democracy run its course, and if we believe in a modicum of rationality on the part of voters, they will choose an alternative course. In their pursuit of their naked self-interest, these super-rich have thus formulated a three-part strategy: deception, disenfranchisement, and disempowerment.[46] Deception: They tell others that policies like the 2017 tax bill to further enrich the rich will actually help ordinary Americans, or that a trade war with China will somehow reverse deindustrialization. Disenfranchisement: They work hard to make sure that those who might vote for more progressive policies can't or don't, either by making it hard for them to register, or by making it difficult for them to vote. And finally, disempowerment: they put sufficient constraints on government so that, if all else fails and a more progressive government were elected, it couldn't do what is needed to reform our politics and economy. One example: the constraints imposed by an increasingly stacked and ideological Supreme Court.

The prognosis—if we don't change course—is more of the same: an increasingly dysfunctional economy, polity, and society. The backlash against science and the foundational institutions that have underlain progress for centuries,[47] including, and most importantly, our truth-assessing and -telling institutions, will continue, leading to still lower growth and more inequality.

An ongoing war or a third way?

Today seems so distant from that moment when President John F. Kennedy said: "Ask not what your country can do for you, ask what you can do for your country."[48] Reagan redirected the country's economy, but he also crystallized a redirection of values toward more materialism and more selfishness. The failure of his approach to yield the fruits that had been promised did not result in the course correction that one would have hoped. It led only to a doubling down on a flawed set of ideas.

As we think about fixing our economic system, we need to dismiss the view that because the US won the Cold War, America's economic system had triumphed. But it was not so much that free-market capitalism had demonstrated its superiority[49] but that Communism had failed.

When the US was competing with Communism for the hearts and minds of those around the world, we had to show that our economic system delivered for all. After the collapse of the Soviet Union, it seemed there was no competition, and the system lost its incentive to deliver for everyone.

For many of the billions in the developing world and emerging markets, China, using its distinctive "socialist market economy with Chinese characteristics," has provided a dynamic alternative vision to that of America—whose standing suffered a major blow with the 2008 crisis, and now, an even greater blow with the rise of Trump. And global awareness that American-style capitalism seems to benefit mainly the top, and is leaving large numbers without adequate health care, hasn't helped America's soft power.

Those who believe in democracy should find this deeply disturbing. There is a battle of ideas going on over alternative social, political, and economic systems, and we should worry about the fact that large parts of the world are turning away from the virtues of our system.

Fortunately, the American style of capitalism is but one of many different forms of democratic market economies, as we saw in the reference to Sweden just above. Other democracies use different forms that seem to be delivering as fast economic growth and more well-being for a majority of their citizens.

We need to bury our arrogance about our economic system. It should be clear by now that it has serious shortcomings, especially when it comes to ensuring shared prosperity. There is a menu of interesting options that we should be considering, recognizing that many of the alternative forms of market economies have strong points from which we could learn.

A misshapen economy creates misshapen individuals and a misshapen society

All of this means that this war of interests—cloaked as a war of ideas, about the best way of organizing society—will not go away soon, with corporations, for instance, trying to get more for themselves at the expense of the rest.

This battle of ideas is not just a sports contest. The reason we should be looking around for how we can fix our economy's shortcomings and create one more attuned to our values is not so much because it will enhance the likelihood that our ideas about markets and democracy will prevail globally, but for what it will do to us, both as individuals and our country.

Standard courses in economics begin with the assumption that individuals have fixed preferences with which they are born; they are who they are, with their likes and dislikes. The idea that tastes and preferences are immutable is, however, sheer nonsense. As parents, we try to shape our children, and though we are not always fully successful we believe that, at least some of the time, we are. The marketing profession tries to shape what we buy. We are shaped by—and shape—our society and culture. And how we structure our economy plays a central role in this shaping, because so much of our relations with others are about economics. Research in behavioral economics has confirmed this. It is not an accident that the bankers exhibited the extent of moral turpitude that has been shown: experiments show that bankers—especially when they are reminded that they are bankers—act in a more dishonest and selfish way.[50] They are shaped by their profession. So too for economists; while those who choose to study economics may be more selfish than others, the longer they study economics, the more selfish they become.[51]

The kind of market economy that America has created has resulted in selfish and materialistic individuals—individuals who often differ from the kinds of ideals we hold up for ourselves and for others. Other forms of economic organization foster more cooperation. All individuals combine self-interest and other-regarding (altruistic) behavior (as Smith himself noted[52]), and the nature of our economic and social system changes the balance between the two.[53] With more individuals who are more selfish, more materialistic, more shortsighted, and with less of a moral compass, our society echoes back these same traits.

The consequences can be even more severe when it comes to politics. A market winner-take-all attitude can, and has been, invading our polity, destroying norms and undermining the ability to reach compromise and consensus. If left unbridled, it will destroy national cohesion.

We are better than that which we seem to be becoming. We may differ in precise details over what we should be striving for—as economists emphasize, there are always trade-offs—but on core fundamentals, there is widespread consensus. To achieve this alternative vision will require collective action. In economics, it will require both regulating the market and doing what the market can't do. We will have to get over the shibboleths that markets on their own are self-regulating, efficient, stable, or fair, or that government is inevitably inefficient. In a sense, we have to save capitalism from itself. Capitalism—together with a money-oriented democracy—creates a self-destructive dynamic, which risks simultaneously destroying any semblance of a fair and competitive market and a meaningful democracy. More is required than just a mild tweak of the system. We have gone too far down the wrong road for that to be possible. We have to construct a new social contract that enables everyone in our rich country to live a decent, middle-class life.

This book then is about this alternative way forward. Another world is possible—based not on the market fundamentalist belief in markets and trickle-down economics that got us into this mess; nor on the nativist, populist Trumpian economics, which repudiates the international rule of law, substituting "globalization with a club," an approach which will actually make America worse off. I am hopeful that in the long run truth will win out: Trump's policies will fail, and Trump's supporters, both the corporates at the top and the workers whose interests he claims to be advancing, will begin to see it. What will happen then is anybody's guess. If there is an alternative way forward, such as that presented here, perhaps they will grasp it.

CHAPTER 2

Toward a More Dismal Economy

Something began happening to America's powerful economic engine around 1980: growth slowed and, much more importantly, the growth in incomes slowed, or often declined. It happened almost without our recognizing it. Indeed, even as the economy was failing to deliver prosperity for large parts of the population, the champions of a new era of financialization, globalization, and technological advances were bragging about the "new economy" that was destined to bring ever-greater prosperity, by which they seemed to mean simply a higher level of GDP. Some of our economic leaders—including successive heads of the Federal Reserve—bragged about the "great moderation," how we had finally tamed the business cycle, the fluctuations in output and employment that had marked capitalism from the start.[1]

The financial crisis of 2008 showed that our seeming prosperity had been built on a house of cards, or more precisely, a mountain of debt. As new data came in giving a deeper picture of the economy, it became increasingly clear that there were long-standing and deep-seated problems. The growth that had been championed turned out to be far slower than that of the decades after World War II. Most disturbing, what growth occurred went to a few people at the top. If GDP goes up because Jeff Bezos's income goes up—but everyone else's income stagnates—the economy is not really doing well. But that is close to the situation in which America finds itself today, and it's the way things have been for four decades, a period over which the average income of the bottom 90 percent of Americans has hardly changed, while that of the top 1 percent has soared. (See Figure 2, where the bottom line is the average pretax income of the bottom 90 percent of the population, and the top line is that of the top 1 percent).

Some economists disdain even discussing inequality.[2] The job of the economist, they say, is to increase the size of the pie. If that is done, all will benefit—as President Kennedy put it, a rising tide lifts all boats. I wish it were true. But it's not. In fact, a rising tide, if it happens too quickly can—and often does—smash the smaller vessels.

FIGURE 2: History of Average US Pretax Income, US, 1974–2014

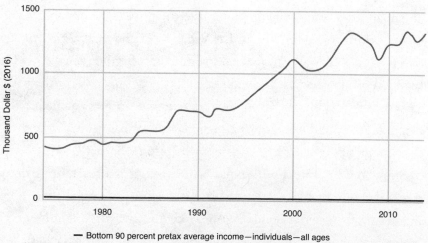

Source: World Inequality Database

Nor is an economy doing well if GDP goes up, but meanwhile the environment is deteriorating and resources are being depleted. A country living off the past and not investing in the future—or destroying its children's environmental heritage—is one in which this generation is doing well at the expense of its descendants.

In each of these dimensions America has not been doing well, either relative to our past or to our competitors. To many Americans this may come as a surprise because it was simply assumed that America was bigger, better, stronger in every way than other countries. That's what our politicians relentlessly tell us. But unless you're committed to a Trumpian other-world, the data speaks consistently: we are not the top-performing country by a long shot, though some data may suggest that the extent to which America misses the top marks may be larger than that suggested by other data.

Among the many explanations for this malaise in the economy, there is one that is fundamental: we didn't grasp the lessons of the previous chapter concerning what was the true source of the wealth of a nation. Too many were seduced into thinking that what was profitable was necessarily what was good, not realizing that profits can be enhanced through exploitation rather than wealth creation.[3] Real estate speculation, gambling in Las Vegas or Atlantic City, or exploitive for-profit schools can make a fortune for a few but can't provide the basis of sustained well-being for society as a whole. Over the past four decades, we didn't invest in infrastructure, in our people, or in technology. Even the country's rate of investment has been low, so low that it hasn't even been keeping up with national output.[4]

Subsequent chapters will explore the various manifestations that this shift from wealth creation to exploitation took—in globalization, financialization, and monopolization. First, however, we should get a better sense of what's gone wrong and why it is that Trump's claims to "make America great again" seem to have such resonance.

Slowing Growth

For the third of a century after World War II, from 1947 to 1980, the US grew at an annual rate of 3.7 percent, while for the last third of a century, from 1980 to 2017, the average growth rate has been only 2.7 percent, a full percentage point lower.[5] This is a major decline, nearly 30 percent.

The 2008 crisis showed, further, that much of the growth that had been recorded in the years before the crisis was not sustainable. It was based on reckless investments, perhaps best exemplified by over-building in the housing market.

International comparisons in standards of living

Part of American exceptionalism is that we have a higher standard of living than others and a higher growth rate—or so we have been led to believe. We are (so it was also believed) more efficient and produc-tive. This belief has an immediate corollary. We should outcompete everyone, that is, they should be buying more of our goods and we fewer of theirs. The implication of this is that if our goods are not "dominating" markets, our rivals must be cheating. Q.E.D. The policy recommendations follow directly from these simple axioms: stop the cheating. If the rules of international trade don't allow us to stop them, then the rules themselves must be crooked. This is the line of reasoning that has led to the imposition of trade barriers, like tariffs, which are taxes on imports, or quotas, which are limits on the amount of goods that can be imported. The spirit of protectionism, protecting domestic producers from foreign competition, is obviously alive and well today.

The only problem with this line of reasoning is that each step is flawed. Here we address the underlying premise—that the US is the most productive economy with the highest standard of living. (We explore the other steps in the logic in chapter 5 on globalization.)

————————

THE REALITY IS that, using the Human Development Index, a broad-gauge measure of standard of living, the US ranks thirteenth, just above the United Kingdom. Once America's inequality is taken into account, it slips to twenty-fourth.[6]

In 2018, the World Bank launched its own "human capital index," reflecting the strength of a society's investment in its people, combining education, health, and just the ability to survive.[7] The United States ranked twenty-fourth, well below Asian leaders like Singapore, Japan, South Korea, and Hong Kong, and well below our neighbor to the north, Canada (ranked tenth), and most of our European competitors. Weak investments in human capital today lead, of course, to low standards of living in the future.

The OECD (Organization of Economic Cooperation and Development), the official think tank of the advanced countries, conducts standardized tests every few years of students from around the world. On such tests, which are also administered to those in some developing countries, Americans rank below average in mathematics—fortieth of the seventy-two countries that participated in the tests—and little better (twenty-fourth) in reading and (twenty-fifth) in science.[8] This dismal performance has been consistent, and while the US has a larger-than-average fraction not meeting the baseline performance, it also has a below-average share of top performers. Canada, Korea, Japan, UK, Norway, Lithuania, and Australia all beat us in college graduation rates among 25- to 34-year-olds—Canada by more than 25 percent, South Korea by almost 50 percent.[9]

Low investments in human and physical capital naturally translate into lower rates of growth of productivity. In comparing outputs across countries, it is important to take into account differences in hours worked. Americans work more hours than those in other advanced countries (an average of 1780 hours per worker per year compared to 1759 elsewhere—but especially many more compared to some European countries like France [1514] or Germany [1356]).[10] It's not so much shorter work weeks but longer vacations. It is these longer hours that account for much of the higher per capita income. Indeed, in terms of productivity—output per hour—US productivity growth has been less than half of that of the average of the advanced countries in the period after the Great Recession, 2010–2016.[11]

We've been growing so much more slowly than China for the last thirty years that not only is China now the largest economy in the world,[12] in the standard measures by which these comparisons are made, but also it now saves more than the US, manufactures more, and trades more.[13]

I often lecture in China, and when I relate the statistics about what has been happening to most Americans other than those at the top, the audiences look at me in disbelief. Forty years ago, China was a poor country, sixty years ago, a very poor one—a per capita annual income of around $150,[14] labeled by the World Bank as "extreme poverty." In just forty years, while incomes for all but the very top in the US have largely stagnated, incomes in China have increased more than tenfold,[15] and more than 740 million have moved out of poverty.[16]

Growing Inequality

While America doesn't excel in growth, it does so in inequality: the country has greater income inequality than any other advanced country; in terms of inequality of opportunity it also ranks well toward the bottom. It should go without saying that this is contrary to America's identity as the land of opportunity.[17]

America's workers are getting a smaller share of a pie that is growing more slowly—so much smaller that their incomes are stagnating. The share of labor, especially if one excludes the top 1 percent of workers—which includes the bankers and CEOs, treated as "workers" for statistical purposes but not what most of us mean when we say "laborers"—has been declining precipitously, in an unprecedented way, from 75 percent in 1980 to 60 percent in 2010, a 15 percentage point decline in a short span of thirty years.[18]

By contrast, a relatively few, the top 10 percent, the top 1 percent, and even more the top 0.1 percent, were seizing a larger and larger share of the nation's pie. The top 1 percent's share more than doubled; the top 0.1 percent's share increased almost fourfold in the past forty years.[19]

Many among the wealthy claimed that all would benefit from the riches bestowed on the top—the benefits would trickle down. But this has almost never been so, and certainly not in the period since the 1980s. Earlier, we talked about how the bottom 90 percent has basically seen their incomes stagnate. Other statistics corroborate this. The discontent in America seemed particularly acute among men, and this was understandable: adjusted for inflation, median income (half above, half below) of a full-time male worker—and those who get full-time jobs are the lucky ones, with some 15 percent of prime-age males now not working—has changed little over four decades.[20] At the very bottom, matters are even worse, with wages, adjusted for inflation, roughly at the level that they were sixty years ago.[21] It is not as if America's overall income has stagnated—GDP per capita has more than doubled over that sixty-year period. And it is not as if American workers' productivity has been stagnating: it increased by even more, by sevenfold over that period. Indeed, something happened to the country after some time between the mid-1970s and mid-1980s: while before then, compensation increased in tandem with productivity, with say a 1 percent increase in productivity being followed by a 1 percent increase in pay, after that a yawning gap opened up, with pay going up by less than a fifth of the increase in productivity—which means a larger share is going to someone other than the workers.[22]

Among workers, too, wage disparities are larger, manifested in every way possible: stagnant or declining wages at the bottom, an eviscerated middle class, and top wages that are soaring. Within firms,

CEO pay has increased enormously relative to that of the average worker. Differences in average pay across firms has also increased. There are multiple causes, often interrelated, of increasing wage inequality, many of which we will discuss below: globalization and changes in technology have weakened the demand for unskilled workers; unions, which had helped equalize wages, are weaker. There has been an increase in concentration of market power, with accordingly an increase in dispersion in corporate profitability—between those with and without such power, with firms with higher profitability sharing some of what they receive with their workers.[23]

For many years, I have been warning that the great divide—the one between the rich and the poor—was not sustainable, and that a fairer distribution of income was in the long-run interests of even the rich.[24]

Scholars like the late Sir Anthony Atkinson at Oxford,[25] Thomas Piketty in Paris, Emmanuel Saez at Berkeley, and Raj Chetty at Harvard have provided a wealth of data documenting what was happening, and in many quarters, these ideas have had resonance. President Barack Obama, in one of his important addresses, described inequality as the country's most pressing problem.[26]

> The combined trends of increased inequality and decreasing mobility pose a fundamental threat to the American Dream, our way of life, and what we stand for around the globe. And it is not simply a moral claim that I'm making here. There are practical consequences to rising inequality and reduced mobility.

Yet, in American politics and economics, there seemed to be even more pressing issues—the recovery from the Great Recession was going more slowly than Obama and his economic team had expected, and the Republicans in Congress had taken a recalcitrant stance that made passing any legislation beyond simply keeping the government open almost impossible. During his presidency, Obama did not, perhaps could not, deal with the issue of inequality, even as he recognized its importance. He deserves credit, however, for the Affordable Care Act ("Obamacare"), which helped deal with one of the cruelest manifestations of inequality, the lack of access to decent health care. Not surprisingly, the problem of inequality did not heal itself on its own—and could not have. Quite the contrary. Matters got worse.

Inequalities in race, ethnicity, and gender

The inequalities just described do not fully describe the deep divides in the country, for it is riven too by those based on race, ethnicity, and gender, no small part of which arises from brutal discrimination. This, more than fifty years after the country passed civil rights legislation intended to eliminate such discrimination. Given our history, addressing these divides is critical if the country is ever to be *one nation*. (Indeed, in many ways, labor market exclusions by race and gender—and then reactions to attempts to create more inclusion—are central to understanding inequalities in America's labor markets.)

There was some improvement in the years following the passage of civil rights legislation, but then the forces that had led to segregation and discrimination mounted a counterattack, progress halted, and in some ways reversed.

Some fifty years ago, in 1968, in the aftermath of race riots throughout the country, President Johnson appointed a commission to determine the underlying causes. Unfortunately, its conclusions still ring true today: "Our Nation is moving toward two societies, one black, one white—separate and unequal."[27] It featured a country in which African Americans faced systematic discrimination, with inadequate education and housing, and totally lacking economic opportunities— for them, there was no American dream. Underlying all this was a diagnosis of "the racial attitude and behavior of white Americans toward black Americans [as the cause]. Race prejudice has shaped our history decisively; it now threatens to affect our future."[28]

A half century after we began the struggle to eliminate discrimination, women's wages are still only 83 percent that of men's, black men's 73 percent that of white men's, and Hispanic men's 69 percent that of white men's.[29]

There are many other dimensions of inequality in America, including those in health, wealth, and most importantly, opportunity. Inequalities in each of these are larger than those in income.

Inequality in health

No statistics summarize better the dire straits that so many Americans find themselves in than those on health. Americans have a lower life expectancy than do citizens of most other advanced countries[30]—more than five years shorter than in Japan—and are dying younger—the Centers for Disease Control has reported decreases in life expectancy every year from 2014 on.[31] This decrease comes despite advances in medicine that, in most of the rest of the world, have led to declining mortality rates[32] and longer life expectancies. Moreover, there are large disparities in life expectancy between rich and poor Americans, and they're getting dramatically larger. Gary Burtless of the Brookings Institution describes what's happened to the life expectancy of a woman age 50 in 1970 and 1990: "In those two decades, the gap in life expectancy between women in the bottom tenth and the top tenth of earners increased from a little over 3½ years to more than 10 years."[33]

THE EXISTENCE OF such health disparities between the US and other advanced countries, and between America's rich and poor, is to be expected, given that until Obamacare came along America did not recognize the right of every American to have access to health care—a right recognized by virtually every other advanced country.

Anne Case and Angus Deaton (the latter was 2015 recipient of the Nobel Prize in Economics) took a close look at publicly available death statistics and showed something that shocked the nation: among middle-aged white men without a college education, mortality rates had increased markedly from 1999 to 2013 (the last year of data the study reviewed). This reversed a trend of decreasing mortality for that cohort, and ran against the trends for most American age and ethnic groups, as well as the trends in most other industrialized countries.[34]

Still more disturbing are the causes of death, what Case and Deaton label as diseases of despair: alcoholism, drug overdose, and suicide. Given the stagnation of incomes in the middle and bottom that I have described—compounded by the enormous losses of jobs and homes that marked the Great Recession—none of this should be a surprise.[35]

A decline in life expectancy of this magnitude unrelated to war or a pandemic (like HIV) had happened only once before in recent memory: among citizens of the former Soviet Union after it broke up, where there was a collapse of the economy and society itself, with GDP falling by almost a third.

Obviously, a country where there is such despair, where so many are on drugs or drinking too much alcohol, won't have a healthy labor force. A good measure of how well society does in creating good jobs and healthy workers is the fraction of working-age population that is participating in the labor force and working. Here, the US does far worse than many other countries. At least some of our poor labor force participation can be directly linked to our poor health statistics. A recent study by Alan Krueger, former chair of the Council of Economic Advisers, found that nearly half of "prime-age men" not in the labor force suffer from a serious health condition, and two-thirds of those are also taking some prescription pain medication.[36] But America's poor health is not the result of an unhealthy climate, nor is it because sickly people have migrated to these shores. There is no epidemic that can explain why Americans are dying younger and are less healthy than those in Europe and elsewhere. Rather, the causality goes at least partly the other way: because our economy has failed to produce good jobs, with decent wages, individuals have essentially given up, and this despair leads to social diseases like alcoholism and drug dependence.[37]

Inequality of wealth

America's wealth inequality is even greater than that in income—the top 1 percent has more than 40 percent of US wealth, almost twice the share of income.[38] (Income refers to what individuals get in any year; wealth, to their ownership of assets—for most Americans, this consists mostly of their home and car, offset by what they owe on their auto loans and mortgage.) Wealth is particularly important because it is crucial in determining access to opportunity and influence.

AROUND THE WORLD, the picture at the top was even worse. Every year, Oxfam releases statistics on the extremes of inequality: how many at the top have as much wealth as the bottom 50 percent of the world, some 3.9 billion people. The number has come down rapidly: by 2017, it was just twenty-six individuals.[39] A few years ago, it would have taken a couple of large buses to contain those with as much wealth as the bottom half. Now, almost unimaginably, a little over two dozen individuals, almost all men, had as much economic heft as all the people in China, India, and Africa combined.

We described earlier two key ways to become rich: create more wealth or grab more wealth from others. In the case of wealth, there's a third: inherit it.

Many among the top—including the Walton family (heir to the Walmart fortune) and the Koch brothers—had achieved that success not by working hard but, at least in part, by the good luck of large inheritances.[40] Americans like to think of wealth inequality here as being different from that in old Europe, based on a landed aristocracy of a bygone era. But we have been evolving into a twenty-first-century inherited plutocracy.

Inequality in opportunity

The statistics on income, health, and wealth inequalities are depressing enough. Even more so is the country's inequality of opportunity, partly because such inequities go so much against our image of ourselves and our beliefs in a fair society.

Income and wealth in one generation translates into wealth in the next, as the Waltons and Koch brothers illustrate. Advantages—and disadvantages—get transmitted across the generations. And with nearly one in five children in America growing up in poverty, this can easily lead to poverty traps. Those born into poverty have a low probability of escaping. In America, being born into the right family and growing up in the right neighborhood have increasingly become the most important ingredients for success in life.[41] The American dream of equality of opportunity is a myth: a young American's life prospects are more dependent on the income and education of his parents than in almost any other advanced country. I tell my students that they have one crucial decision to make in life: choosing the right parent. If they get it wrong, their prospects may be bleak.

Of course, a few people do make it from the bottom to the top; but the fact that it's so well covered in the press reinforces the point: these are the exceptions, not the rule. Indeed, far more than other countries, America has *a low-income trap.* Those whose parents are in the bottom of the income distribution are likely to wind up in the bottom. A child of someone at the top who does poorly in school is likely to wind up in a better position than a child of someone toward the bottom who does well.[42]

The combination of low growth and low mobility has been devastating: as Opportunity Insights, a research project at Harvard University, points out in what it labels "The Fading American Dream," "children's prospects of earning more than their parents . . . fell from approximately 90 percent for children born in 1940 to around 50 percent for children entering the labor market today."[43] And the Pew Mobility Project, a research project supported by the Pew Foundation, has similarly found that only half have greater wealth than their parents at the same stage of their life.[44]

Conclusions

The American economy, and those of many other advanced countries, has not been working well—and this is especially so if by "working well" we mean increasing standards of living of most citizens. Low growth, stagnating incomes, and growing inequality are, of course, deeply interrelated, and they all are, at least in part, the result of policies begun under President Reagan some four decades ago, policies based on deep and pervasive misunderstandings about what makes for a strong economy. Not surprisingly, extremes of inequality, and inequalities arising from lack of opportunity, are particularly corrosive of economic performance. Lack of opportunity means that those born of poor parents are not living up to their potential. This is morally wrong, but it also means that America is wasting its most precious resource, the talents of its young people.

The slogan "leave it to the market" never made sense: one has to structure markets, and that entails politics. Those on the Right grasped this, and beginning with Reagan, they restructured markets to serve those at the top. But they made four key mistakes: they didn't understand the eviscerating effects of ever larger inequality; they didn't understand the importance of long-term thinking; they didn't understand the necessity of collective action—the important role that government has to play in achieving equitable and sustainable growth; and most importantly, they failed to understand the importance of knowledge—even as we were championing ourselves as an innovation economy—and that of basic research, the foundations on which our technology rests. They thus downplayed key factors that were essential to the success of capitalism over the past two hundred and some years. The result is largely what one should have expected: lower growth and more inequality.

With a good sense now of the depth of the problem, we explore in the next chapters two of the key contributors to these dismal outcomes: we confused the two ways in which individuals become wealthy—through wealth creation, increasing the size of the national economic pie, or through exploitation; and we didn't recognize the various facets of exploitation, beginning with market power. Too much of the nation's energy was devoted to exploitation, too little to true wealth creation.

CHAPTER 3

Exploitation and Market Power

S tandard economics textbooks—and much political rhetoric—focus on the importance of competition. Over the past four decades, economic theory and evidence have laid waste to claims that most markets are by and large competitive and the belief that some variant of the "competitive model" provides a good, or even adequate, description of our economy.[1] Perhaps long ago, the picture of innovative, if ruthless, competition, of myriad firms struggling to better serve consumers at lower costs, provided a good description of the American economy. But today we live in an economy where a few firms can rake in massive amounts of profits for themselves and persist unchecked in their dominant position for years and years.

Our new tech leaders have ceased even paying lip service to competition—Peter Thiel, for a short while one of Trump's advisers and one of the great Silicon Valley entrepreneurs, put it bluntly: "competition is for losers."[2] Warren Buffet, one of the country's wealthiest men and smartest investors, also understood this well. In 2011 he told the Financial Crisis Inquiry Commission[3]:

The single most important decision in evaluating a business is pricing power. If you've got the power to raise prices without losing business to a competitor, you've got a very good business. If you've got a good enough business, if you have a monopoly newspaper or if you have a network television station, your idiot nephew could run it.[4]

On an earlier occasion, he had explained to his investors that an entry barrier was like being surrounded by a moat:

[We] think in terms of that moat and the ability to keep its width and its impossibility of being crossed. We tell our manager we want the moat widened every year.[5]

Buffett is correct in his assessments, and the noncompetitive world he so candidly describes is bad news. The trouble is, barriers to competition are everywhere. As we explain below, there has been a great deal of innovation in the creation, leveraging, and preservation of market power—in the tools that managers use to increase the moat that surrounds them and with which they can use the resulting power to exploit others and increase their profits. It is understandable why our business leaders don't like competition: competition drives profits down, to the point at which firms receive a return on their capital at a level that is just enough to sustain keeping investment in the business, taking into account its risk. They seek higher profits than that which a competitive market would afford—hence the necessity of building bigger moats to forestall competition and the enormous innovation in doing so.

What is needed now is innovation in countering these innovations—restoring competition and creating a more balanced economy. In the last part of this chapter, we show how that can be done.

The Big Picture

Let's begin with a simple question: Is there any reason why US telecom prices, including broadband, should be so much higher than those in many other countries—and the service so much poorer?[6] Much of the innovation was done here in the United States. Our publicly supported research and education institutions provided the intellectual foundations. Telecom is now a global technology, requiring little labor—so it cannot be high wages that provide the explanation. The answer to this puzzle is simple: market power. The growth in market power holds much of the answer to the puzzle presented in the last chapter,[7] how seemingly the most innovative economy in the world has had so little growth, and so little of that growth has trickled down to the benefit of ordinary citizens. Market power allows firms to exploit consumers by charging higher prices than they otherwise would and by taking advantage of consumers in a variety of other ways. Higher prices hurt workers just as much as lower wages. In the absence of market power, the forces of competition would drive excess profits to zero, but as we shall see, it is these excess profits that are at the root of America's growing inequality.[8]

Market power also allows firms to exploit workers directly, by paying lower wages than they would otherwise, and by taking advantage of labor in other ways. Market power gets translated into political power. The huge profits generated by market power allow corporations—in our money-driven politics—to buy influence that further enhances their power and profits, for instance by weakening unions and the enforcement of competition policy, giving free rein to banks to exploit ordinary citizens, and structuring globalization in ways that further weakens workers' bargaining power.

Creating wealth vs. grabbing wealth

There are two ways that countries can get wealthy: taking wealth from other countries, as the colonial powers did, or creating wealth, through innovation and learning. The latter is the only true source of wealth creation for the world as a whole.

So too for individuals. Individuals can get wealthy by exploiting others—in societies without a rule of law, typically through brute force; or with an unjust rule of law, by slavery. But in the modern American economy, they do it in much more subtle ways. They can do it by the exercise of market power, charging high prices. They can use opaque pricing structures, as in the health care sector. They can engage in predatory lending, market manipulation, insider trading, or any one of the abusive practices that have become the hallmark of the financial sector (and which we discuss further in chapter 5).[9] A major form of "grabbing wealth" is corruption. In less developed countries, corruption might take the form of cash in plain white envelopes. In "corruption American style," it becomes much more sophisticated, such as passing laws that ensure that one gets overpaid for what one sells to the government (defense contractors and drug companies) or that one underpays for natural resources that rightfully belong to the public (oil and mining companies or timber firms using public lands).[10]

Alternatively, individuals can get wealthy by innovating, creating new products, and, during the short period before others imitate or add value through further innovation, making high profits. Such wealth creation adds to the size of the nation's economic pie. This is the sort of wealth creation that we need.

The exploitive way of getting wealthy is just wealth redistribution—often entailing taking money from the bottom of the pyramid and moving it to the top; and indeed, in the process, wealth is often actually destroyed. Our financiers did this through their predatory lending, abusive credit card practices, market manipulation, and insider trading. Later in this book, we'll see other ways that the rich have learned to exploit others.

Market power and the division of the national pie

Free-market economists like to describe the division of the national income pie as the working-out of impersonal market forces—akin to the forces in physics that determine our weight. No one seeks to repeal the law of gravity; and if the scale shows one is too heavy, one doesn't blame gravity, but only one's eating habits. But the laws of economics are different from those of physics: markets are shaped by public policy, and most markets are far from competitive. Public policy shapes, in particular, who has how much market power.

The advocates of free markets like to cite Adam Smith and his argument that in the pursuit of their own self-interest, individuals and firms are led as if by an invisible hand to the advancement of societal interest. They forget Smith's admonishment that "People of the same trade seldom meet together, even for merriment and diversion, but the conversation ends in a conspiracy against the public, or in some contrivance to raise prices."[11] It was the recognition of this ever-present danger that led Congress some 125 years ago to pass antitrust laws that forbade conspiracies to reduce competition and restricted anticompetitive practices.[12]

The national income pie can be thought of as being divided into labor income, the return to capital, and everything else. Most of the rest, economists refer to as "rents." Land rents are the most obvious example, but returns to natural resources, monopoly profits and returns to intellectual property (to patents and copyrights) also are considered as "rent." The big difference between, say, income from work and rents is this: if workers work more, the size of the national pie increases. In perfect markets, they get as a return to their increased efforts just what they have added to the national pie. By contrast, the owner of land or some other rent-producing asset gets paid simply because he owns the land or the asset. The supply of land can be fixed—nothing that the owner has done has added to the national pie—and yet he can receive a large income. What he receives is just money that otherwise would have gone to others. So too for a monopoly: when its power increases, the monopolist takes away more monopoly profits (or monopoly rents). Here, however, the national pie may at the same time shrink, because to exploit his market power, the monopolist limits production, to make the goods the monopoly produces more scarce.

Thus, at best, rents are unhelpful to growth and efficiency, at worst harmful. They can be harmful because they distort the economy, because they "crowd out" the kinds of "good" economic activity that is the basis of true wealth creation. We naturally describe the pursuit of higher incomes through acquiring more rents as *rent-seeking*. If talented individuals in society are attracted to rent-seeking—whether making more money through the exertion of monopoly power or scamming others in the financial sector or enticing them into gambling or other nefarious activities—then fewer talented individuals will be engaged in basic research, providing goods and services that individuals really want and need, and other activities that increase the real wealth of the nation. Moreover, if those who save for their retirement or for a bequest to their descendants invest in rent-producing assets like land, there will be a lower demand for new, truly productive assets, such as plants and equipment that enhance workers' productivities.

It follows that if one sees rents increasing, one should be worried, and especially so if the rent-generating activities are harmful, whether it's increased monopoly power or increased exploitation of ordinary consumers. And that's the story of the American economy today.

The diminishing share of labor and capital and the increased share of rents

A stark aspect of growing inequality is the diminution in the share of the national income that goes to workers (described in the previous chapter). But the share going to labor is also getting smaller.

The share of capital is the fraction of national income that goes to those who have saved and accumulated wealth in the form of, say, machines and buildings or intellectual property (sometimes referred to as intangible capital). While there is no clear data source to which we can easily turn, we can make inferences with considerable confidence. For instance, from national income data, we can trace the increase in the capital stock. Each year a country may invest more, but each year, some of the old capital wears out. We can thus estimate the net addition to the capital each year, and from that, the total amount of capital in the economy at any point in time.

To estimate the total "income of capital," we multiply this value of capital by its rate of return. Unfortunately, again, there is no simple source to which we can turn for the "rate of return on capital." Typical data series on *observed* returns confound the actual return to capital—to saving and investment—with returns to market power. Our objective here is to attempt to separate out the two. The logic is actually simple. We can easily ascertain the return on safe assets—the interest rate government has to pay on government bonds. The question is: What is the additional amount necessary to compensate for risk, i.e., the "risk premium?" The risk-free return on capital has decreased as a result of the increased global supply of savings from emerging countries like China, and has especially decreased with the advent of the 2008 crisis, when real interest rates (interest rates adjusted for inflation) around the world were pushed to zero or below. So too, overall the risk premium has been reduced as a result of improvements in the ability to manage risk.[13] Adding together the safe rate of return and the risk premium, we get the overall rate of return to capital, and with both components lower today than in earlier periods, the overall rate of return to capital is also lower. Multiplying the value of capital estimated earlier by the rate of return to capital yields the overall income of capital.

The ratio of income to capital, thus estimated, to national income has gone down significantly. Multiple studies have confirmed these findings, some taking a close look at the corporate sector, others focusing on manufacturing, others at the economy as a whole. [14]

If the share of labor income and the share of capital income have both gone down, it implies that the share of rents must have gone up—and significantly so. In the US, while there has been some increase in land and intellectual property rents, a big source of rent increase is in profits—profits in excess of what would have been earned in a competitive economy.[15]

Precisely the same results can be seen by looking at the problem in a different way. National wealth is the total value of a country's capital stock (described earlier, including plant, equipment, and commercial and residential real estate), land, intellectual property, and so forth. Studies have noted that in most advanced countries national wealth has increased far more than the increase in capital. Indeed, in some countries, including the US, the wealth–income ratio is increasing even as the capital–income ratio is decreasing.[16] The critical difference between wealth and the real value of the capital stock is the value of rent-generating assets. The value of these assets has increased enormously, even relative to GDP.[17]

As we look at the various sources of "rent wealth," we see that one large piece of the increase is the growth of excess profits derived from the exercise of market power. And a large piece of the increase in the capitalized value of profits is that of the hi-tech companies. Mordecai Kurz of Stanford University has recently shown that about 80 percent of the equity value of publicly listed firms is attributable to rents, representing almost a quarter of total value added, with much of this concentrated in the IT sector. All of this is a marked change from thirty years ago.[18]

Explaining the Increase in Market Power and Profits

This increase in profits should not come as a surprise. There are two sides of this coin: the power of workers has been eviscerated, with the weakening of unions and especially with globalization, described in the next chapter.[19] And in market after market, the number of competitors is falling or the fraction of sales that go to the top two or three firms is increasing, or both. There has been increasing market concentration[20]—a full 75 percent of industries witnessed increased concentration between 1997 and 2012[21]—and with this increasing market concentration comes increasing market power.[22] Firms have used this market power to increase prices relative to costs—what are called "markups."[23] This then translates into high profits. The result is that our large firms are seizing a larger and larger share of the national income pie and the profit rate of firms is reaching new highs, from an average of around 10 percent return to 16 percent in some recent years.[24] By one estimate, just twenty-eight firms in the S&P 500 contributed 50 percent of corporate profits in 2016, reflecting more concentration of market power today than in the past.[25]

Further evidence of increased market concentration and power

The evidence that our economy is becoming less competitive is all around us. Some is obvious: We see it in the limited choices we face for cable TV or the internet or telephone services. Three firms have an 89 percent market share in social networking sites, 87 percent in home improvement stores, 89 percent in pacemaker manufacturing, and 75 percent of the beer market; four firms have 97 percent of the dry cat food market, 85 percent of the jelly market, and 76 percent of domestic airlines revenue.[26] But the evidence exists too in little niches throughout the economy, in dog food, batteries, and coffins.[27] In some cases, market concentration may not be transparent: a single company owns a large fraction of pharmacies, but operates them under different names.

When there is one firm in an economy, we say there is a monopoly. When there are so many firms that none has any power to set price, we say there is perfect competition. With perfect competition, were a firm to charge even a small amount above the going price, its sales would drop to zero. In the real world, there is almost never a sufficiently large number of firms that the competitive model provides even a remote approximation of reality. On the other hand, there are few situations where a firm has no competitors. The real world is the murky area between perfect competition and pure monopoly. Even with a few competitors, firms can have some power over price. If they raise their prices over the costs of production, they lose some sales, but not much—it is still profitable for them to do so.[28] Typically, the fewer the competitors, the weaker the competition, and the higher prices relative to costs.[29] The power to sustain prices above costs reflects market power.

In response to criticisms of tech giants' market power, one hears the objection that while Google may dominate the online search market, it still must compete for advertising dollars with Facebook, and similarly, Apple must compete with Samsung in the smartphone market. In a market, power, as I have noted, is almost never absolute; it is always constrained. Yet it is absurd to pretend that there is not market power just because there is *some* competition. And so long as there is some market power, there is scope for exploitation and excess profits.[30]

MARKET POWER SHOWS up in ways other than just higher prices and profits—including the way companies treat their customers. Many, for instance, force their customers to forego the use of our public legal system for the adjudication of disputes—what should be the right of every individual in a democratic society—and instead use secretive arbitration panels that are stacked in favor of the companies.[31] Indeed, most of us have unwittingly signed away our rights when we accept a credit card, when we open up a bank account, when we sign up for the internet, or when we choose a telecom provider, with virtually all of them imposing similar provisions. The virtue of a competitive market economy is supposed to be that it gives one choice. In fact, in this and many other arenas, there is no effective choice.[32]

There are still other manifestations of the existence and depth of market power. In a competitive market, a firm can't charge different customers different prices for the same thing—price is determined by the (marginal) cost of production, not by the value the customer places on the good. Yet such price discrimination has become commonplace in our digital economy, as we discuss further in chapter 6.

Innovation in creating market power

There can be little doubt that there has been an increase in market power. The question then is why. I described earlier Warren Buffett's view that the best way to ensure sustained profits is for firms to surround themselves with moats that create barriers to entry, preventing profits from being eroded by the competition that new entrants would provide. Among the most profitable recent "innovations" in the United States are those enhancing the ability to create and widen these moats and the ability to exploit the subsequent market power.

In the standard economic model, creating a better product does not ensure sustained profits. Others may enter, and compete away those profits. When the dust settles, firms should only get the normal return on their capital, just the return required to compensate them for the use of their money and the risk they bear. There should be no *excess* returns. Not surprisingly, this is an outcome that firms don't like. So an essential part of the strategy of innovative firms is to create barriers to entry—what Warren Buffet called moats—so others won't come in and compete away their profits.

Firms like Microsoft led in the innovation of new forms of barriers to entry and clever ways of driving out existing competitors,
late twentieth-century advances building on the shoulders of anticompetitive giants that had gone before them. The saga of the 1990s
internet browser wars is instructive. At the time, Netscape was one
of the boldest innovators in the sector. Worried that the upstart company might somehow impinge on its near monopoly on operating
systems for personal computers, Microsoft sought to drive it out. The
firm developed what many thought was an inferior product, Internet
Explorer. Internet Explorer couldn't really win on its merits, but with
its existing power in the market of operating systems for personal computers, Microsoft could muscle it into almost every personal computer
in America. It bundled its browser with its operating system, giving it
away for free. How could one compete with a browser provided at a
zero price? But this measure proved insufficient, so Microsoft created
what was called FUD—fear, uncertainty, and doubt—about whether
there would be interoperability problems with Netscape. Warnings
to users made them worry that installing Netscape would hurt the
functioning of their computer.[33] Through these and other anticompetitive practices, Microsoft drove out Netscape. By the beginning of
the twenty-first century, Netscape had fallen almost completely out
of use. Even after Microsoft's anticompetitive practices were barred
by authorities on three continents, its dominance continued, until
eventually, new entrants (such as Google and Firefox) broke into the
browser market.

Today, it is the new tech giants that abuse market power, with
European competition authorities repeatedly finding that companies
like Google have engaged in anticompetitive practices, first in favoring its own services in internet searches, and then in abusing its power
in the mobile phone market, with the EU levying record-setting fines
in the two cases of $2.8 billion and $5.1 billion, respectively.

Abusing the patent system is another avenue for reducing competition. Patents are a temporary barrier to entry. No one can produce a product that is identical to a patented good. When most Americans think of how patents are supposed to be used, they may imagine the small-time inventor who gets legal protection in order to prevent big companies from stealing her idea. These days, the situation is not nearly as simple, and patents have often become an effective barrier to entry. Many innovations today require hundreds, if not thousands, of patents. And as a firm creates a new product (say, a new chip) there is a risk of unwittingly intruding on one of a myriad of patents. Only a large firm would have the resources to research all the existing patents. Moreover, large firms often do deals with each other, allowing them to share each other's patents, knowing that otherwise they would be mired down in never-ending litigation. But this presents real problems for a new entrant. New entrants are not part of this club. They know that there is a real risk of being sued no matter what they do and how innovative or careful they are. They don't have the financial resources to win in court. Many potential innovators are no doubt discouraged from even trying, as they consider the threat of expensive lawsuits that would bankrupt them even if they have little merit.[34] Even the threat of a patent suit can send chills down the spine of a young innovator.

A quick search of "patent infringement" shows numerous cases, in the hundreds of millions of dollars, between Qualcomm and Apple, Apple and Samsung, and so forth. The only sure winners in all of these suits are the lawyers; the only sure losers are consumers and small firms unable to enter the fray. Such is American-style capitalism in the twenty-first century.

Our "innovative" firms do not rest their anticompetitive practices there. They have pioneered new contractual arrangements to leverage their market power. In credit cards, these new contractual forms do not allow, for instance, stores to charge customers who use credit cards with high rewards—and high merchant fees—for the use of these high-cost credit cards. Credit card companies have effectively short-circuited price competition.[35] The lack of competition means that the dominant firms (Visa, MasterCard, and American Express) can charge merchants fees that are a multiple of the costs of providing the service.[36] Of course, these costs eventually get passed on in the prices of the goods and services that individuals buy with these cards, so even when the credit cards provide rewards, it's not even obvious that the credit card customers are better off. But this does mean that those who pay cash and therefore can't avail themselves of the rebates provided by the credit cards wind up subsidizing high-income individuals who use premium credit cards, including American Express.[37] As a portion of the cost of a transaction, 1, 2, or 3 percent may seem small, but multiplied by the trillions of dollars of transactions, it amounts to tens of billions of dollars—money that goes directly from the pockets of consumers into the coffers of the financial institutions.[38]

Each industry has exhibited creativity in finding its own way to maintain market power. Our pharmaceutical companies have been particularly innovative in keeping out generic firms, which lower prices and hence Big Pharma's profits. They used to just bribe the generics not to enter, but that was rightly found to violate the antitrust laws.[39] They have found ways of effectively extending the life of the patent—a practice called evergreening.[40]

Still another example of creativity in maintaining market power has been especially employed by the new tech giants: preemptive mergers—buying potential competitors before they could be a competitive threat and before an acquisition would receive careful scrutiny by the government for reducing competition. These young entrepreneurs are willing to cash in, often for a large amount beyond their wildest dreams, rather than take the risk of getting into a battle with Google or Facebook.[41]

Further reasons for the increase in market power

There are multiple other reasons for the increase in market power, besides the innovativeness of our corporate sector in figuring out how to create and maintain that power. Some of the increase in market power is just the result of the evolution of our economy. This includes a shift in demand to segments where local market power, based on local reputation, is significant. There may be only one Ford dealer in an area, or one John Deere tractor servicing agent. To the extent that customers take their vehicles or tractors back to the dealer for servicing, this provides a kind of local market power from which companies like John Deere derive much of their profits even if competition has driven profits and prices down on the manufacturing part of their business.

So too, industries in which there is what is called a "natural" monopoly are attaining increasing importance. Natural monopolies arise when there is some cost savings from having a single firm dominate a market, for instance in situations where average costs are lowered with the scale of production.[42] In any locale, it pays to have only one company supplying electricity or water. A hundred years ago, many of the key industries like steel and automobiles were dominated by just a few behemoth firms. Competition was limited because entrants simply couldn't reach the scale required to get costs down. But globalization has expanded the scale of the market so much that even though it's hard to be, say, a competitive auto producer making fewer than several hundred thousand cars, the global market is so big that there are still many firms that can reach the requisite scale.[43]

Today, it's in the "new economy" that competition is limited. In much of the new innovative economy, the basic cost is the up-front research and development. The extra cost of serving an additional customer is nil.[44]

Changing the rules of the game

Much of the increase in market power, however, arises from changing the implicit rules of the game. Among the important rules are those designed to make sure that markets remain competitive, the antitrust laws referred to earlier. New, lower antitrust standards have made the creation, abuse, and leveraging of market power easier.[45] And our antitrust laws haven't kept up with the changing economy.

Lax enforcement of existing rules plays a role, too[46]—a record low number of antitrust cases was brought to trial during the administration of President George W. Bush, and Obama did little better. In 2015, mergers and acquisitions—firms getting together to get ever bigger and more powerful—reached an all-time high of $4.7 trillion—and though not all of these harmed competition, many did. Inadequate competition policy allows those with some market power, like Google, Facebook, and Amazon, to leverage that power, enhancing it, extending its reach, and making it more durable.

Growth and Market Power

It's easy to see how market power leads to more inequality. But it also plays a role in the economy's slow growth and poor economic performance. Monopoly power is, of course, a distortion of the market system—it leads to a less efficient economy.[47] Recent estimates by David Baqaee of the London School of Economics and Political Science and Emmanuel Farhi of Harvard show just how large is the cost to the economy—eliminating the markups to which lack of competition gives rise would increase the productivity of the US economy by about 40 percent.[48]

The creation of barriers to entry is an integral part of market power. By contrast, a dynamic competitive economy is marked by the entry (and exit) of firms, with the fraction of new firms typically high.

The percentage of firms in the American economy that are young is much lower than in many other countries, well outpaced both by "old Europe" (e.g., Spain, Sweden, and Germany) and newly emerging countries like Brazil, and lower than it was in our past. This is consistent with the view of an economy where competition is in decline, and where successful firms manage to construct large entry barriers—surrounding themselves with large and deep moats.[49]

The marked increase in market power hurts productivity of the economy. But it also can have significant effects on consumer demand. As money moves from the bottom of the economic pyramid to the top, aggregate consumption is lowered simply because those at the top consume a smaller fraction of their income than those below, who have to spend virtually all of their income just to get by.

Moreover, investment is weakened, because the *extra* return from producing additional output is lowered as monopoly power increases. With monopolies, as more is produced, prices have to be decreased, so the increase in profits can be far less than in competitive markets, where prices are essentially unaffected by any given firm's level of production. This helps explain an anomaly in recent years: while profit rates have been very high, investment rates (as a share of GDP) have fallen from 17.2 percent in the 1960s and 1970s to an average of 15.7 percent from 2008 to 2017. And this lowered private investment bodes poorly for future growth.[50]

There is a further effect that has already been noted: innovation that should be directed at creating more efficient ways of producing better products is instead directed at better ways of creating and maintaining market power and exploiting consumers. While our financial firms have excelled in the latter arena, they are not alone, as Nobel Prize winners George Akerlof and Robert Shiller demonstrate forcefully in their 2015 book *Phishing for Phools: The Economics of Manipulation and Deception.*[51] We've described, for instance, how our cigarette, pharmaceutical, and food companies have profited from producing products that are addictive, and not only not needed, but are also actually harmful.

We used to think that high profits were a sign of the successful working of the American economy, a better product, a better service. But now we know that higher profits can also arise from a better way of exploiting consumers, a better way of price discrimination, extracting "consumer surplus" (the excess of what individuals would be willing to pay for a product from what he would have to pay in a competitive market). The main effect of such exploitation is to redistribute income from consumers to our new super-wealthy and the firms they own and control.

Workers' Weakened Market Power

Firms' exploitation of market power is but half the story. We now face an increased problem of monopsony power, the ability of firms to use their market power over those from whom they buy goods and services, and in particular, over workers.[52] Monopsony refers to a situation where there is a single buyer in a market, or a single employer. Just as there are few markets where there is a single seller (a monopoly), there are few markets where there is a single buyer. When we referred earlier to monopoly power, we meant that firms had *significant* market power, enough that they could profitably raise price well above the competitive level. We argued earlier in this book that changes in the economy had led to an increase in market power, at least in many important sectors of the economy. Similarly here: what we are concerned with is the diminution of workers' bargaining power, and with that their wages.

The standard competitive model has "atomistic" labor markets where wages are set to match the demand for labor with its supply. No one has market power. A worker's quitting has no consequence on the firm—it just reaches into the labor market to find an identical worker at the same wage; and more importantly, a worker's being fired has no consequences for the worker, who just finds an equivalent job at the same wage.

But this is not the world we live in. The firm can easily find a replacement worker, perhaps not quite as good, but almost. On the other hand, the worker is typically unable to quickly and easily find an alternative equivalent job, especially when the unemployment rate is high. If there is a job available, it may be in another city, requiring the individual to move. The disruption is costly to the worker and his family. Any long period without a job is simply not an option. There are mortgage, car and other large payments due every month. In short, there is a huge asymmetry of market power in favor the employer.[53]

JUST AS MARKET POWER in the product market (the market for goods and services) allows firms to raise prices from what they otherwise would be, and well over the cost of production, in labor markets, market power enables firms to push wages below what they would otherwise be.

WHILE IT'S ILLEGAL to do so, many of our leading firms have gotten together, usually in secret, to keep wages low; and it is only through litigation that these misdeeds have been brought to light. Under Steve Jobs, Apple got together with Google, Intel, and Adobe to agree not to "poach" each others' employees—that is, they agreed not to compete. The affected workers sued against this anticompetitive conspiracy; the suit was settled for $415 million. Disney and a host of film studios similarly paid a huge settlement in a lawsuit charging them with an illegal antipoaching conspiracy. Even fast food franchise agreements have antipoaching provisions. Competition, they knew, would drive up wages. Many contracts have restrictions on an individual accepting a job from a competitor, the effect of which too is to reduce competition and wages.[54]

Just as Adam Smith was well aware of the dangers of firms colluding to raise prices, he was concerned about their getting together to suppress wages[55]:

> Masters are always and everywhere in a sort of tacit, but constant and uniform, combination, not to raise the wages of labour above their actual rate [. . .] Masters, too, sometimes enter into particular combinations to sink the wages of labour even below this rate. These are always conducted with the utmost silence and secrecy.

He seems to have fully anticipated the actions of our twenty-first-century business leaders, whether it's in Silicon Valley or in Hollywood.

Further evidence of employer market power

We see evidence of employer market power every day, with employers forcing workers to work split shifts (four hours in the morning, three hours off, and four hours in the evening); or giving them opportunities only for part-time employment when they would like to work full time, just so they won't have health benefits; or moving around their schedules from week to week, notifying them only at the end of the previous week (called on-call scheduling). We see evidence of employer market power in the demands they impose on workers to work overtime—often without paying overtime rates.[56] These employer policies wreak havoc with family life, and make the individual feel powerless.[57]

A variety of changes in institutions (the weakening of unions[58]), rules, norms, and practices have weakened workers' bargaining power. For instance, when unions negotiate a better deal for workers, all the workers in a factory benefit—including those who don't belong to the union. But some workers would like to "free ride," to enjoy the benefits of the union without paying for them. That's why unions often negotiate what are called "union shops," requiring all workers to contribute to support the unions. All can then participate in voting, for instance, on what should be the union bargaining position, on what is most important to workers.

Companies naturally want to get workers as cheaply as possible, and thus don't like unions. They want to be able to fire and lay off workers at will—ensuring a docile work place and forcing workers to bear the costs of economic fluctuations. They know that any single worker has no bargaining power in dealing with the firm and its management; but workers collectively may have bargaining power.[59] So it is natural that employers want to weaken unions in any way they can. An easy way of weakening unions is to make it more difficult for them to collect dues—encouraging workers to free ride, to enjoy the benefits of the union such as the higher wages without contributing to its support. And of course, without resources, the unions will be less effective in getting what workers want and need. Thus, in many states companies have turned to government to outlaw union shops in what are called right-to-work laws, but are more aptly called right-to-free-ride laws. [60]

The weakening of unions has not only led to lower wages for workers[61] but also eliminated the ability of unions to curb management abuses within the firm, including managers paying themselves exorbitant salaries at the expense not only of workers but of investment in the firm, thereby jeopardizing its future. What John K. Galbraith had described in the middle of the twentieth century as an economy based on countervailing power has become an economy based on the dominance of large corporations and financial institutions—and even more, of the power of the CEOs and the other executives within the corporation.[62]

Curbing Market Power: Updating Antitrust Laws for the Twenty-First Century

In the late nineteenth century, the United States faced a situation similar to that of today with growing market power and increasing inequality. Congress responded by passing a slew of laws to limit market power and its abuse. It passed the Sherman Antitrust Act in 1890. This was followed in the next twenty-five years by other legislation trying to ensure competition in the market place. Importantly, these laws were based on the belief that concentrations of economic power would inevitably lead to concentrations in political power. Antitrust policy was not based on finely honed economic analysis. It was really about the nature of our society and democracy.[63]

For a while, antitrust laws worked. Big monopolies were broken up. Mergers that would have resulted in new monopolies were constrained. But in the ensuing decades, antitrust was taken over by an army of lawyers and conservative economists who narrowed the scope of antitrust. They weren't concerned with the broader consequences of market power either for our economy or our democracy. They simply wanted to give free rein to corporate and business interests.

Some academic economists tried to provide an intellectual defense for this pure power grab. At the University of Chicago, Milton Friedman gathered around himself a group of economists who argued that one didn't need to worry about monopoly because economies were naturally competitive.[64] In an innovative economy, monopoly power would be temporary, and the contest to become the monopolist spurred innovation and consumer welfare.[65] Their central precept was that government was bad and the private sector was good. Government attempts to interfere with the wonderful workings of the market—even curbing monopolies—were both unnecessary and likely to be counterproductive. Thus, enforcers of antitrust laws worried more about the downside risk of finding a practice noncompetitive when it was really a reflection of the complex ways in which efficient markets often worked than about the risk of allowing a non-competitive practice to persist.[66]

The Chicago School had a disproportionate influence on our politics and our courts. It led to the weakening of antitrust, as courts simply assumed that markets were competitive and efficient, and any behavior that might seem anticompetitive was in fact nothing more than efficient responses to new market complexities. Enormous burdens of proof were placed on anyone trying to claim that a firm had engaged in anticompetitive practices. As one former member of the staff of the Federal Trade Commission (the government agency charged with ensuring a competitive marketplace) put it: "We have to devote all of our energies to proving that water is wet, so that we don't have any resources to attack the real problems in competition."

Take one common form of anticompetitive behavior, called predatory pricing. A large, well-heeled dominant firm lowers prices or takes other actions to drive out its rivals. It loses money in the short run, but more than makes up for it in the long. After the entry of an upstart new airline, American Airlines would increase capacity and lower prices on some route that it would want to dominate. It typically didn't take too long before the upstart cried "uncle" and left. Once gone, capacity was reduced and prices increased. It was a smart move, called "predation."

In the "Chicago" theory, any attempt to raise prices above costs would instantaneously be met by an onslaught of new firm entry (so it was claimed). Accordingly, it would never pay for a firm to engage in predatory pricing because it would never be able to recoup its initial losses by setting prices at a higher-than-competitive level. Courts, buying into the Chicago doctrines, placed a heavy burden of proof on those who claimed that a firm was engaged in predation, so heavy that it became almost impossible to successfully bring a predatory pricing case.[67]

What is needed now is a change in these *presumptions*, with their associated burdens of proof, based on the hypothesis that markets are fundamentally competitive. Anticompetitive practices—actions that reduce competition in the market—should be presumed to be illegal, unless there is strong evidence that (a) there are significant efficiency gains and that a significant proportion of the benefits of these efficiency gains accrue to others than the firm and (b) these efficiency gains could not be achieved in a less anticompetitive manner.[68] We discuss a number of other changes in presumptions below.

Government will also have to be more active in resorting to a broader range of tools, not just limiting mergers and enjoining certain anticompetitive practices. It's been a long time since the government broke up a dominant firm like Standard Oil, but perhaps it's time to look at whether Facebook should divest itself of Instagram and WhatsApp. Mergers that lead to major conflicts of interest should be prohibited (as when an internet provider acquires a firm creating entertainment content), and if they've already been allowed, there should again be divestiture. Similarly, firms with market power should be proscribed from entering business activities where there is a conflict of interest with their existing customers.[69] These new policies are sometimes referred to as structural reforms.

As we noted above, the effects of market power, once established, can be long-lived, so until a competitive marketplace is restored, government may need to regulate, to ensure that there is no abuse of market power. The Durbin Amendment to the Dodd-Frank financial regulation bill, for instance, gave the Federal Reserve Board authority to regulate the fees debit cards charged to merchants, though it left the even higher fees that credit cards charge unregulated.[70]

Checking market power however it arises

What is needed then is a renewed commitment to constraining excesses of market power, wherever they exist and however they arise, to try to restore competition in the economy. It should be a violation of antitrust laws to engage in the abuse of market power, no matter how acquired. Anticompetitive practices, whether arising from monopsony or monopoly power, should be outlawed, period.

In the United States, a firm that gained its market dominance legitimately, without engaging in anticompetitive practices, has great latitude in its use of its market power—not just imposing higher prices but imposing anticompetitive contracts. By contrast, in Europe, such a firm can still be accused of abuse of market power.

Valeant, a major drug company, the only FDA-approved manufacturer of the out-of-patent drug Syprine, a life-saving drug for those with a rare liver condition called Wilson's disease, used its market power in 2015 to raise prices of a pill which sells for a dollar in some countries so that a year's supply cost $300,000.[71] This is but one item on a long list of abuses in this sector alone.[72]

Standard antitrust doctrine, as it has evolved, typically focuses on consumers, with a short-term perspective, and, as we have noted, with a strong presumption that markets are naturally competitive. Thus, as courts have viewed predatory actions, driving out competitors to establish a dominant position on the basis of which firms can raise prices, they have looked at the short-term benefits of lower consumer prices, with little concern about the long-term harm.

This short-term consumer perspective also runs into problems when it comes to monopsony. Walmart's size gives it such clout that it can drive down the prices it pays to suppliers. Especially in those places in the US where there is high unemployment and few employers, it has the power to set its wages and working conditions at levels below what they would be in a competitive economy. It's bad for the economy, even if Walmart shares some of the gains from its market (monopsony) power with its customers. Thus, looking at market power only through the eyes of the impact on consumers is wrong. Walmart is distorting the economy in its ruthless quest for profits; and what it gains (including what it shares with its customers) is less than what the rest of the economy loses.

Mergers

Our evolving economy has led to other challenges to standard anti-trust practice. Traditionally, antitrust laws have focused on the creation of market power through mergers and acquisitions. But in sector after sector, mergers have been allowed even as market concentration has reached dangerous levels—airlines and telecom provide good illustrations—suggesting that the restraints need to be tightened.

Firms claim, of course, that the mergers and acquisitions that they propose will benefit the economy as a result of economies of scale and scope—larger firms are more productive, so they allege. But the real reason for many mergers—both horizontal (among firms in competing lines of business) and vertical (where a firm merges with a supplier or customer of its service) is enhancing market power. Firms should be required to present more compelling cases for the efficiency gains from a proposed merger. If prices of goods go up after the merger, this is a red flag that what's driving the merger is the increase in market power.[73]

Conflicts of interest that arise with mergers also need to be looked at with greater circumspection: when, for instance, an internet company merges with a provider of online entertainment, one would expect that it would use its market power in the internet to give itself advantages over competing entertainment providers, even if it promises to be "neutral." We will have a more dynamic and competitive economy if we proscribe such mergers that give rise to inherent conflicts of interest; the claimed gains in static efficiency are dwarfed by the long-run anticompetitive effects.[74]

Further, regulation of mergers must take into account the likely future shape of markets. Today, mergers are only prevented when there is a significant decrease of competition *in the market as it exists today.* But in a dynamic sector, what matters is the effect of the merger in the market as it is likely to evolve. The tech giants understand the rules, and have been gaming the system. They engage in what we referred to earlier as preemptive mergers, acquiring firms while they are still small enough to pass antitrust scrutiny, thereby eliminating future challenges to their dominance. Facebook acquired Instagram (for $1 billion in 2012) and WhatsApp (for $19 billion in 2015—more than $40 per user of the platform). Facebook had the technical know-how to build analogous platforms. If it didn't, it could have hired engineers who did. There was really only one reason that it was willing to pay so much—to forestall competition.

Such preemptive mergers need to be forbidden. A merger that has a reasonable chance of reducing competition in the foreseeable future should be prohibited.[75]

New technologies and new challenges

Even if there had been nothing wrong with antitrust law as it evolved in the second half of the twentieth century, it is clear that it has not been able to keep up with the challenges posed by our evolving economy, the new technologies, the new contracts, and the new innovations in creating and extending market power.

We now understand better, for instance, how a range of practices and contract provisions undermine competition: a guarantee by a dominant firm that it will meet the price of any competitor undermines entry—an entrant knows that he can't win. Earlier, we discussed several provisions in labor contracts that undermine competition for workers.[76] Arbitration clauses inhibit both workers and customers getting adequate redress for exploitive behavior. Contracts between merchants and credit card companies and between airlines and the computer reservation systems undermined competition and led to exorbitant profits. All of these should be seen for what they are—anticompetitive—and outlawed.

The tech giants know how to wield their power in many arenas.[77] Amazon used the enticement of thousands of jobs to get cities across the country bidding to have it set up its second headquarters in those cities through, for instance, lower taxes—shifting the tax burden onto others, of course. Small firms can't do this, and so it gives an enormous advantage to Amazon over local retailers. We need a legal framework that prevents these races to the bottom.[78]

Intellectual property rights and competition

There is one area where government sanctions monopolies: when a patent is given, the innovator gets temporary monopoly power. As we move to a knowledge-based economy, intellectual property rights (IPR) are likely to play an increasing role.

The monopoly power means that knowledge is not being used efficiently and prices are higher than they otherwise would be. A well-designed IPR regime balances these large costs with dynamic benefits arising from the incentives for innovation that it is supposed to provide. But in recent years, that balance has been upset, as corporations have successfully lobbied for changes in IPR providing corporations increasing market power—so much so that now, it is even questionable whether America's IPR regime stimulates or stifles innovation.[79] An obvious example is the extension of the life of copyright. There is no evidence of any innovative benefit of the extension to seventy years beyond the death of the author. This provision in the Copyright Term Extension Act of 1998 was called the "Mickey Mouse" provision—it was supported heavily by Disney, which controlled the copyright to Mickey Mouse—but beyond that, there was no societal benefit, and considerable cost in terms of the free flow of knowledge.[80]

In fact, there is evidence that our current IPR regime not only leads to high prices but also stifles innovation. When the Supreme Court ruled that one could not patent naturally occurring genes, the consequences were dramatic: the tests for a critical gene related to breast cancer, which previously had been patented, quickly became much cheaper and much better.[81]

Historically, antitrust authorities have been sensitive to the power of patents to create, amplify, and increase the duration of market power. In 1956 they forced AT&T to put its patents into a pool, accessible by others. One of the proposals put forward to curb Microsoft's monopoly power was to limit the life of its patents.[82] Curtailing intellectual property rights in these ways can not only increase competition but also innovation.

Broadening the reach of antitrust: Market power beyond products—the marketplace of ideas

When considering market concentration, media is a sector that deserves special consideration.[83] Traditionally, the effect of media concentration has simply been measured by market power in often narrowly defined advertising markets. Mergers across media (between television stations and newspapers) leading to markedly reduced access to different viewpoints have been allowed to go forth simply because there is competition in the "relevant" market for advertising. This is wrong. In no arena is competition more important than in the marketplace for ideas. A well-informed citizenry is essential for a well-functioning democracy.[84] A media that is controlled by only a few companies or wealthy individuals will result in their views dominating the national discourse.

Yet a large share of the electorate get their political information from a small number of news sources, typically television networks. Today, in too many communities across the country, an extreme conservative perspective dominates the media.[85]

Competition does make a difference. An alternative newspaper in a city can keep both the city council and the dominant newspaper in check. Moreover, a consolidated media is easy to capture by wealthy individuals. Accordingly, media company mergers and abuses of market power need to be held to an even higher standard than those in other sectors.[86]

A particularly invidious example of market power is the oligopoly in academic publishing. Chapter 1 highlighted the central role of knowledge in increases in our well-being. Advances in knowledge, in turn, require the dissemination of ideas. But in our market-based economy, this has been entrusted largely to the market, and the form that has taken is a highly concentrated and highly profitable oligopoly, with some five publishers accounting for more than half of all papers published, and for 70 percent of those in the social sciences. The irony is that the publishers get the articles for free (in some cases, they even get paid to publish them), the research reported is typically funded by the government, the publishers get academics to do most of the editorial work (the review of the articles) for free, and educational institutions and libraries (largely government-funded) then pay the publishers. Their high prices and excess profits, of course, mean that there is less money to fund research.[87]

Conclusions

The idea that markets are a powerful way of organizing the production of goods and services has been deeply influential. It has provided the intellectual underpinnings of capitalism. But two centuries of research have now brought us to a better understanding of why Adam Smith's invisible hand can't be seen: because it's not there.[88] More often than not, firms' incentives are to create market power, not just better products—and we've seen that American firms have excelled in doing so. They've used this market power to exploit their consumers, their workers, and the political system, in ways that have resulted in lower growth, even in a supposedly innovative economy. Even worse, this growth benefits only a fraction of the country. Indeed, our corporate leaders have even figured out how to exploit their own shareholders, taking advantage of deficiencies in our rules of corporate governance to pay themselves outsized compensation.[89]

Our economy has changed a great deal since our antitrust laws were first introduced and even since the Chicago School interpretations came to prevail; our understanding of economics has changed too; and today we can better grasp the failures of the existing legal framework. But the underlying political and economic concerns about power and exploitation that drove the original legislation are still present—even more so. Competition law has been excessively narrowed, and excessively influenced by presumptions concerning a competitive marketplace. Today, our competition laws and antitrust practices need to be reformed, to incorporate the realities of the twenty-first century and the insights of modern economics.

Curbing market power, however, is about more than just economics—about the power to raise prices or lower wages, or to exploit in other ways consumers and workers. Market power, as we have repeatedly seen, gets translated into political power: one cannot have a true democracy with the kinds of large concentrations of market power and wealth that mark the US today.[90] But there is a broader societal consequence: the flip side of power is *powerlessness*. Too many Americans feel powerless against their health insurance company, their internet provider, the airlines they travel on, their telephone company, their bank. And they resent it. It has deep consequences for them as individuals, for our politics and for every aspect of our society.[91] In so many areas they have no choice: for instance, as employees or customers of their banks, they have no choice but to sign away their rights to a public trial in the case of a dispute; as we have seen, they have to accept a business-friendly arbitrator.

This chapter has shown that there are easy ways of curtailing market power. We've focused our discussion on how to make the markets for goods and services more competitive. There are also important changes required in our legal framework to curb the power firms have over workers—most importantly, by facilitating workers acting together to advance their interests. So too, when firms exploit consumers, as they so often do, there need to be better ways by which they can act together to seek redress—just the opposite of what has been happening as courts and Congress have narrowed the scope for class action suits.[92] We also need to curb the power corporate leaders have to advance their own interests at the expense of the other stakeholders in the future of the corporation, including shareholders, workers, and the communities in which the firm operates.[93] Measures to achieve this include greater transparency and more voice in decision making.[94]

In all these reforms, we seek not perfection, but to curb the extremes of twenty-first-century American capitalism. Presidents Carter and Reagan, and those following, rewrote the rules of capitalism in ways that led to a more unstable, less efficient, and more unequal economy—and an economy marked by pervasive market power.[95] The time is ripe to rewrite those rules once again. Doing that is a challenge because it entails politics, and our economic inequality has been translated into political inequality. We turn to that in Part II. But first, we take a closer look at how the globalization and financialization of our economy has contributed to the creation of market power and exploitation—and how changes in technology may make matters still worse.

CHAPTER 4

America at War with Itself over Globalization

Globalization sits at the center of America's economic crisis. On one side, critics of globalization blame it for the plight of America's suffering middle class. According to President Trump, our trade negotiators got snookered by those smart negotiators from other countries. We signed bad trade deals that led to the loss of American industrial jobs.[1] This criticism of globalization has found enormous resonance, especially in the parts of the country that experienced deindustrialization.

By contrast, globalization's advocates claim that all of this is sheer nonsense. America has benefited from globalization. Protectionist policies put at risk all that has been gained through trade. In the end, they say, protectionism will not help even those who've lost their jobs due to globalization or seen their wages collapse. They, the US, and the entire world will be worse off. Globalization's advocates shift the blame for deindustrialization and the American malaise elsewhere: the real source of job loss and low wages for unskilled workers has been improved technology, and globalization is getting a bum rap.

For more than twenty years, I've been criticizing the way that globalization has been managed—but from a completely different angle.

From my perch as chief economist at the World Bank, it was obvious that the global rules of the game were tilted—not against, but in *favor* of the United States and other advanced countries at the expense of developing countries. The trade agreements were unfair—to the benefit of the US and Europe and to the detriment of developing countries.

The idea that our trade negotiators got snookered is laughable: we got almost everything we wanted in late-twentieth-century trade negotiations.[2] Over the opposition of those from developing countries, we secured strong intellectual property protections—which protected the intellectual property of the advanced countries, but not that of developing countries. We've succeeded in forcing countries to open up their markets to our financial firms—and even to accept those highly risky derivatives and other financial products that played a central role in our own financial collapse.

It's true that American workers have been disadvantaged—low-skilled workers in particular have seen their wages reduced, in part because of globalization. But that is partly because American negotiators got what they asked for: the problem was with how we managed globalization and with what we wanted—trade agreements simply advanced corporate interests at the expense of workers in both developed and developing countries. We as a country didn't do what we should have to help workers whom globalization was hurting. We could have ensured that globalization benefited all, but corporate greed was just too great. The winners didn't want to share their gains with the losers. Indeed, they liked it that wages were pressured down as American workers had to compete with workers from developing countries. It increased corporate profits all the more.

It might seem that President Trump and I are on the same side of this battle against globalization, but that is wrong. Fundamentally, I believe in the importance of the rule of law—of a rules-based system for governing international trade. Just as we need a rule of law within our economy—without that, no society can function—so too, we need a rules-based international system.[3] Trump, by contrast, wants to return to the rule of the jungle: when there is a trade dispute between two countries, they "duke it out," and the stronger country wins. His misguided view is that since we are stronger than any single country we would win all of these battles, and we could then create an international trade regime that is a maidservant to US interests. He misses two critical points: why would anyone else join such a system, to be taken advantage of, rather than focus on trading and other economic relations with partners that behave and treat others decently? And other countries can, and would, get together, and while we're not much different in economic size than China and Europe (though within a short while China is slated to be more than 30 percent larger than the US), if the other two got together against us—or any of the other two are joined by large numbers in the "third world"—our seeming power advantage would quickly disappear.

TRUMP IS WRONG to blame globalization, whether unfair trade rules or unwanted immigrants, for the country's woes, but globalization's advocates are also wrong in arguing that globalization has played no role in the plight of the large parts of the population that have seen their incomes stagnate or decline, and that it's just technological progress that's to blame. The real onus of blame, though, should be on ourselves: we mismanaged the consequences both of globalization and of technological progress. If we had managed these well, both could have generated the blessing that their advocates claimed.

WE NEED BETTER, fairer international rules. But what America needs most is better management of the changes being brought about both by globalization and technology. There is an alternative—the progressive agenda that I lay out later in this book.

THIS CHAPTER DESCRIBES briefly why globalization hasn't lived up to its promises, and why President Trump has only made matters worse. I sketch out an alternative globalization, which will work better both for the rich countries and the poor and especially for workers in both—but not necessarily for the large multinationals who've taken over the globalization agenda.

The Pain of Globalization

Globalization has affected both jobs and wages. It's simplest to see its effects on low-skilled workers. When an advanced country like the US imports low-skilled, labor-intensive goods, the demand for low-skilled labor in the US falls, simply because we produce less of those goods here. If there is to be full employment, wages for low-skilled workers—adjusted for inflation—have to fall.[4] And if wages don't fall enough, unemployment increases. It's really that simple. Anybody who believes in the law of supply and demand should understand why globalization (in the absence of government programs to ameliorate its effects) hurts low-skilled workers.

The same goes for labor more generally: the US imports labor-intensive goods, and thus trade liberalization (opening up US markets to foreign goods by reducing tariffs or other trade barriers) reduces the overall demand for labor, and thereby also reduces (real) wages in equilibrium. Again, if wages don't fall, employment will.

Trade advocates similarly stress that trade increases the country's GDP, as it takes advantage of its comparative advantage (whether a result of specialization or resource endowments), and somehow, mystically, everyone will be better off—another instance of the belief in trickle-down economics. Even if the country as a whole is better off, it just means that everyone *could* be better off; the winners could share their gains with the losers so all would benefit; but it doesn't mean they *will* share their gains—and in selfish capitalism American-style, they don't.

Moreover, advocates of globalization emphasize how exports create jobs, but they fail to mention the number of jobs destroyed by imports. If trade is roughly balanced, and if imports are more labor-intensive than exports, then overall, trade destroys jobs.

If monetary policy responds by lowering interest rates, and the lower interest rates increase investment or consumption, full employment might be restored. But sometimes monetary policy doesn't work, or at least work well enough to achieve full employment. That helps explain why after the admission of China to the WTO in 2001, American unemployment increased and wages fell in those places that produced goods that were competitive with things being imported in growing volume from China.[5]

Even when monetary and fiscal policy work to return the economy *eventually* to full employment, globalization often leads to job destruction in the short run, as the loss of jobs from an onslaught of imports occurs faster than job creation from additional exports, especially when banks aren't lending much to new enterprises seeking to take advantage of the new opportunities offered, say, by a new trade agreement.[6]

Moreover, trade agreements and tax laws have effectively encouraged firms to move manufacturing abroad, destroying jobs at home. Not only are taxes lower, but also our trade agreements typically give American firms more secure property rights abroad than they have at home.[7] Such agreements typically protect firms against changes in regulations—protections that they do not have in the United States. If a changed regulation hurts a firm's bottom line, today or in the future, under the provisions of standard investment agreements, it can sue, and the suit will be heard by a corporate-friendly arbitration panel.[8] Historically, one of the reasons that firms located in the US as opposed to a developing country, where wages are so much lower, was that they felt "more secure." The government wouldn't just take away their property on a whim. Security of property rights has been one of the country's strengths. These trade agreements changed that, however. An American investor putting his money into Mexico or some other country covered by similar provisions is *more* protected: not only can't the foreign government take away his property without compensating him, but it also can't even change a regulation. In contrast, the US government can change regulations without providing any compensation. The US thus gave away its crucial institutional advantage arising from its rule of law and the security of property rights.

Why would a country so readily give away so much of its comparative advantage? The corporations demanded these provisions because they were in the corporations' *short-term interests.* These provisions gave them not only cheaper labor abroad but also at home, because they weakened workers' bargaining power. The threat of firms moving abroad became all the more credible. If corporations wanted to weaken workers' bargaining power, they couldn't have chosen a better way of doing so.[9]

Globalization hurt ordinary Americans in another way—depriving the country of tax revenues. Corporations were successful in ensuring that their profits wouldn't be taxed twice—in foreign countries where they operate and in the United States. But nothing was done to ensure that they would be taxed at least once. Globalization provided a way by which corporations could game countries against each other. Corporations persuaded governments that, unless they lower the corporate tax rate, they will relocate abroad. There are some footloose firms that have actually done this, giving some credibility to the argument.[10] Of course, having achieved lower corporate taxes in one country, they turn around to other nations, saying that if they don't lower their taxes businesses will leave. Not surprisingly, corporations love this race to the bottom.[11]

The argument that we had to lower corporate tax rates to compete with others was invoked by Republicans as they slashed the corporate tax rate from 35 percent to 21 percent in 2017,[12] just as it had been used earlier, in 2001 and 2003, as taxes on capital gains and dividends were cut. The earlier tax cuts didn't work—they didn't lead to higher savings, an increase in labor supply, or higher growth,[13] and there is no reason to expect that the 2017 cut will either. In fact, there are reasons to believe that Americans' incomes will be lower as a result of the tax cut ten years hence.[14] What really matters in attracting firms are things like a well-educated labor force and good infrastructure, and for these, you need taxes. The corporations want to free ride on others who they hope will finance these basic public investments.

As if this race to the bottom weren't bad enough, our corporations took advantage of arcane provisions in tax laws—typically put into the legislation by corporate lobbyists—to drive taxes actually paid lower and lower, well below the "official" tax rate, in some cases close to zero. America's effective corporate tax rate (taxes paid as a ratio of total profits) on multinationals plummeted, and by 2012 was just over half of the official top rate.[15] Google and Apple pretended that vast amounts of their profits originated from a few employees working in Ireland, and those profits were taxed at 0.005 percent.[16] It would be easy enough to get rid of these loopholes, and that was the original promise of the 2017 tax bill. But with the corporations in the driver's seat in writing the new tax law, this wasn't done. In fact, matters were made worse. Previously, there had been a provision, called an alternative minimum tax, which limited the extent to which corporations could scam the tax system. What was needed was to tighten this provision; instead, it was eliminated.

But for our corporations and our ultra-rich, low tax rates and massive loopholes weren't enough. "Fiscal paradises," secrecy havens like Panama and the British Virgin Islands, were created to avoid and evade taxes.[17] It would be an easy matter to close down these fiscal paradises. All that would be required is to cut their banks off from the US financial system unless they agreed to the transparency and other regulations that apply to US financial institutions. The economics of this and other reforms described here is easy: as we repeatedly note, the difficulty is the politics, the influence of the rich who will do what they can to keep their "benefits." Our banks and those in Europe helped create these fiscal paradises as part of their "services" to rich clients and themselves.[18]

Is globalization or technology the real culprit?

As was noted, the defenders of globalization blame changes in technology for workers' declining wages and the loss of jobs. Technology may decrease the demand for workers, especially for those with limited skills, and that too may cause lower wages and higher unemployment.[19] Many economists have tried to parse out what fraction of the increased unemployment or decreased wages is a result of globalization. With the two so intertwined, I think that's essentially impossible. The key observation is that, even if there had been no changes in technology, globalization on its own would have wreaked havoc on America's workers—in the absence of help from the government. And with changes in technology themselves putting workers under so much stress, globalization just compounded workers' misery.

Instead of helping American workers, though, government, especially in the US, has in many ways done just the opposite. Globalization weakened workers' bargaining power, but then legislation affecting unions and workers' rights weakened it further. Increasing minimum wages to keep up with the growth of the economy might have protected those at the bottom, but instead, minimum wages were not increased even in tandem with inflation.[20] In short, policy, technology, and globalization all are inextricably linked together in generating today's problems; the fact that unions were powerless against the forces of technology and globalization no doubt greatly weakened them—why pay dues to unions that can't even keep real wages from falling? The weakening of unions contributed to unbalanced trade agreements and stagnating minimum wages. There was no one to fight for workers, no one to counterbalance the enormous influence of our corporations. The trade agreements were both a reflection and a cause of growing imbalances in economic power. The way globalization was managed added insult to injury: the plight of workers suffering from deindustrialization as a result of technological change was simply made worse.

Twenty-First-Century Trade Agreements

Over the past sixty years, tariffs have been vastly lowered. Today, trade negotiations typically focus on other issues, including regulations and other "non-tariff" trade barriers,[21] intellectual property, and investment. The Trans-Pacific Partnership (TPP), embracing 44 percent of global trade, signed in 2016 but which Trump abandoned on his first day in office, illustrates that point. Dropping the word "trade" from the title was a hint that trade, as we conventionally look at it, was not at the core of the agreement.[22] The net effect on US growth, when fully implemented, would have been only 0.15 percent of GDP, according to estimates from the government itself. Other less biased estimates thought that even that low figure was a gross exaggeration.[23]

If TPP and other recent agreements are not centrally about trade, what are they about? They are about investment, intellectual property, regulations, a host of issues that are of concern to businesses. The fight over these new issues is markedly different from the traditional conflict in trade negotiations over tariffs. Then, lower tariffs pitted the interests of producers in one country (who wanted protection) against those of another (who wanted to be able to enter a new market), with consumers the big beneficiary from lower prices. More recently, the conflict is often not between commercial interests in one country and those in another, but consumers in both countries and commercial interests in both. Ordinary citizens want to be protected against unsafe and unhealthy products that are bad for the environment; firms around the world simply want to maximize profits, and less scrupulous firms want the government to join them in the battle, driving another race to the bottom. The quest for regulatory harmonization (having common "standards") typically means harmonizing at the lowest possible level. The benefits of such harmonization are at best limited, and the costs can be significant, especially when corporations get their way and the common standard is a low one. Many Europeans worry about genetically modified food (GMO). They want it banned, or at the very least, clearly labeled. The US says that labeling will discourage Europeans from buying American products—and they're right. Accordingly, the US says that labeling is a trade barrier; but in that, they're wrong: each country should have the right to protect its citizens, its environment, and its economy in ways that it believes are appropriate. The *intent* of the GMO disclosure is not protectionism; it reflects genuine concerns of its citizens. Similarly, a big thrust of US trade policy over the past quarter century has been to force countries to open their markets to derivatives (the financial products which played such a central role in the 2008 crash)—to enhance the profits of American financial firms, even if such products impose dangerous risks on these countries' economies. The intent of many countries in restricting derivatives is not *protectionism*, but protecting their economies against a really dangerous financial product. I believe governments should have the right to such protections, and I empathize with countries that oppose trade agreements that try to restrict governments in these ways.

Intellectual property

Among the important trade issues today is intellectual property. Big Pharma—the makers of the expensive brand medicines—have tried to use intellectual property provisions of trade agreements to block the much less expensive generic medicines, doing what they can, for instance, to force a delay in entry of this competition.

Getting a strong international agreement on intellectual property has been the dream of multinational corporations, and in 1995 they got some of what they wanted in the "Trade-Related Aspects of Intellectual Property Rights" (TRIPS) agreement.[24] The objective of the agreement wasn't to spur innovation. In chapter 3 we saw how intellectual property rights gave rise to monopoly power, enhancing profits, and poorly designed IPR regimes don't even spur innovation. TRIPS was really about increasing profits of Big Pharma and firms in a few other industries.[25] It was about ensuring a flow of money from poor developing countries and emerging markets to the US.[26] Not surprisingly, then, it wasn't a balanced agreement, even within the domain of intellectual property; it didn't recognize the intellectual property of developing countries, either that of the genetic resources that resided in their rich biodiversity that so many were working so hard to preserve, or in traditional knowledge.[27]

Protectionism Is Not the Answer

While globalization, and especially poorly managed trade liberalization, has contributed to deindustrialization, unemployment, and inequality, Donald Trump's protectionist policies won't solve any of these problems. Indeed, his mindless undoing of the global rules-based system may make some of them worse. Renegotiating trade agreements will neither reduce the trade deficit nor lead to a return of manufacturing jobs. This is because the trade deficit is determined largely by macroeconomic factors, not by trade agreements. Macroeconomic factors determine the exchange rate—which is simply the value of one currency in terms of another—and the exchange rate is critical in determining exports and imports. When the value of the dollar is high, we export less and import more.[28]

When a country, such as the US, saves so little that even its meager investment exceeds its savings, it has to bring in capital from abroad to finance the deficiency. When capital comes into a country, the exchange rate is driven up as investors convert their currencies to the local one. That is, when capital comes into the US, the value of the dollar increases relative to, say, the euro. American goods and services are then more expensive for Europe, causing a commensurate decline in American exports. It also means that the costs of European goods are lower, so the US imports more. This is the real rub: as the US imports more, jobs in the import-competing industry disappear. That's what gives rise to the demand for "protection"—protection from foreign imports, either by limiting the amount that can be imported or by taxing foreign imports (imposing tariffs). In highly competitive markets, even low tariffs can effectively shut out foreign sales.[29]

Because the overall trade deficit is just equal to the shortfall of domestic savings over domestic investment, the policies that matter in determining the trade deficit are those that affect overall national savings or investment. Thus the 2017 tax bill will have more impact on it than any bilateral trade agreement. Here's how it works: when the 2017 tax bill was passed, it enormously increased the government's future deficit and simultaneously increased the amount of capital the US would eventually have to import from abroad to finance it. This last will increase the value of the dollar (from what it otherwise would have been) and thereby the trade deficit. It's a simple relationship: an increase in the fiscal deficit typically leads to an increase in the trade deficit.[30] And this will be true regardless of Trump's success in negotiating trade agreements.

Trade agreements do matter, but more for the pattern of trade than for the trade deficit. Changes in the pattern of trade, in turn, affect the *bilateral* trade deficit (the trade deficit between any two countries), even as they leave the *multilateral* trade deficit (the overall trade deficit, the difference between the total value of US exports and imports) largely unchanged. If the United States imposes, say, a 25 percent tariff on China, the US would import less apparel from China and more from some other country, say, Malaysia. And since comparable Malaysian clothes are slightly more expensive than those made in China (if they were not, we would already be importing clothes from Malaysia), the cost of apparel in the United States would increase. American standards of living would, in turn, decrease.

Importantly, regardless of Trump's success in renegotiating trade agreements, there is likely to be only limited return of manufacturing production to the United States.[31] Even if the production does return, it will be in our highly capital-intensive plants, using few workers. Further, there is no saying the new jobs will be in the same places as the ones lost. Protectionism will thus not solve the problem of those who have lost manufacturing jobs.

Consider the new trade agreement between US, Canada, and Mexico. It is designed to lead to slightly lower imports of Mexican auto parts. Even if the provisions work as intended, American cars will become more expensive and less attractive. We might gain a few more jobs in the production of car parts, but we would lose jobs in the production of cars because sales of American-made cars would decline.

To take another example, let's look at the highly publicized tariff the United States put on Chinese solar panels in 2018. It won't lead to the revival of the coal industry. It's not even likely to lead to the creation of an American solar panel industry. China has already gotten such a lead in the efficient production of solar panels that it will be difficult for the United States to catch up, especially taking into account the cost of American labor. More likely, solar panels used in the United States will continue to be manufactured in China, but the tariffs will make them more expensive and thus less attractive to American consumers and businesses. This will destroy jobs in installing solar panels—a nascent but booming sector that employed more than twice as many Americans as there are coal miners before new, higher tariffs were placed on solar panels. Predictions that tariffs would lead to less employment in these green jobs seem to have been borne out, and that means environmentally friendly energy production has been reduced.

Jobs were certainly destroyed in the process of globalization, but they will be destroyed again in the process of the reckless deglobalization proposed by Trump. The world has created efficient global supply chains, and wise nations take advantage of them. For America to walk away from these supply chains will make our firms less competitive. Most importantly, there are large costs of adjustment. Adjusting to globalization was hard, and we—and especially our workers—paid a high price. But we will pay another high price as we try to adjust to deglobalization.[32]

Global Cooperation in the Twenty-First Century

While protectionism won't help the US, or even those who have suffered from deindustrialization, it can have profoundly negative effects on America's trading partners and the global economy. During the past seventy years, the international community has created a rules-based system that facilitates commerce and cooperation. The US played a central role in the creation of this system. We did this not out of altruism, but because we believed that such a system was better for the entire world, including the US. It was believed that commerce and interchange would promote understanding across borders, and that would contribute to peace, making less likely the wars that had been a scourge over the previous century. It was also good economics: a rules-based, well-managed globalization held out the potential of benefiting all countries. And overall, the US overall economy was helped—the problem was that we didn't make sure that the fruits of that growth were equitably shared.

Trade wars and global cooperation

Now this rules-based global trading system is under attack. When President Trump first suggested he'd undertake a trade war with China, those both in and outside of the US seemed incredulous that it would happen. After all, it seemed too much against the interests of both sides, and especially corporate interests, which seemed to have long dictated US international economic policy. But Trump was never known either for rationality or consistency. The initial trade skirmishes in steel, aluminum, washing machines, and solar panels blossomed in 2018 into a full-scale trade war, with the US imposing tariffs on more than $200 billion of Chinese goods, and China retaliating. Trump is confident that the US will win, simply because the US imports from China more than it exports to China. But that reasoning is fallacious for several reasons. What matters are the instruments available to each side, the resolve, the capacity to do harm to the other side and to undo the harms that the other side would do, and the support within the country. Because China still is a more controlled economy than the US, it not only can target better what it does, but it can also better provide countervailing measures for those sectors that otherwise would be harmed. China has wanted to move away from dependence on exports, and the US is simply accelerating the process—and increasing China's resolve to advance its technological capacities. Moreover, the fraction of China's exports that are actually "made in China" is much smaller than for US exports, so a dollar decrease in China's exports has a much smaller impact on its economy than a dollar decrease in US exports has on the US economy.[33]

China also begins this trade war with its people more united behind its government; the US begins this trade war with large fractions, perhaps a majority, opposed.[34] And finally, there are many other economic and noneconomic actions that China could take, from squeezing American firms operating in China to acting more aggressively in the South China Sea.

Of course, everyone is likely to be the loser in the end, with the negative repercussions of protectionism extending far beyond direct economic channels. We need international cooperation on many fronts besides trade. For example, we need South Korea's and China's help in dealing with North Korea; we need Europe's help in dealing with Russia. Such help is less likely to be forthcoming if our countries are engaged in trade wars.

Globalization in a world with multiple value systems

Underlying the threat of a trade war are some deep grievances about the global trading system that go beyond those who have suffered as a result of the way it has been managed. Many advocates of globalization have assumed that we could have a free trade regime covering countries with deeply different systems of values. Values affect our economy—and comparative advantage—in pervasive and important ways. It is possible that a less free society could actually perform better in, say, an important arena like artificial intelligence. Big Data is crucial, and China has less inhibitions on the collection and use of data. Could or should Europeans complain that America's use of convict labor (prisoners make up almost 5 percent of the US industrial labor force) gives it an unfair advantage, since prisoners typically receive far less than the minimum wage? Or that America's failure to impose constraints on carbon emissions gives it an unfair advantage?

A quarter century ago, as the US and the West became increasingly engaged in trade with China, there was the hope that this engagement would accelerate their process of democratization. As was noted earlier, the West, and especially the US, interpreted the collapse of the Iron Curtain as the triumph of our economic and political system; it was only a matter of time until everyone, with perhaps the exception of a few rogue countries like North Korea, would see the light and adopt American-style democracy and capitalism.

But that was before the 2008 financial crisis, which showed the limits of American-style capitalism; before the election of Trump, which showed the limits of American-style democracy; and before China's President Xi abolished term limits for himself, which suggested that China might not be moving as fast as we hoped away from authoritarianism, and might in fact be moving in the other direction. China's distinctive economic model—some called it state capitalism, China refers to it as a "socialist market economy with Chinese characteristics"—had proven remarkably robust, and the country weathered the 2008 global crisis better than any other. Even though growth has now slowed, China's growth rate has been more than three times that of Europe, and twice that of the US. Its success, combined with its large foreign aid programs, were proving alluring to many countries in the third world trying to decide on an economic model for themselves.

Forty years ago, when China began its transition toward a market economy, no one could have imagined that this impoverished country would in less than half a century have a GDP comparable to that of the US. China's success in some advanced areas, like artificial intelligence and cyber security, has raised concerns not just about economic competition but about national security. Business interests too have become less enthusiastic about China: while they once had seen the country as a gold mine, higher wages, stronger environmental and other regulatory standards, and more intense competition from Chinese companies, all meant that China was no longer as profitable as it had once been, and future prospects seem even less bright.

American firms complain that it is unfair for China to demand joint ventures (which include sharing of intellectual property) as a condition of entry. China responds that no one is forcing any firm to enter China; they enter, knowing the conditions.[35] China is a developing country—albeit a large one—with a per capita income a fifth that of the US. It is working hard to close the gap between it and more advanced countries, especially the gap in knowledge, and in a few areas, some of considerable importance, it has managed to do so. There is no international law or even norm proscribing joint ventures, with all that entails.[36]

China's success today, however, is broad-based, and not just dependent on joint ventures with companies from the West or stealing intellectual property. In some areas like social media and artificial intelligence, it is already at the forefront. The number of patents it is receiving is increasing dramatically.[37] In many other areas, it has already largely closed the knowledge gap separating it from the advanced countries. The Trump administration in its trade with China is trying to close the barn door after the horses have escaped.[38]

As we put behind us ludicrous ideas that trade with China will quickly lead to a democratic China, there is a real question: How can there be fully open trade with a country with such a different economic system? What does it mean to have a "level playing field," for instance, with a country with little regard to privacy concerns but with a willingness to engage in censure and block websites that it finds politically distasteful? In a more muted form, this issue has long been debated. The emerging markets and developing countries argue that there can't be a fair global trading system as long as the US and EU insist on subsidizing agriculture—the sector on which billions of poor people around the world depend for their livelihood. The US claims that hidden subsidies permeate the Chinese economy; China claims that such subsidies are present in all economies—including in the large agricultural subsidies, the massive bailouts to the financial sector, and the enormous research expenditures of the defense department, some of the benefits of which (like Boeing passenger planes) get translated into consumer products. Europe too has objected to these hidden airplane subsidies, just as the US complains about the more transparent European assistance to Airbus.

WE ARE NOW confronting the reality that different countries will organize their economies in fundamentally different ways, reflecting their values and beliefs. Not everyone wants American-style capitalism, with its corporate power and inequality. And certainly, not everyone wants China's level of intrusion in the economy or its lack of concern for privacy. A values-free system of unfettered globalization can't work; but neither will a system in which the rules of the game are dictated by one country or another. We will have to find a new form of globalization, based on some version of peaceful coexistence, recognizing that even if we have markedly different economic systems, there are still large areas where we can fruitfully engage in commerce. We will need a minimal set of rules—some version of a rule of law, what might be thought of as a basic set of rules of the road. We can't force others to adopt our regulatory system, nor should we be forced to adopt theirs. And it will be a lot better for all of us if these rules are global, multilateral, and can be agreed upon by all countries.

Fixing Globalization

Protectionism isn't the answer either to the problems facing the US or the rest of the world. But neither is doubling down on globalization as it's been managed. Doing the same thing we've done for the last third of a century won't work any better in the coming decades. That is likely to result in still more suffering, still more political turmoil.

We've seen how in the past, globalization has been managed on a set of false premises: that everyone is a winner (without government intervention, there are large losers); and that globalization is *simply* a matter of good economics (in fact, the way it's been managed has advanced a corporate political agenda that has weakened workers' bargaining power and increased corporate power, especially in certain sectors). In the name of globalization—to keep countries competitive—workers have been told that they must accept lower wages, worse working conditions, and cutbacks in essential government services that they depend on. How can such policies possibly lead to an increase in workers' living standards? We now know that the growth benefits in the advanced industrialized countries have been exaggerated, and the distributive effects underestimated.

Of course, those emerging markets, like China, that have managed globalization well have enjoyed enormous success. China avoided the instability associated with short-term capital flows—hot money that could come in and out overnight. It encouraged foreign investors, and did so in a way that allowed it to narrow the knowledge gap that separated it from more developed countries. It encouraged exports, maintaining overall a stable exchange rate, and at earlier stages in its development (though not recently), keeping the value of its currency slightly lower than it otherwise would have been. Most importantly, while it allowed inequality to grow, it made sure that almost everyone benefited from globalization (moving, as we noted earlier, 740 million people out of poverty).

It is tempting to say that their growth has been at the expense of the advanced countries; but that would be wrong. The standard argument that trade can be mutually beneficial *to both countries* is, by and large, correct (if governments manage risks and opportunities well); but large groups within a country can be worse off unless government takes offsetting measures. In the US, government didn't take the required measures, and the results are what we should have expected.[39]

Globalization's impact goes far beyond economics. Much has been made of the increases in life expectancy as medical knowledge spreads globally; or the global recognition of gender rights, as ideas spread globally. We've seen how global tax avoidance and evasion has robbed countries of the revenues needed to provide basic public services. At the same time, the way globalization has been managed has often undermined communities, and in some cases, even nation-states. Local storekeepers are often the pillars of a community. But these local stores are now being driven out by large chains with their distinct advantage in buying cheap goods abroad. The loyalties of the managers of these stores are with the company more than with the community, and the managers often don't stay in one place long enough to plant roots.

The rules of globalization have been far from ideal. They have protected corporations' interests at the expense of workers, consumers, the environment, and the economy. Big Pharma has won more protection for its expensive drugs, at the expense of lives all over the world. Big corporations have gotten an intellectual property regime that has tilted the playing field in their favor over small businesses, and put profits over lives and the environment, and even over long-term growth and innovation. As we've made it easier for multinationals to avoid taxes, more of the tax burden falls on workers and small businesses. So too, providing more secure property rights for investments abroad through our investment agreements than those at home makes no sense.

There is an easy list of reforms: our investment agreements should focus on one thing—making sure that American firms are not discriminated against.[40] The intellectual property provisions of our trade agreements too should focus on ensuring access to generic medicines, not ensuring high profits for Big Pharma. In addition, we should worry more about the use of globalization for tax avoidance and evasion.

Almost surely, we would get better international trade rules if we arrived at them through a more open and democratic process. Currently, the agreements are negotiated by the US Trade Representatives (USTR), behind closed doors—but not fully closed. Corporate representatives are effectively at the table, as the USTR discusses with them what to negotiate for although members of Congress are often shut out, with the USTR even refusing to share its negotiating position.[41]

Most importantly, though, whatever the rules, we have to help ordinary citizens adjust to the changing economy, whether the changes come from globalization or technology.[42] Markets on their own are not good at making transitions, in transforming the economy. Countries that have helped their people with the transition, such as some of those in Scandinavia (for instance, Sweden and Norway), have a more dynamic economy, a polity that is more open to change, and a higher standard of living for their citizens. This requires active labor market policies that help people retrain and find new jobs; and industrial policies that ensure that new jobs get created as fast as old jobs get destroyed and that help places that are suffering from large job losses find new economic opportunities.[43] It also requires good systems of social protection so that no one falls between the cracks. But those managing globalization and our economies have demanded cutbacks in these programs—allegedly to compete in a globalized world—just when we need them most.

It's easy—at least from an economics perspective—to rewrite the rules of globalization and to manage globalization better. Later in this book (in chapter 9) I explain some of the ways in which both globalization and changes in technology can be better managed—so that all, or at least most, citizens benefit and few if any are left behind.

CHAPTER 5

Finance and the American Crisis

Finance was central to the creation of today's economic, social, and political malaise: in the economic crisis that America endured for almost a decade as well as in the increase in inequality and the slowing of growth. Resources—including some of the most talented young people—went into finance rather than into strengthening the *real* economy. A sector that should have been a means to an end, the more efficient production of goods and services, has become an end in itself. No modern economy can perform well without a well-functioning financial market that serves society, and that's why it's essential to reform the financial sector so that it serves society, rather than the other way around.

Since the founding of the Republic, there has been a worry that powerful banks could undermine popular democracy—that was why so many opposed the creation of the First National Bank, and President Andrew Jackson declined to renew it when its twenty-year charter came to an end in 1836. Those worries have proven more than justified in recent years, as became clear with attempts to regulate the banks, to prevent a recurrence of the 2008 crisis. More than three-quarters of Americans believed strong regulation was needed. Yet, with five lobbyists for every congressperson, the country's ten largest banks had as much or more influence than 250 million Americans. It took two years to pass what was known as the Dodd-Frank Bill (finally signed into law in 2010), which was intended to rectify the problems that had led to the crisis, and the bill was a far cry from what was needed. Hardly was the ink dry than this army of lobbyists went to work to scale it back—with enormous success in 2018, when the vast majority of banks were removed from the tighter oversight that had been enacted.[1]

The bank bailout of 2008 itself showed the power of the banks. They had caused the crisis, yet government provided massive largesse to the banks and the bankers—without any sense of accountability for the crisis that they had created, and with miserly help for the workers and homeowners who seemed but collateral damage in the financiers' war of greed. The diary of those who met with Obama and his Treasury Secretary, Tim Geithner, as they developed their plan to resuscitate the economy demonstrates who was at the table, and who was not. Ordinary homeowners who were struggling were not at the table; the big financial companies were.[2]

It was necessary to save the banks, to keep the flow of credit going (akin to the lifeblood of the economy). But one could have saved the banks without saving the bankers and the banks' shareholders and bondholders; one could have played by the rules of capitalism, which require that when any firm, including a bank, can't pay what it owes, its shareholders and bondholders lose all before taxpayers are asked to pony up anything.[3]

Moreover, as we poured money into the banks, saving their bondholders and shareholders, we could have imposed conditions on the banks—that they use that money to help homeowners and small businesses and not to pay the bankers big bonuses. We didn't. Obama and his team put their trust in the bankers—who had over the previous decade given us every reason *not* to trust them; they believed that if they gave enough money to the banks, their bondholders, and share-holders, somehow it would trickle down; all would benefit. It didn't work out that way—in the first three years of the recovery, 91 percent of the growth went to the top 1 percent of the country. Millions lost their homes and jobs as the bankers who had brought on all of this basked in their millions in bonuses. What we got was neither efficient nor fair; but what we got was what one would expect in a democracy in which the scales are tilted toward banks.

Stopping the Financial Sector from Harming Society

Most of the efforts at financial reform on both sides of the Atlantic have been directed at stopping the banks from harming the rest of society, which banks have done on a grand scale not only through their reckless lending but also through their predatory lending, abusive credit card practices, and exploitation of market power. In the years after the 2008 crisis, we've discovered that they behaved more badly than we could ever have imagined: Wells Fargo, America's third larg-est bank by assets, opened up accounts for individuals without their consent, multiple banks engaged in market manipulation in foreign exchange and interest rate markets, and the rating agencies and most of the investment banks committed massive fraud.

The pervasive moral turpitude presents the most important and difficult challenge going forward: changing the norms and culture of finance.[4] The bankers knew that our legal system was not up to the task of dealing with massive fraud or breach of contract, where the banks simply refused to honor contracts that they'd signed.[5] Sue us, they seemed to say. The banks knew that at best those seeking justice would find the process slow; at worst, they hoped that specious argu-ments would prevail with a banker-friendly judge. If they lost, they simply had to pay what was due. But perhaps they would win. Perhaps the party they cheated, with shallower pockets than the big banks, would give up, and settle for a fraction of what was owed. For the bankers, it was a one-sided bet. For those who had relied on their contract guarantees, it was far different: justice delayed is justice denied.

MOST IMPORTANTLY, our economic system can't work if there is no trust, and this is especially important for banks. We trust them to get us back our money when we want it and we trust them not to cheat us when we buy complex financial products from them. Again and again, our bankers have shown that they are not trustworthy, thereby undermining the functioning of the entire economy. The bankers' shortsightedness led them to abandon any pretense of "reputation." But just as Peter Thiel had declared that competition is for losers, so Lloyd Blankfein, the head of Goldman Sachs, made it clear that the reputation for honesty and trustworthiness—what had traditionally been viewed as a bank's most important assets—was a quaint relic of the past. Goldman Sachs had created a security that was designed to fail. As they sold the product to others, they actually took bets that it would do so (called "selling short"); but of course, didn't tell their customers that it was designed to fail and that they were using this knowledge to bet against it. If you think that's immoral, you are probably part of 99 percent of humanity who thinks in an evidently anachronistic way, better suited for a world gone by. Blankfein put an end to this notion of bankers to be trusted as he said (in effect) that anyone who trusted a banker was a fool.[6]

THE FINANCIAL SECTOR's shortsightedness—almost never looking beyond the next quarter—has also weakened the economy.[7] Shortsightedness allowed banks to sacrifice their long-term reputation, in their short-run pursuit of today's profits, as they cheated investors (as in the case of Goldman Sachs) or ordinary depositors (as in the case of

Wells Fargo). It was the same shortsightedness (or the expectation that they could get away with it) that led many of the investment banks and credit rating agencies to commit fraud.

A Dysfunctional Financial Sector, a Dysfunctional Economy

One of the financial sector's central functions is called intermediation, bringing together those who have excess funds with those who need more funds. This is a time-honored process: in a simple primitive agrarian economy, a farmer with excess seeds could offer them to a neighbor. In a modern economy, intermediation consists of taking money from the households who are saving for their retirement or to make a down payment on a house or to finance their children's college education and bringing it to the corporate sector to be invested.

As banking has evolved, increasingly, intermediation has shifted away from a relationship between savers and firms wanting to expand and create new jobs. Rather, banks intermediated between savers and households that wanted to spend more than they made, for example, through credit card lending. Credit card lending was so profitable because it was so easy to take advantage of consumers, charging them usurious interest rates, late fees (even when they weren't late), overdraft fees, and a host of other charges. This was especially true as deregulation proceeded, eliminating constraints on banks' predatory behavior. Banks could rake it in from all sides, using their market power to impose high fees on both consumers and merchants *simultaneously*. Moreover, in their lending, banks could more easily exploit consumers than they could firms; there was more easy money to be made there than by lending to small and medium-sized enterprises (SMEs). So SMEs found it increasingly difficult to get money, especially from the large banks. Indeed, in 2016, years after the crisis, lending to SMEs (*unadjusted* for inflation) was still some 14 percent

below what it was in 2008. In some European countries, the decrease
was even larger.[8]

So too, banks did a poor job in one of the central areas where
intermediation was necessary—between long-term savers and long-
term investors. Around the world, many of the savers are long-term—
pension funds; university and foundation endowments; and sovereign
wealth funds, which hold a country's money for future generations.
Many of the most important investment needs are also long-term, for
example, infrastructure and retrofitting the world's energy system to
reflect the reality of climate change. But standing between long-term
investors and long-term savers are shortsighted financial markets. The
bankers were simply not up to the task of making long-term resource
allocation decisions. They wanted short-term projects that yielded
quick returns. And they were not up to the task of creating financial
products that would help manage long-term risks.

Increasingly, *public* multinational development banks, like the
World Bank, the Asian Infrastructure Investment Bank, the New
Development Bank (also called the BRICS Bank[9]) and the African
Development Bank, which focus on long-term development, have
stepped into the breach. But they are undercapitalized and can't fully
make up for a dysfunctional private financial system.

Less intermediation and more gambling, more efforts in creating market power

Banks also turned to activities which were much more lucrative than
intermediation—for instance, taking on big gambles. What at Las
Vegas might simply be called a bet, on Wall Street takes on a fan-
cier name, a "derivative" (just a bet, for instance, on what's going to
happen with interest rates, exchange rates, or oil prices) or a "credit
default swap," a bet on whether a firm or another bank is going to go
into bankruptcy or near it. These are not like quarter slot machine
bets; they are typically mega-million dollar bets. This betting market

exists because it is effectively partially insured by the government. If the loss is too great, the government will bail the bank out. It's another way that the banks engage in one-sided gambles—if things turn out *on their side* they walk away with the profits; if not, the government is backstopping them. And it is only because the government is backstopping them that the other side is willing to enter the gamble, because they know the contract will be honored come what may.

The Dodd-Frank Bill tried to stop this kind of government-underwritten gambling that had proven so costly. This kind of speculation had resulted in the $180 billion bailout of a single company, AIG—more corporate welfare in one fell swoop than had been provided to all of America's poor through our welfare programs aimed at children over a period of more than a decade.[10]

The brazenness of the banks' response to attempts to curtail their gambling at public expense was breathtaking: in 2014, Citigroup lobbyists wrote the provision restoring banks' right to gamble, with government effectively underwriting losses, and got it placed as an amendment to a piece of legislation (funding the government) that just had to get passed.[11]

Amazingly, banks have refused even to bear the risks associated with issuing mortgages. Ten years after the financial crisis, a dozen years after the housing bubble burst, the government still has to underwrite the vast majority of mortgages. The bankers want the fees from issuing mortgages, but don't want to take the responsibility for their failures of judgment. They want the government to pick up the losses from bad lending. It is ironic that in a country that supposedly holds capitalism dear, the private sector says the simple task of creating mortgages and bearing the associated risk is beyond them. Every proposal to reform the mortgage market has faltered on banks' insistence that they are not able or willing to bear the risks associated with issuing mortgages.

Another lucrative diversion for banks is "mergers and acquisitions," facilitating mergers—helping the large firms get ever larger, thereby exacerbating already high levels of market concentration and power. A single merger or acquisition can generate hundreds of millions of dollars in fees for the banks. In chapter 3, we discussed the economic and social implications of these agglomerations of powers—and the banks have been accomplices, if not instigators, in this transformation of the economy.

Still a third, very lucrative line of business of the banks is particularly unproductive for society: helping multinational corporations and rich individuals avoid paying the taxes that are due, moving money around from high-tax jurisdictions to low-tax jurisdictions, skirting the law, if not disobeying it.[12] At the same time, banks have resisted efforts at reforming the global tax and financial system. Tens of billions of dollars escape taxation every year.

Here's an example of how banks facilitate tax avoidance. Apple, working with the financial sector, used its ingenuity not just to make well-loved products but also to avoid taxes. Some of Apple's shareholders, seeing the treasure chest of money on which it was sitting, wanted it now. If this money had remained abroad, under the old (pre-2017) tax law, Apple wouldn't have had to pay taxes; but were it to be brought home, corporate taxes would have to be paid on the profits. So Apple turned to financial markets. By borrowing to pay a dividend, it could have its cake and eat it too: it avoided repatriating its profits and the taxes that would then be due. But its shareholders got what they wanted, cash in their pockets.

Here, as in the earlier example of tax avoidance we described as Apple shifted profits to Ireland, there was a total absence of a corporate conscience: Though its own growth rested on technologies developed or financed by the US government, Apple, like the banks, was willing to take but not to give, even as it made a huge pretense of corporate responsibility. To me, the first element of corporate social responsibility is to pay your taxes.

More disintermediation

Even beyond failing to perform its traditional role of intermediation, bringing money from the household sector to the corporate sector, the financial sector today is doing just the opposite, taking money *from* the corporate sector and bringing it to the household sector, so the rich can enjoy more of their wealth now. One way they do this, with marked tax advantages,[13] is for banks to help firms buy back shares from the market by lending them money to do this, as the example of Apple illustrates. Money flows *out* of firms. The firm has less money to invest in its future. Fewer jobs will be able to be created. The recipients, of course, are the owners of the stock, disproportionately the very wealthy.[14] So large are these buybacks that in recent years, they have consistently exceeded nonfinancial firms' investment (their capital formation)—a big difference from the years after World War II when buybacks were negligible.[15] After the Republicans' tax bill passed in December 2017, there was a surge in buybacks, with 2018 on pace to set records.[16]

From Traditional Banking to a Dysfunctional Financial System

The financial sector has not always been as dysfunctional as it is today. As it grew, from 2.5 percent of GDP in 1945 to 8 percent at the time of the crisis, the economy didn't perform better. Indeed, growth slowed and the economy became more unstable—culminating in the worst crisis in seventy-five years.

The deficiencies in the financial sector appeared only gradually over the past quarter century, as it evolved away from traditional banking. Traditional banking, as we have noted, entailed individuals turning over their savings to the bank, which lent it to enterprises, which in turn used the money to hire more workers or to buy more machines. The money went to those most able to make good use of the funds. The bank didn't try to squeeze the last penny out of the borrower: it knew that charging a high interest rate would discourage responsible borrowers and encourage excessive risk taking.[17] Moreover, the bank had a long-term relationship with the borrower, so the bank could help see the firm through good times and bad. This kind of banking is called relationship banking.

Modern banking has changed this in multiple ways. In traditional banking, bankers were boring but highly respectable people, pillars of their communities, who wanted to ensure others of their probity— they wanted to convince others that they deserved trust sufficient to allow the bankers to take care of their money. They bore the consequence of bad lending: if they didn't do a good job, and those they lent to couldn't repay, they lost their capital.

In the new "originate-to-distribute" model, which came to dominate banking in the twenty-first century,[18] banks originate the loans, but pass them onto others, who bear the risk of bad lending. They make their profits not from the spread between the rate borrowers paid them and the rate they paid depositors but from fees charged at every stage in the process.

Lending backed by government guarantees

The amount of loans that a bank can lend out is not limited to the amount it has on deposit. In this way, it's markedly different from the simple agriculture situation described earlier in the chapter. Then, a "seed bank" could give seed to a farmer wanting to plant more only if some other farmer had given the bank seed to lend out. But for several hundred years, banks have realized that they can create accounts, knowing that only a fraction of them will be called in at any one time. We evolved into a system of what is called fractional reserve banking, where the amount that banks hold in reserves is just a fraction of what they owe. Today, this system works because we rely on government to ensure that the reserves are sufficient, that what is not in reserves has been prudently managed, and to step in when there is a shortfall.

Even if lending was not the most lucrative of the banks' activities, bankers made a pretty penny lending out money—not only because what they lent out carried a higher interest rate than what they paid to depositors, but also because they could create loans essentially out of thin air. The bank could just enter into its books that an individual had a deposit (a right to spend money) of, say, $100,000. The bank, in a sense, owed the borrower this money. But lending the money meant that at the same time the bank had created an asset of equal value, the loan itself. The borrower values the deposit because others will accept a check written by him or her. The reason that others are willing to accept such a check, though, is that the bank is backed by the US government. In effect, banks make their money by cashing in on—by taking advantage of—the trust in the US government. That means that when they fail, taxpayers foot the bill. Since banking is so profitable, and the more they lend the more they make, bankers have an incentive to persuade government that they don't need much reserves.[19] That's been one of the big battles in the post-2008-crisis world. The smaller the reserves, the greater the banks' profits—but the more risk that is put on taxpayers. From a societal point of view, though, it's more than just a matter of shifting risk to government away from the bankers and banks. With higher reserves required and banks thus with more at stake, bankers will be more prudent in lending, better loans will be made, and our economy will perform better.

The misalignment of private and social interests

Of course, bankers are not interested in the overall performance of the economy; they're interested in making profits. Here again, private and social interests are not well aligned. Thus, in testifying before Congress on the origins of the financial crisis, former chairman of the

Federal Reserve Board Alan Greenspan said that he had assumed that the bankers would manage risk better. This was the great "flaw" in his reasoning—a flaw that cost the global economy trillions of dollars. [20] He was surprised. I was surprised that he was surprised: anyone understanding economics and the incentives that the banks and bankers faced could easily understand that they had incentives to engage in excessive risk taking. Greenspan should have known this.[21]

The financial sector itself became a victim of a set of doctrines that became fashionable in the Reagan era: firms should pursue their shareholder interest; doing so would lead to the well-being of all stakeholders and our economy more generally.[22] And shareholder interests came to mean not long-term investors, who care about the fortune of the firm over a period of years or decades, but short-term speculators, who cared only about the stock price today, squeezing every dollar of short-run profits, with little regard to the long-run consequences. Incentive structures were put into place to encourage this short-term perspective—and they worked, to create the largest financial meltdown in 75 years.

Contagion to the rest of the economy

The maladies of the financial sector, on their own, are bad enough. Unfortunately, too many others imitate what they do. They try to emulate its high pay and the incentive structures that contribute to shortsighted behavior, valuing today's stock market performance over long-term growth. Moreover, firms are inevitably sensitive to the perspectives of their funders; and if their funders are shortsighted, they too will be. Hence, the financial sector has played an important role in the spread of one of the major maladies in capitalism American-style: one can't make long-term investments in people, in technology, and in factories on the basis of a quarterly horizon. An economy with a short-term horizon is an economy with a slow growth rate.

Conclusions

The financial sector exemplifies in so many ways all that is wrong with our economy. The sector has been the example par excellence of rent-seeking—the bankers increased their wealth at the expense of the rest of society, in what clearly turned out to be a negative sum game, where what the rest of society lost was far larger than what the bankers gained. They exploited the financially unsophisticated, but there is no honor among thieves: they also exploited each other. The economy was hurt in so many ways: resources that could have gone into wealth creation were devoted to exploitation, as the financial sector grew and grew in size, attracting some of the country's most talented individuals. But all the country had to show for it was slower growth, more volatility, and greater inequality. The financial sector illustrates too what's wrong with unfettered markets: bankers' unbridled pursuit of their self-interest didn't lead to the well-being of society, but to the largest financial crisis in 75 years.

In America's money-driven politics, the bankers had used their wealth to get rules that allowed them to make ever more money at the expense of others, through deregulation, and when that failed miserably, they used their influence to get the largest public bailout in the history of the world, while letting those that they had preyed on, homeowners and workers alike, to largely fend for themselves.

The love of money may not be at the root of all evil, but certainly finance is the root of many of the countries' maladies. The shortsightedness and moral turpitude of our money-focused bankers spread, infecting our economy, our politics, and our society. In many ways, it has changed who we are, making so many Americans more materialistic, more selfish, and more shortsighted.

Across the political spectrum, American voters are fed up with the big banks and the misbehavior of the financial sector. Obama's failure to hold the banks accountable for their misdeeds—while giving them a near-trillion-dollar bailout—contributed to the disillusionment with government and the rise, first of the Tea Party movement, and eventually Trump.[23] Trump's "drain the swamp" slogan was supposed to refer to the influence of Wall Street as much as anything, even as Trump went on to stack his cabinet with unprecedented numbers of rich financiers.

The public's fury with the big banks is justified. Banks have used their market power to harm society, taking the economy hostage. In the absence of market and political power, they couldn't have gotten away with any of their misdeeds. In an efficient, competitive market, firms that impugned their reputation in the way all of our major banks have done wouldn't survive. Yet not only have they survived, they are now earning record profits.[24] And rather than punishing the bankers for their misdeeds, we bailed them out, in some cases even rewarding them. There have to be consequences, both for the institutions and for individuals, of behavior that is as reckless and as reprehensible as that evidenced by the financial sector over the past decades. An argument can be made that our political system is now paying the price of the failure to deal effectively with the misdeeds of the financial sector: it showed politicians, in both parties, more attuned to the bankers than to those that both the political and financial system were supposed to serve.

Still, finance is vitally important to the economy. We need credit to start and expand businesses and to create jobs. Finance is crucial, but there is nothing inherent about its functioning that requires the financial sector to be as gargantuan as it has become. Today, we have too big of a financial sector doing too much of what it shouldn't be doing and too little of what it should be doing. It's used its power not so much to serve society but to extract profits for itself.

We've grasped the multitude of methods used by those in the sector to harm us—though almost every day reveals new forms of ingenuity and new examples of moral depravities. There is a general understanding of the set of regulations that would reduce efficiently the harms that the sector imposes on the rest of us, both through direct exploitation and through reckless lending. Doing this is not that hard.[25] One needs comprehensive regulations preventing banks from being too big and too interconnected to be allowed to fail, from engaging in excessive risk taking, market manipulation and the exploitation of their market power, and abusive and predatory behavior.

The most important failing of the banks, however, was not the multiple ways they cheated and exploited others or the excessive risk taking that brought the global economy to its knees, but their failure to do what they were supposed to do—provide finance, at reasonable terms, for businesses as they sought to make investments that would allow the economy to grow. Many of these projects are long-term, yet banks' short-term focus led them to center their attention on easier sources of profits. The many efforts to prevent banks from doing harm missed this critical issue: ensuring that the financial sector actually does what it's supposed to do.

By circumscribing the riskier and more abusive ways the financial sector makes profits, we will encourage it to do more of what it should be doing. But that won't be enough. We also need to make the financial sector more competitive.

In countries all over the world, the government has to take an active role in providing finance for small and new businesses, for long-term investments, including infrastructure, for high-risk technology projects, and to underserved communities—even with nondiscrimination laws, our banks have practiced discrimination. Even in the most capitalistic of countries, the US, the government has long been an active player in the provision of finance. It may have to take a still more active role—how much more active will depend on how well we succeed in reforming our regulations and how well the banks do in reforming themselves. Providing finance through the public sector, for instance for mortgages, will also provide competition for the private sector, and this may be more effective in curbing the sectors' exploitation than attempts to force more competitive and responsible behavior through regulation.

The difficulty is not the economics, but the politics: in a money-driven political system, the source of money—finance—will inevitably have great political power. Unfortunately, the banks will fight tooth and nail against both regulations that curb their bad practices and those that encourage good behavior, so that while the economics is easy, the politics is not. At the same time this illustrates the worry expressed in the early days of the Republic, concerning the excessive political influence of a large financial sector—and it illustrates a central theme of the final part of this book: if we are to achieve the necessary economic reforms, we need to reform our politics.

CHAPTER 6

The Challenge of New Technologies

S ilicon Valley and the advances in technology associated with it have become symbolic of American innovation and entre-preneurship. Larger-than-life figures like Steve Jobs and Mark Zuckerberg brought products to consumers around the world—products that they love and which make it possible for us to connect better with each other. Intel has produced chips that make our products "think" faster—do calculations faster—than the best brains in the world. Artificial intelligence (AI) can now beat humans not only in simple games like chess, but in more complicated ones like Go, where the number of possible moves is greater than the atoms in the universe.[1] Bill Gates, it would seem, illustrates the best of the American spirit—having accumulated an estimated $135 billion, he began giving massive amounts to charity, as he used his energies to fight diseases around the world and attempted to improve education in the United States.

And yet, for all these virtues, there is a darker side to all of these advances. They create legitimate concerns about job loss. Further, the new industries are prone to numerous abuses, from market power, to invasions of privacy, to political manipulation.

Full Employment in a Hi-Tech World

There is great angst about the job market. In the twentieth century, we created machines that were stronger than humans. Now, we're able to make machines that are more efficient than humans in routine jobs. AI now presents an even greater challenge to humans. We can make machines that not only perform programmed tasks better than humans but also *learn* better, at least in certain domains.

Thus machines can outperform people in many key jobs. Better education and job training for workers may be a short-term palliative for many, but computers can and are replacing radiologists, so not even a doctor's degree provides a safe harbor. It is anticipated that within a few years, self-driving cars and trucks will replace drivers; if true, this is of especial concern, because truck driving today represents a very large source of employment for men who have a high school diploma or less.

The worry is that these labor-replacing machines will drive down wages, especially of low-skilled workers, and increase unemployment. The natural answer has been to increase workers' skills. But in many areas, this won't suffice: with AI, robots can learn complicated tasks more quickly and perform better than even well-educated humans.

There are those who say not to worry: Look to the past. Markets always created jobs, as the economy restructured. Besides, these techno-optimists claim, the pace of change has been exaggerated. Indeed, it doesn't even show in the macro-data: productivity increases in recent years are significantly lower than in the 1990s, and in the decades after World War II. Robert Gordon of Northwestern University in his bestselling book *The Rise and Fall of American Growth: The US Standard of Living Since the Civil War* argues that the pace of innovation has actually slowed.[2] Yes, we have Facebook and Google, but these innovations pale in comparison with the importance of electric-

ity, or even indoor toilets and clean water that played such an important role in improving health and longevity.

These past experiences may, however, not be a good guide for the
future. More than a half century ago, John von Neumann, one of the
leading mathematicians of the mid-twentieth century, suggested that
there might be a point[3] where it becomes less expensive to produce a
machine to replace a human than to hire and train a human. These
machines will, in turn, be produced by other machines that learn how
to produce them. What matters to firms' decisions to use machines
instead of human workers is not just the increase in productivity but
also the relative ease and cheapness with which the right machine can
be designed, manufactured, and managed. Machines, for instance,
don't go on strike. One doesn't need a human resources department to
make sure that they are not disgruntled. Machines are unencumbered
by emotions. Von Neumann's forecast has already been realized for
certain tasks; as we noted, machines can already outperform radiologists. But the range of tasks and the amount of job replacement may
accelerate rapidly, given the advances in AI in just the last five years.[4]

Some of the advances in AI will not lead to replacing labor, but
will increase human performance. These are sometimes called IA—
intelligence-assisting—innovations. Such innovations can increase the
demand for labor and drive up wages, and in the past, much of the
innovation has been of this form. But I wouldn't count on this continuing. There is the possibility that, as bad as the jobs problem has
been in the past, it could get worse. Technology could evolve in ways
that the economics literature refers to as entailing "polarization," with
a relative increase of jobs requiring very, very high levels of skills, with
the rest of the growth in employment being in very low-skilled jobs
with correspondingly low wages.[5]

As machines replace labor, unemployment increases, a situation
captured well by an apocryphal but often told story of the heads of

the Ford Motor Company and the autoworkers union looking down
on the floor of a new plant, where much of the work was being done
by robots. "How are you going to get those robots to pay your union
dues?" the Ford executive needled. "These robots won't be joining
your union." To which the union head replied, "How are you going
to get them to buy your cars?"[6]

The lack of jobs will give rise to a lack of demand, and the economy could (without strong government intervention) settle into a state
of what has been called secular (long-run) stagnation. The ultimate
irony is that, were this to happen, advances in technology may lead to
economic suffering, rather than the increased prosperity that should
have resulted. Some argue that this is precisely what happened in the
United States in the lead-up to the Great Depression.[7] Rapid innovation in agriculture led to rapidly falling prices for some commodities
in the years before the Great Depression began.[8] As a result, net farm
income (income after expenses) fell more than 70 percent in real terms
between 1929 and 1932.[9] The rapid decrease in income and the corresponding diminution in farmers' wealth, as the value of rural land
and homes decreased, had several big consequences: the unemployed
farmers couldn't afford to move to the cities, and as their incomes fell,
they worked harder and produced more, which had the perverse effect
of driving down prices even further. Moreover, with reduced incomes,
they couldn't buy the goods produced in the cities, like cars.[10] Thus,
farmers' suffering was quickly felt in the cities, and the consequences
then reverberated back: lower incomes in cities meant lower demand
for agricultural goods, lower prices, and more suffering on the farms.
The economy was caught in a low-level equilibrium trap, from which
it emerged only as a result of World War II, where massive government
intervention—the war effort—resulted in the movement of individuals
from the rural area to the cities and training them for the new urban
jobs: ushering in the post–World War II era of prosperity.

The lesson of this experience is that if innovation is not well managed, rather than bringing prosperity to all, it could have just the opposite effect. Today, as a result of advances in economics, we know better how to manage an economy confronting innovation. The key is maintaining full employment. We can do this using fiscal policy (cutting taxes or increasing spending—increases in public investment can be a particularly effective way of stimulating the economy) when monetary policy (lowering interest rates or increasing the supply of credit) fails to do the trick. Both monetary and fiscal policy stimulate aggregate demand, and with enough stimulus, the economy can always be restored to full employment.[11]

The "jobs" problem of hi-tech is thus a political problem. Blind ideology, especially when combined with nasty politics, may make undertaking sufficient fiscal stimulus politically difficult.[12] We saw this in the Great Recession. The Federal Reserve brought interest rates down to zero, but this didn't suffice to restore full employment. Even so, Republicans and other fiscal hawks refused efforts to provide adequate fiscal stimulus. The refusal is particularly galling, because at the time, government could obtain funds at *negative* real interest rates (taking into account increases in prices), and thus it was an especially good time to make the public investments the country badly needed.

Relying excessively on monetary policy has one further problem: with the cost of capital so low, it pays firms to invest in labor-replacing machines. Firms have to decide where to allocate scarce research and investment dollars, and they do so focusing on factors that represent a large share of costs. With the Federal Reserve keeping interest rates so low for so long, capital costs relative to labor were especially low— and not surprisingly, then, attention got drawn toward reducing labor costs. The demand for labor, already not enough to maintain full employment, was weakened further.[13]

Lower wages and increased inequality

Even getting us to full employment may not be enough. If machines *replace* labor, then by definition, the demand for labor at any given wage is reduced, so to restore the economy to full employment wages must fall. This is just a straightforward application of the law of supply and demand. But it means that, without government intervention, large parts of the economy will be worse off.[14]

Of course, in principle, technological advances should be able to make all of us better off, as is also true for globalization. The size of the national pie has increased; there's more to go around; and so everyone can get a bigger slice. But with machines replacing labor, it won't happen on its own: the decreased demand for labor, and especially unskilled labor, will lower wages, so that workers' income will decrease even as national income increases. Trickle-down economics won't work, just as it didn't work for globalization.

But government can make sure that everyone, or at least most people, are better off. There are at least four sets of policies that will be required: (1) Ensuring that the rules of the economic game are fairer, that the game is not stacked against workers—and most importantly, that the big tech companies don't use the new technologies to increase corporate market power, in the manner described later in this chapter. Strengthening the bargaining power of workers and weakening the monopoly power of firms would create a more efficient economy with greater equality. (2) Intellectual property rights can be designed so that the fruits of the advances, most of which rest on foundations of basic research funded by the government, are shared more widely. (3) Progressive tax and expenditure policies can help redistribute income.

Finally, (4) we need to recognize the role of government in helping restructure the economy from manufacturing to a service-sector economy. This change parallels the structural changes that occurred a century ago when the economy moved from agriculture to manufacturing.

In the present-day structural transformation, government may have to do even more than it did then, because in many of the expanding service sectors, like health and education, government finance is central, and understandably so. If government, for instance, hired more workers to care for our aged, sick, and disabled and to educate our young, and paid those people decent wages,[15] it would drive up wages throughout the economy. If we, collectively, valued our children, our sick, and our aged, we would want to spend more on them. If, for instance, we want better-educated children, we need more teachers who are better paid. Higher pay will, in particular, attract more qualified people into teaching. Doing this will require more tax revenues—but the larger pie, the increased income, brought about through technological advances, ensures that we can impose such taxes and still leave our capitalists and innovators well off, better off than they are today.

In short, the unemployment, decreasing wages, and increasing hardship for workers that result from advances in technology could easily be addressed, if there were only the political will to do so. We'll return to how best to do this in Part II of this book.

Market Power and AI

Earlier chapters noted the increase in market power in many sectors of the economy, and that both the poor performance of the economy overall and the growth of inequality could be linked to this growth of market power. These problems, and their consequences, are especially severe in the new technology industries for reasons that were explained in chapter 3.

Big Data—the massive amount of data that companies like Amazon, Google, and Facebook can gather on each individual—and AI raise the specter of an even greater increase in market power. If a firm (like Google or Facebook or Amazon) has a large, perhaps even dominant, position in an area where they can collect data, they then know more about the individual than others, provided they don't share that data with others—and they have no incentive to do so. The advocates of Big Data argue that it can be used to design products that better meet what customers want and tailor them to customers' needs. There is hope too that the information provided will have enormous benefits for tailored health care. The search engines claim they can use the data to better target advertising, so one is more likely to receive information that is useful.[16] These are the positive possibilities of Big Data. But the dominant firms can also use that data, through AI, in ways to enhance their market power and profits at the expense of customers.

The potential consequences of the market power held by the new technology giants are greater and more pernicious than anything we saw at the turn of the twentieth century. Then, the market power of companies like Swift, Standard Oil, American Tobacco, the American Sugar Refining Company or US Steel allowed them to raise the price they charged for food, steel, tobacco, sugar or oil. Now, it's about more than just price.

The existence of the new technology giants' market power is seen most dramatically every time Facebook changes its algorithms, the way it determines what individuals see and in what order. A new algorithm can bring on the quick decline of a media outlet, or can create, and then possibly end, new ways of reaching large audiences (as in Facebook Live).

Because of their market power, the tech giants deserve the full attention of the competition authorities, who will need not just to deploy standard tools against them, but will also have to create new tools to combat their innovative ways of extending and exercising market power. At the very least, as we noted earlier, we should consider breaking out WhatsApp and Instagram from Facebook. And we need to restrict the scope for conflicts of interests, such as arise when Google opens up its online store to compete with those who advertise on its platform.

Almost surely, though, we'll have to go further, restricting, for instance, access to data and the uses to which it can be put. In the following paragraphs, I describe some of the promising ideas.

Big Data and customer targeting

Because AI and Big Data enable firms to assess how much each individual values different products and is therefore willing to pay, they give these firms the power to price discriminate, to charge more to those customers who value the product more or who have fewer options.[17] Price discrimination not only is unfair, but it also undermines the efficiency of the economy: standard economic theory is based on the absence of discriminatory pricing.[18] Everyone pays the same price. But with AI and Big Data, different people can pay different prices.

Thus, AI and Big Data enable technology firms to extract a larger fraction of the value of what society produces for themselves, leaving the rest of society—ordinary consumers—worse off. Staples, for instance, has been shown to know whether individuals living in a particular zip code have a store selling comparable products nearby; if not, they can charge a higher price for internet orders.[19] Insurance companies know the zip codes in which their customers live, and can charge accordingly—not based just on the risk of those in the zip code but on market power and their ability to charge more. In practice, in both examples, consumer products and insurance, the zip codes where higher prices were charged house predominantly minorities— thus, AI and Big Data have proved to be new instruments for racial discrimination.

The twenty-first-century digital economy has enhanced the ability of firms to target those whom they can take advantage of in other ways.[20] They can prey on individuals' weaknesses. AI could, for instance, detect someone with an addictive personality who might fall into the clutches of a gambling casino, and incentivize him to go to

Las Vegas or the nearest casino. As sociologist Zeynep Tüfekçi is fond of pointing out, it could exploit each of our weaknesses, an irrational desire for new shoes or handbags or trips to warm beaches, and feed us information that leads us to dissipate our incomes, our emotional self prevailing over our more deliberative self.[21] Research by Nobel Prize winner Richard Thaler has described what might be viewed as a war going on inside many individuals between these different identities. These new technologies intervene in this war on behalf of our lesser selves. The fear is that Big Data and AI will allow firms to have near perfect insight into these dynamics, and adjust their practices accordingly to maximize profits.

Big Data is also invaluable in many areas of research. The more data a genetics firm has, the better able it is to analyze an individual's DNA and to detect the presence of certain genes. Profit-maximizing firms thus want to gather as much data on individuals as they can—and not to share that data. In this pursuit of profits, lives lost are just another form of collateral damage, as the following story illustrates. Beginning in 1990, there was a great international effort to decode the human gene sequence, the Human Genome Project. It was successful—by 2003 the task had been completed. But a few private firms realized that if they raced ahead, they could beat the project, and get a patent on any gene that they decoded, and that could be a gold mine. For instance, Myriad, a Utah firm, got the patent on two genes, called BRCA1 and BRCA2, and developed a test to identify those carrying them. This was valuable because a woman with these genes had a high probability of getting breast cancer. Myriad charged outrageous prices—between $2,500 and $4,000, the price of a whole genome sequencing. This put the test out of the range of many individuals. And not only were Myriad's prices high, but like all tests, theirs was imperfect. Meanwhile, scientists at Yale University developed a test claimed as more accurate, that they were willing to provide at a much lower price. Myriad, as the "owner" of the patent, refused to allow them to do it. The reason was not just the lost profits, it was also that they wanted the data. This particular story has a happy ending: The Association for Molecular Pathology sued Myriad, arguing that naturally occurring genes should not be patentable. On June 13, 2013, in a landmark case, the US Supreme Court unanimously agreed. Since then, prices of the test have come down and the quality of the test has gone up, a striking piece of evidence on the adverse effect of patents on innovation.[22]

To accomplish this kind of exploitation, of course, firms have to have an enormous amount of data on each of us, which means a loss of privacy. Some say, only people who have done something wrong should be worried about a loss of privacy. That's wrong. Anyone with a large set of data on anyone else might be able to construct a partial release of information that would suggest, at the very least, a compromise of integrity. Dictators and authoritarians have long understood the power of information. That's why secret services from East Germany's Stasi to Syria's secret police have made it a top priority to keep extensive dossiers on anyone of political relevance. To accomplish this required vast networks of spies. Big Data and information technology allow both firms and governments to create with ease an electronic dossier far fatter than anything the Stasi ever dreamed of. They enhance the ability of any authoritarian government to become a totalitarian government.

Some take comfort that Big Data is not in the hands of government but in private hands, those of Google, Facebook, or Amazon. I don't. Once we think about the problems of cybersecurity, the boundary between the public and private becomes less distinct. Edward Snowden's revelations taught us of the enormous amount of data that the government is already collecting on us, and made it fairly clear that whatever data the private firms have, the NSA could easily get hold of.[23] And revelations about how Facebook has been using some of its data and allowing others (for example, Cambridge Analytica) to use its data, and the security measures it has taken to protect the data shouldn't make us any too comfortable either.

George Orwell's dystopian novel *1984* and a more recent one, *The Circle*, by Dave Eggers, illustrate our fears of a Big Brother government having control over us—and Big Data provides it with the ability to control that which was well beyond Orwell's imagination.[24]

In short, we should be concerned about our loss of privacy. Privacy is about power. The Big Data companies understand this, but it's not apparent that the same is true for those they prey upon.

THIS POWER CAN be used and abused in multiple ways. Those like Facebook, Amazon, and Google with access to vast amounts of information can, as we have noted, use their information advantage to strengthen their market position vis-à-vis rivals and leverage their market power into other arenas. The huge advantage of having more data means that competitive entry will be even harder, perhaps impossible. Both economic theory and history tell us that an entrenched monopolist has less incentive to innovate. It will devote more of its energies to ensuring that its market power is extended and enhanced than to figuring out how to better serve others.[25]

Even more disturbing has been the use by Facebook of its data for purposes of political manipulation, and not just by Russia in the United States.

Regulating data and its use

There are large societal consequences for market power, privacy, and security of having huge amounts of data in the hands of a relatively few firms. We should be concerned. In thinking about how to react, the government could play a number of roles, for instance, in assigning ownership of data and regulating how data can be used. [26]

Europe has taken some first steps.[27] Of course, the tech giants complain that European officials are taking these actions because they are anti-American. They are wrong. Europe is taking these actions because the law requires them to maintain a competitive marketplace and because throughout Europe there is a healthy concern for privacy. The United States has been slow to follow suit, at least partly because of the tech giants' political influence.[28]

One set of proposals for curbing both the power and the abuses of the current tech giants is to give ownership of an individual's personal data to the individual himself. That would mean that any firm that wants to use the data could obtain it, at a price; and the individual could proscribe any exploitive uses. It would mean too that at least some of the value of the data would accrue to the individual, rather than to the tech firms. There have been some attempts to at least give an individual some control over his own data this way—in Europe, individuals must explicitly give Google permission to use their data. Free-market advocates support such a solution: let the individual him- self decide. Thus, some internet companies have offered to give a small discount on the prices they charge if individuals allow them to use their data, and most customers agree to do so. The head of one company crowed to me about how cheaply his company was able to obtain data which was of such value to the company, and which it was so successfully monetizing.

Some say, let it be. The individual is freely deciding whether to let others have his data. But there are many areas where we as a soci- ety decide to intervene in individuals' unfettered decisions. There are other settings where we forbid individuals to engage in behavior that harms only themselves, such as participating in pyramid schemes or selling organs. The same arguments apply to data, but even more strongly, since one's data, in combination with that of others, can enhance firms' ability to exploit everyone in the economy. Individuals don't really appreciate what is or could be done with their data, espe- cially if that data wound up in the wrong hands. They don't know the extent to which those companies that have their data exercise adequate security. Most don't even know what the liability laws are or what the consequences are of a data breach. Given America's biased legal system, getting justice will be costly, at the very least. And the Equifax scandal illustrates the deceptiveness of America's corporate sector. This firm, that had collected data on individuals, typically without their permission, had a massive data breach in 2017, allowing information on 150 million Americans to be stolen in one fell swoop. Not only had they failed to secure the data, but they also later attempted to make money out of the breach itself, forcing individuals to sign a waiver just to find out whether their data had been breached.[29]

Regulation of firms' use of data could take a number of forms. Soft regulation would simply require transparency and a review of what the firm discloses about its privacy and security policies for accuracy. Harder regulation would entail stronger oversight and prohibitions, proscribing certain uses and sale of data. For instance, we could, at the very least, make sure that individuals know what is being done with their data. There can be restrictions on putting together ("agglomerating") data sets, recognizing that the dangers, for instance, of the invasion of privacy and exploitation of individuals increase with the amount of data that a firm has. Each individual could be required to give "informed consent" about the use of his data. The problem is defining what that means, and ensuring that the individual's intentions are honored. Many have been shocked by the extensive use of their Facebook data, even though they thought they had high privacy settings.

Government could go further, assigning a minimal price as compensation for a firm using personal data or even prohibiting companies from storing an individual's data for more than the time necessary for the transaction(s) in which they are currently engaged.[30]

We could have a review process, where any firm holding a large amount of data about individuals would have to disclose to a review panel how that information is being used. Given the remarkable record of dishonesty on the part of some tech giants, there would have to be strong punishments for any deceit.

There are still further steps that could be taken: We could impose a tax on the use or storage of data. (The technologies that allow the gathering, storage, and use of mass data also allow for its easy taxation.) We could require that data only be stored in an aggregate form, without individual identifiers (called anonymizing data), allowing researchers to glean information about behavioral patterns, but not to target individuals.[31]

And we could go even further, treating data as a public good, demanding that any data that is stored (in either processed or unprocessed form) be available to everyone, reducing the ability of the current tech giants to use their data advantage to further entrench their monopoly power. But here, the privacy issues raise a conundrum: The control of Big Data by a few big tech companies reinforces their market power. If we want to break this market power by making the data available to others, then we get a large, common pool of data. But a larger common pool means a greater loss of privacy and more opportunities for exploitation, with entrants competing on how to use the information to extract more value, which includes using that information to take advantage of consumers in the ways described above. It opens up the possibility of more abuse of the data. Almost surely, the solution will entail limiting the use and agglomeration of data.

New technologies and the threat to democracy

Even more troubling than the potential threats to our economy and our privacy posed by the new technologies are those posed to our democracy. The new technologies are double-edged swords. Proponents have highlighted the positive: the creation of a larger public space in which everybody's voice can be heard. But we have seen a far more sinister side, as, for instance, Russia has repeatedly interfered in democratic elections, seemingly in an attempt to undermine confidence in Western democracy. The new technologies can be used for manipulation, not only to enhance economic profits, but also to foster certain views, and cast doubt on others. Those with more money can do this better—and the family of Robert Mercer and others who funded Cambridge Analytica in their secretive and subversive attempt to manipulate the 2016 election have shown how it can be done. Thus, the new technologies have opened a new avenue through which power and money begets more power and money.

A host of reforms have been proposed, none convincingly up to the task. Some put greater onus on the platforms. Germany, perhaps not surprisingly given its history, has taken a strong position on the dissemination of hate speech. In some cases, simply introducing delays—slowing down the internet, reducing the chances of misinformation going viral or trending—may work. In the meantime, fact-checking processes may be set in motion; labeling items that are being re-sent as fact-checked or not, may help.

Requiring disclosure of sources of paid advertising attempting to circulate as real news on social media would also help—and so would proscribing foreign supported advertising aimed at our elections. This should be done, even if it costs Facebook and Twitter some lost profits. To prevent banks from being used as a conduit for money related to terrorism or money laundering, we require banks to "know your customer." We should impose similar requirements on Facebook, Twitter, and the other tech platforms. This policy change alone would, if adequately enforced, have gone a long way to stop Russia's interference in America's elections and the elections of other countries.

The social media platforms are effectively like publishers; they both distribute news and carry ads. Newspapers are liable for what they publish, but the tech giants have used their political influence to escape a corresponding liability.[32] If they had comparable liability, they would take greater care in what information they distribute, investing more in screening, and we would have a safer and more honest internet.[33]

We can also attempt to create more discerning consumers of information. Some countries, like Italy, are extending public media education (including about social media), making individuals more aware of assertions that are blatantly false.[34]

An active, publicly supported media can also play a role in publicizing the attempts, for instance, of Russia to interfere with US politics. Russia has perhaps been as effective as it has been simply because it has been unseen. As we noted, there is no more important arena for collective action than ensuring the integrity of the processes by which we make collective decisions and the information on which those decisions should rationally be made. This is a public good, requiring public support. Many countries (like Sweden and the UK) have active, independent but publicly funded media that have earned the people's trust; nonetheless, many on the Right want to scale these successful media back—perhaps because they are afraid of the truth, and because they prefer media controlled by the rich (e.g., Murdoch and his Fox News), who are more likely to side with them. These efforts should be resisted; and those countries that do not have an effective independent and well-funded public media should explore creating these institutions.

Unfortunately, those who would use the new technologies for manipulation understand the limitations of our regulatory framework, and work hard to exploit any gaps. It is a war, and at this juncture, those who would undermine democracy seem to be winning.

The reason, to a large extent, is the handcuffs we put on ourselves, in our attempts to protect free speech. Even the US Supreme Court, well attuned to the principle of freedom of speech, has noted that one cannot cry fire in a crowded theater (*Schenck v. United States*, 1919). In this war for an informed public, to block the corrosive effects of those who would use disinformation to weaken our democracies, the measures we have described here are small compromises. Further actions may be needed.

In the end, the market power and potential for abuse of a platform like Facebook may be simply too large for societal well-being. When Standard Oil became too large and powerful, we broke it up. But in that case there were no significant economies of scale, and so the economic costs of doing so were limited. Facebook, on the other hand, may be what we referred to earlier as a natural monopoly.[35] It may be both hard to break it up and hard to regulate what it does. Further, breaking it up may make regulation even more difficult. There may be no alternative to declaring Facebook a public utility, with all the tight public oversight that that entails.[36]

Critics of such measures worry about the impact on innovation. While I believe that we could simultaneously have strong regulations and still provide good incentives for innovation, we need to ask how concerned we need to be about possible adverse consequences of these regulatory and other measures on innovation. As I noted earlier, the overall social value of these innovations may be far less than what our Silicon Valley entrepreneurs would have us believe. Tighter public oversight (or even ownership) might enable us to redirect innovation in a more constructive way. Figuring out a better way to target consumers with advertising or to extract more consumer surplus can be important for firms—it can be an important source of profits. But this is another instance where social and private returns are not aligned. The social return to discriminatory pricing and other forms of consumer exploitation is in fact negative.[37]

In the US and elsewhere in those countries with a strong democratic tradition, I believe strong judicial and congressional oversight of whatever actions have to be taken to tame the social media—to ensure against the loss of privacy, political manipulation, and market exploitation—with civil society participation in an open and transparent process, could work, even if in countries with weaker institutions and a weaker commitment to democracy, one would be worried about abuses. Moreover, we could develop an effective regulatory regime that will sustain innovation where it matters.[38] These may be existential matters for our democracy and our society in coming years.

Globalization in the Era of AI

Differences in views about privacy and cybersecurity across the world may represent the most important impediment to globalization in the future. Some have suggested that we are moving toward a "splinternet," with China, the US, and Europe moving toward different legal frameworks.[39] If AI and Big Data are as important as some claim, China, with its absence of concerns for privacy, may have a huge advantage. American firms will argue that because Chinese firms are given a leg up on US firms due to China's lack of concern about privacy, they need some form of protection. But by the same token, European firms may demand protection from American firms because of our looser privacy and security laws.

Under the influence of our tech giants, America may demand (and under Trump, it is demanding) that everyone accede to American standards, that Europe should repeal its regulations designed to protect privacy.[40] This, however, is a particularly provincial perspective. There are good reasons that Europeans are concerned with privacy. There is no reason for Europe to give in to what the American government wants, whether what it wants is driven by the genuine concerns of American citizens or the power of Big Technology in America's pay-to-play politics. Going in the direction of China is (and should be) unacceptable. I fear Big Brother. It is better that we join Europe in having strong privacy protections and, if necessary, figure out ways to offset any advantage that others have from unbridled access to Big Data.[41]

Conclusions

This chapter has shown how some of the new technologies may exacerbate all of the problems presented in previous chapters—in particular those associated with jobs and wages, inequality and market power. They also introduce several new ones, including those involving privacy and cybersecurity. While the "solutions" are not clear, what is clear is that matters can't just be left to the market.

Earlier chapters discussed the ways in which the market economy—our capitalist system—is shaping us. It is making at least large numbers more selfish and less moral. So too, one of the most troublesome aspects of some of the new technologies is how they are changing *who we are* both as individuals and as a society.

There is increasing evidence of the multiple ways in which the new technologies are affecting individuals and their interactions with others. Attention spans may be getting shorter. And the hardest problems can't be solved with short attention spans. Personal interaction may be less common, and when we interact, we interact with those who are more similar. Thus, our society gets more polarized, with each of us living in our own echo chamber. In such a world, finding common ground is increasingly difficult, and so, accordingly, is social cooperation. There is more scope for bullying—bringing out the worst in us, and allowing that to happen in private, where there are not social correction mechanisms in place. So while we may be better connected with others in a superficial way, the depth and quality of social interactions may be deteriorating.

Even those in the tech community have begun to be worried. Where this will lead us no one knows. But it is already clear: the division of the US into warring camps, seeing the world through totally different lenses, even arguing for the validity of "alternative facts" makes the construction of consensus policies and a viable politics increasingly difficult.[42]

The central theme of this book is that none of this has to be—at least to the extent that it is. Advances in technology *should* be a blessing. They *should* better enable us to ensure that everyone has access to the basic requisites of a decent life. But these advances can, and likely will, lead to the immiseration of large fractions of the population unless we take strong collective action. The next chapter elaborates on why we have to act *together*. The problems can't and won't be solved by markets or individuals on their own.

CHAPTER 7

Why Government?

The basic principle that individuals working together can do far more than individuals working alone has long been recognized. Perhaps the necessity of large-scale "collective action" was first realized in ancient rice-growing societies, which depended on irrigation. Everybody benefited from the construction and maintenance of irrigation canals, and these had to be collectively organized and financed. Moreover, in the many places where water was limited, there had to be rules for the fair sharing of the water that was available—again, something that had to be done collectively. In other places, it was defense, the protection of the community from marauders, that led to forms of early collective action. The community, working together, could provide a kind of protection that individuals, by themselves, could not.

The Constitution of the United States shows that the citizens of the newly independent states understood the need for collective action. As the preamble states:

> **We the People** of the United States, in Order to form a more perfect Union, establish Justice, insure domestic Tranquility,

provide for the common defence, promote the general Welfare,
and secure the Blessings of Liberty to ourselves and our Posterity,
do ordain and establish this Constitution for the United States
of America.

These were all things that it was necessary to do *together*. There was
a common good in coming together, and doing so not just through
voluntary associations but through *government*, with all the powers that
that implied. Societal well-being was advanced not just by farmers and
merchants pursuing their own interests in a libertarian dream, but
also through a strong government, with clearly specified but limited
powers.

This need to act collectively sometimes seemed to conflict with
American individualism, the notion that we (or at least the most successful among us) are self-made and we would be even more successful
if only we weren't restrained by government. This notion is largely
a myth. In a literal sense, no one is self-made; the biological process
just doesn't allow it. But even our greatest geniuses realize that what
they do is built on the works of others.[1] A simple thought experiment
should induce a note of humility: What would I have achieved if I
had been born to parents in a remote village in Papua New Guinea
or in the Congo? Every American business benefits from the rule of
law, the infrastructure, and the technology that has been created over
centuries. Steve Jobs could not have created the iPhone if there had
not been the multitude of inventions that went into it, much based on
publicly funded research over the preceding half century.

A well-functioning society thus requires a balance between individual and collective action. In the first decades after their revolutions,
the Soviet Union and Communist China lost that balance. The worry
today is that we are losing that balance on the other side.

In this chapter, I want to explore both the need for and limits of
collective action. The previous chapters explained what's gone wrong

with globalization and financialization. We've described the consequences of the growing power of corporations and the weakening situation of workers. We've seen how these have led to slower growth with increasing inequality, and large fractions of the population actually doing worse over time. And we've seen how advances in technology have the potential to make matters still worse. But we've argued that none of this was inevitable. These changes could have been managed differently, and had they been managed differently, there would have been more winners and fewer losers. Markets on their own did what the rules of the game allowed them to do, what those rules incentivized them to do. What is needed are different rules of the game—we need collective action to *reform* our market economy. Each of the chapters has provided specific suggestions. This chapter attempts to tie all of these together by articulating a set of principles that should guide us in thinking about the role of collective action. After setting out the general principles, we'll see that in our evolving economy, there is an increasing need for government—rather than the retrenchment that so many on the Right seek.

The Need for Collective Action

Over the past half century, economists have come to a deeper understanding of the circumstances in which some form of collective action is needed to ensure the attainment of societal objectives—and which markets by themselves fail to produce efficient or fair outcomes.[2] This book has repeatedly stressed, for instance, the pervasive discrepancies between social and private returns—for instance, in the absence of regulations, individuals will fail to take into account the cost of their pollution in their economic calculus. Markets on their own produce too much pollution, inequality, and unemployment, but too little basic research.

There are certain things, like national defense, from which we all benefit; these are called "public goods,"[3] and have to be provided collectively. If we rely on private provision of a public good, there will be an undersupply. People or companies think only of their own gain, not of the broader societal benefits.[4]

While defense is the most obvious example, there are many others: just as rice-growing economies benefit from the infrastructure of a good canal system, so too we all benefit from a high-quality infrastructure of roads, airports, electricity, water, and sanitation.

Advances in knowledge are also public goods. Chapter 1 emphasized how advances in knowledge are the most important sources of increases in standards of living. We all benefit from innovations like transistors and lasers. That is why basic research has to be funded by government.

One of the most important public goods is an efficient and fair government, something from which we all benefit.[5] Public support of individuals and institutions engaged in the public interest—including an independent media and think tanks—is necessary if we are to achieve good government.

There are many other areas where markets fail to do what they should and where collective action can improve well-being. The reason we have a variety of social insurance programs (from retirement annuities, to health care for the aged, to unemployment insurance) is simple: these are big risks that, accordingly, have large impacts on individual well-being, but before the government came along, the market either didn't provide insurance against these risks, or did so only at very high prices with high transaction costs.[6]

Dynamic economies are always in transition, and markets don't manage these transitions well on their own. We are now moving from a manufacturing economy to a globalized, urbanized, service and innovation economy, with marked changes in demography.

So too, coordinating a large, complex economy is difficult. Prior to active government policies managing the macroeconomy, there were frequently long periods of extended unemployment. Keynesian policies have made downturns shorter and expansions longer. Today, every large country has a government-run central bank, and most take seriously the notion that it is the task of government to stabilize the economy.

Even if markets were efficient and stable, the outcomes might be (and often are) socially unacceptable, with too many people on the verge of starvation, too much of the wealth of the country going to a few. A fundamental role of government is ensuring opportunity and social justice for all. Deficiencies in capital markets mean that those unfortunate enough to be born in poor families won't, on the basis of their own or their parents' resources, ever be able to live up to their potential. It's unfair, and it's inefficient.

Government involvement in all these activities is essential. That should not be controversial. How government *organizes* these activities is, however, more complicated. In some areas, government has proven to be a far more efficient producer than the private sector—such as the provision of annuities through Social Security or the provision of health insurance through Medicare.[7]

In some cases, public–private partnerships, for instance in the provision of infrastructure, have proved an effective way of delivering services. The private party provides the capital to build the road on public land, managing, say, the road for 30 years, and eventually turning it over to the public. Often, however, these partnerships consist of the government bearing the downside risks and the private sector walking away with the profits. When the firm underbids, it walks away from the contract; when the firm bids more than its cost, it keeps the profits. It's a one-sided bet.[8]

The principle behind these examples is that we need our government to keep an open mind about the best way of organizing the production and delivery of services. Ideology here and elsewhere is unhelpful. The near-religious belief that private firms are always and everywhere better than government is wrong and dangerous.[9]

Regulation and Writing the Rules of the Game

There are many areas where it is best to leave production to the private sector. That doesn't, however, mean the private sector should be able to do whatever it wants. It needs to be regulated. We have to understand why and when we need regulation, how best to manage the regulatory process, and why it is that in many areas, the problem today is not overregulation, but underregulation.

In an interdependent society, there *has* to be regulation.[10] The reason is simple: what one person does affects others, and without regulations those effects won't be taken into account.[11] A firm that pollutes is shortening the lifespan and increasing the risk of lung disease of everyone who breathes the air—admittedly often by a small amount, but when multiplied by millions of firms, the pollution adds up. Obviously, a firm with no moral conscience that just focuses on making profits would rather not spend the money required to curb its pollution.

The Ten Commandments were a set of regulations designed for a simple society to ensure that individuals could live peaceably together. Stoplights are a simple regulatory mechanism, allowing traffic going in different directions to take turns. To see the benefits of this and other regulations, just go to any major city in a developing country, and observe the chaos that results in their absence.

The set of regulations required for the functioning of a modern society are obviously complex. Banks know how to take advantage of others through predatory and deceptive lending. Large banks engage in excessive risk-taking, knowing that they are too big to fail, so that if they run into a problem, they will be rescued—2008 was only the latest instance in which government had to bail them out. It's natural, then, to try to keep banks from undertaking excessive risk or from taking advantage of others. The banks argued for deregulation—stripping away the regulations that prevented them taking advantage of others and undertaking excessively risky actions. At the same time, they successfully clamored for laws that said that, in the case of bankruptcy, their derivatives—the risky products that played such a large role in bringing down the economy in 2008—should be paid before workers or anybody else. In doing so, they achieved what they really wanted: a set of laws and regulations that privileged the banks over everyone else. So too, in the 2008 and other crises, banks clamor for government bailouts.

Thus, the deregulatory movement that the banks did so much to push was really about constructing a pro-big-bank regulatory structure. The question should always be *which regulations*, not *deregulation*. No country, no economy, can function without laws and regulations. The banks wanted rights without responsibilities, a set of regulations and policies that gave them the freedom to exploit others and engage in excessive risk taking, but not bear the consequences of their actions.

One person's "freedom" can be another's "unfreedom." One person's right to pollute conflicts with another person's "right" not to die from pollution. Financial market liberalization gave banks the right to exploit others—and in a sense, it opened up their right to extort money from all of us, as the resulting financial crisis forced the country to pony up a trillion dollars or so.

Every society has learned the painful way that there are those who seek to get rich not by inventing a better product or making some other contribution to society, but by exploitation—exploitation of market power, exploitation of imperfections of information, exploitation especially of those who are vulnerable, poor, or less educated. To take one classic example: meatpackers tried to take advantage of consumers, selling them rotten meat, until Upton Sinclair exposed this in his 1906 book, *The Jungle*. The book caused such furor that the industry then *asked* to be regulated so confidence in meat could be restored. To take another example, there is almost universal recognition that a person would do anything to prevent his children from starving to death, or to buy them necessary medicine—including bor-rowing at usurious interest rates. That's why so many countries and religions have laws and precepts preventing usury, and why the more humane wealthier societies try to do what they can to prevent people from being in these extreme positions where they can be so exploited by others. More generally, there is and should be concern when there is too great an asymmetry in bargaining power.

Critics of regulation contend that our legal system is enough of a deterrent to exploitation, that the example of convicted criminals like Bernie Madoff who took advantage of others is sufficient. That is not the case: we need regulations to make it more difficult for the bad behavior to happen in the first place. It is better to prevent these actions than to clean up the mess after they occur because the damage can never be fully repaired—as the Madoff example itself makes abun-dantly clear. So too, we should have regulations to prevent predatory behavior, like the for-profit colleges that take advantage of individuals' natural desires to get ahead, but do not deliver anything of value; or the predatory lending that marked the pre-crisis mortgage market or that marks payday lending today.

In short, we need regulation to make markets work like they're supposed to—in a competitive way, with transactions between well-informed parties, where one party isn't trying to take advantage of another. Without confidence that markets are reasonably well-regulated, markets might even disappear. Who would buy a stock if there were a good chance that it was nothing but a scam?

The regulatory process

Designing a good, efficient regulatory system is difficult, but we've done a remarkably good job of combining expertise with checks and balances. We want to avoid politicization of the regulatory process as far as possible. Congress sets the goals and objectives of regulations, with responsibility for the details of the regulation left to independent but accountable agencies, which in turn implement the intent of Congress as impartially as possible (at least, that's the theory). We've even created regulations to ensure that regulations are made and enforced fairly and efficiently. For instance, for all major regulations our system requires a cost-benefit analysis—weighing the benefits of the rule against the costs. Typically, the benefits are a multiple of the costs. The regulation has to be put out for "notice and comment," a transparent process in which those who have concerns about the regulation can raise their objections. Commentators can suggest improvements and alterations. (Of course, the special interests weigh in far more than the general public, resulting in a more pro-business regulatory framework than might be ideal.)[12] Then the agency proposing the regulation has to respond to the comments, eventually issuing a final version. And those who do not like the regulation can challenge it in court, arguing that it is not consistent with the objectives set forth by Congress, that it violates some other governmental rule, regulation, or precept, or that the process of issuing the rule was not done properly. In short, we have imposed enormous democratic safeguards into our regulatory process. This doesn't mean that every rule is ideal. Often there is far from perfect information about where a market will be evolving, and the world turns out to be different from what we expected. Sometimes the world changes, and a rule that made sense at one time won't at another.[13] But all human institutions are fallible. We've done a creditable job of creating a framework that works.[14]

Restoring regulations, both individually and as a principle

Right now, on balance, our economy needs more regulations, at least in certain key arenas. Our economy has been changing fast, and our regulations need to keep pace. Twenty years ago, for instance, we didn't realize the dangers posed by carbon emissions; now we do, and we need regulations to reflect that. Twenty years ago, obesity was not the problem it is today. Now, we need to protect our children from the sweet and salty foods, designed to be addictive, that are contributing to this epidemic. Twenty years ago, we didn't have the opioid crisis that has in part been manufactured by the pharmaceutical industry. Twenty years ago, we didn't have a rash of for-profit educational institutions exploiting their students and the government loans for which they qualify.[15]

The conflict over net neutrality provides a vivid example of the need for regulation and the ways in which corporate interests manipulate the system for their own advantage.

Net neutrality says that the controllers of the internet (there are three major internet providers in the US—Comcast, Charter, and AT&T—hardly a competitive market) have to treat all those who want to use the internet equally—and, in particular, they are not allowed to give an advantage to anyone in terms of internet speed.[16] In 2015, net neutrality became the law of the land when the Federal Communications Commission (FCC) issued its Open Internet Order, which made the internet, in effect, regulated as a public utility, and as such prevented discrimination among users (hence the term "net neutrality"). But just two years later, in December 2017, Ajit Pai, Trump's FCC chairman, repealed the Open Internet Order. Providers now have no legal limitations on throttling the speeds they give different online businesses.[17]

Net neutrality's demise came too recently to say what the outcome will be. But the worry—shared intensely by many consumers and economists who see the internet as essentially a public utility—is that with the law of the jungle, the strong and powerful prevail. Big firms will strike better deals with the internet providers; and the internet providers will give themselves the advantage. They will leverage their market power in the control of the internet into market power in the provision of content (such as entertainment) over the internet.

Streaming video services provide a good example of how the loss of net neutrality could hurt competition—disadvantaging even large and seemingly powerful firms. Netflix is very data-intensive—its appeal to its customers relies on the quick and seamless transfer of video, requiring a fast and large flow of data into their homes. Thus, slowing down the internet speeds that Netflix has access to would deal a serious blow to its viability as a business. If an internet provider has its own video streaming service that competes with Netflix, it could give itself the advantage by choking off Netflix's access to bandwidth.

Absent net neutrality, the monopoly internet provider also has the ability to extract from users like Netflix a large fraction of their profits, demanding a premium payment from Netflix for access to high speeds. If Netflix did not give in, that is, unless Netflix paid the ransom, the internet provider could randomly slow down service, even when there was no capacity problem.

Net neutrality's detractors like to claim that the market will sort out this kind of issue: if consumers aren't getting what they want, they'll switch to another internet provider that streams Netflix reliably at fast speeds. But with only three major national internet providers, customers have limited choice; indeed, in many parts of the country, consumers who want broadband internet have only one choice.[18] Even if in the long run there would be entrants offering more reliable internet service, as John Maynard Keynes said in another context, in the long run, we're all dead: Netflix wouldn't be able to wait. The knowledge that the internet providers have such market power puts a damper on innovation in the entire industry. The result is more inequality, less innovation, and slower growth.[19]

Government Failure

We've explained why collective action is needed. But that doesn't mean that it's easy or always successful. Collective action takes many forms and occurs at many levels. A host of nongovernmental organizations and charities work to provide for the public good. Our not-for-profit universities like Harvard and Columbia, heavily supported by voluntary contributions, are among our most successful organizations, producing knowledge and imparting it to successive generations.

Still, the single most important institution for collective action is government.[20] But here's the rub: the powers that enable government to improve societal well-being can be used by some groups or individuals within society to advance their interests at the expense of others. This is sometimes termed "government failure," in contrast to market failure. Critics of government action claim, wrongly, that resorting to government to cure market failures is a cure worse than the disease and that government failure is pervasive. As this book has argued, there is no way we can do without government; we can't go back to the jungle. We have to have government action. The question is how best to ensure that what the government does serves the interests of all of society. The most successful countries are those that have figured out good answers to this question, and have strong and effective governments. For instance, the East Asian countries that made a dramatic transition from poor developing countries to powerful emerging markets in the space of a few decades had governments that played a central role in their development.[21] Similarly, government has played a central role in the development of the US economy throughout the nation's history.[22]

By studying when government involvement has succeeded as desired and when it has failed, economists have obtained a much better understanding of how to prevent government failure. Many of the failures are associated with what is called "capture," private firms and rich individuals using their money and influence to get the government to advance their interests. We have to be constantly on guard against this possibility, and set up rules and institutions to make it more difficult.

The Founding Fathers also recognized that a critical and independent media is an essential part of any healthy democracy. Still another essential feature of a successful democracy is transparency.

Many critics of the views I've put forward in this book combine a skepticism about government with an overarching—and unjustified—faith in markets. Earlier, I referred to the notion of market fundamentalism (sometimes also referred to as neoliberalism): the ideas that unfettered markets on their own were efficient and stable, and that if we just let markets work their wonders and grow the economy, everybody would benefit (called trickle-down economics). Previous chapters have debunked these ideas—as if the 2008 crisis, the episodic high levels of unemployment, and our massive inequality weren't proof enough. All of these problems would be far worse were it not for large government interventions.

At the most basic level, as has been noted, markets have to be structured by rules and regulations—at the very least, to prevent one party or group from taking advantage of others or imposing costs on others (for instance, through pollution). Those rules and regulations have to be set *publicly*.

And then there are many things that markets on their own won't do—from preserving our environment to investing enough in education, research, or infrastructure or, as we've seen, providing insurance against many of the important social risks that they face.

The ongoing debate over the role of government

The *real politik* of twenty-first-century America is that those who seek to preserve our standards of living and the values I articulate in this book will have to persuade the rest of the country that there are alternative policies more consistent with their interests and values than the course the country is currently on, that is, Trump's nativism and protectionism, or the "market fundamentalism" course that Reagan set the country on some four decades ago. Unfortunately, too often, social issues, like abortion and gay rights, have gotten in the way of our ability to address the basic economics—of how we can get to growth with equality.[23]

Today, though, a major impediment to the acceptance of the ideas
I've put forward is the lack of trust in government. Even if collective
action were desirable, those on the Right have encouraged a widespread distrust in government.

There can only be trust if there is a belief that the political system
is fair, and that our leaders are not just working for themselves. Nothing destroys trust so much as hypocrisy and gaps between what leaders promise and what is delivered. Well before Trump, our elites and
political leaders (in both parties) created the conditions for mistrust,
with policies that seemed only to help themselves. The real winners
of the policies that they had pushed throughout the 1980s and 1990s
were the elites: the claim that all would benefit was sheer self-serving
nonsense. So too, in the Great Recession of 2008 that these policies
brought on, the same elites saved themselves: the bankers kept their
bonuses and jobs, while millions lost their homes, tens of millions
their jobs.[24] Something had gone badly wrong and it wasn't just an act
of nature, a once-in-a-thousand-year flood. And yet, though almost
every day revealed a new misdeed by our banks and our bankers,
almost no one was held accountable. If it wasn't illegal, it should have
been. The government picked a few "demonstration" cases, a small
Chinese bank here, a mid-level banker there. But the leaders of the
banks, those who had been so amply rewarded for the "successes" of
the banks, their billions of dollars of profits, seemed immune. They
claimed credit for the banks' profits, but not for their sins.[25]

We had created a system where the inequalities in justice seemed as
wide as those in income, wealth, and power. No wonder that so many
Americans were angry.

It was not inevitable, though, that the anger would take the form
that it did. It could have been directed against those who were most
responsible for the plight faced by the vanishing middle—those who
had advocated unfettered globalization and financialization, but who
simultaneously opposed progressive taxes and transfer programs and

assistance for workers who lost their jobs as a result of globalization or were hurt by financialization, financial deregulation, and their aftermath.[26] Why it took the form it did—an attack on people who were *more* aligned with their interests, though not perfectly so—is a question that will surely be debated for years to come. Perhaps it was because the "Clinton" and "Obama" Democrats seemed most hypocritical; at least the Republicans didn't make a pretense of caring for ordinary workers. Perhaps it was just bad luck: the arrival of a demagogue able to articulate a story about the betrayal of ordinary Americans by the "enlightened" elites and use that to engineer a hostile takeover of the Republican Party. It was not, however, a truly hostile takeover, for the vast majority of the party went along with Trump's bigotry, misogyny, nativism, and protectionism, and even an unprecedented increase in peacetime nonrecession deficits in order to get what they wanted—tax cuts for the rich and corporations, and deregulation. In making their bargain with the devil, they had made their values and priorities clear.

How ideas spread, taking hold at one place or at one time, is in many ways a mystery. Nothing seems inevitable, even if there are preconditions that make one outcome or another more likely. It was not inevitable that Germany would go through the nightmare of Hitler, and at many points there were opportunities for the business elite to stand up to him. We can't be sure what would have happened if they'd done so, but there is at least a chance that the course of history would have been changed. Will someone a half century from now be writing a similar sentence about America's business community today?

The Increasing Need for Government

Our twenty-first-century economy is markedly different from that of the twentieth century, and even more from that about which Adam Smith wrote at the dawn of the Republic. These changes have made it imperative that government take on a far larger role than it did in those earlier eras. In the following paragraphs, I describe six of the ways in which the economy has changed, each of which calls for more collective action.

The innovation economy. The production of knowledge is different from the production of steel or other ordinary commodities. Markets on their own will not invest sufficiently in basic research, the wellspring from which all other advances come—which is why government has taken on the central role at least in financing it.

The urban economy. As we've industrialized and moved into the postindustrial era, we've urbanized. There are distinct advantages of urban agglomerations, but they are hard to manage well. In close quarters, what one person does can have large effects on others. Without traffic rules there is gridlock and untold accidents; without environmental and health regulations cities would be the unpleasant places they used to be, with short life spans and rampant disease. Noise pollution would make life even more unpleasant. "Unplanned" cities in emerging markets give us a picture of how unbearable cities without zoning can be.

An economy bounded by planetary limitations. In Smith's day, there was little awareness of environmental fragility. Today, we are encroaching on the limits of our biosphere. Markets, on their own, have shown themselves capable of making cities unlivable: think of London's pea soup smog or that of Los Angeles. The market didn't clean these cities up on its own: it was government regulations that forced changes in behavior. At a small cost to each individual and firm, there were enormous benefits for all.

The complex economy. Managing an economy in the Adam Smithian world of farms and pin factories is different from managing a postindustrial globalized and financialized innovation economy. Then, economic fluctuations were largely related to weather. For two hundred years, however, there have been large business fluctuations that have inflicted enormous societal costs. The 2008 crisis was not an act of God; it was man-made, something our system did to *us*. Our system failed us—and in many ways, we are still reeling from its economic and political consequences. A more complex system, with more interrelationships, with each market participant trying to squeeze out the last dollar of profit, turns out to be a more fragile economic system.[27]

The economy in flux. Our economy is always changing. We've moved from an agricultural economy to a manufacturing economy to a service-sector economy. We've globalized and financialized. Now, we'll have to learn to manage a complex, urban economy, within our planetary boundaries and with a rapidly aging population, presenting new challenges for the distribution of income and well-being across generations. As I've noted, markets don't manage transitions well on their own: That's partly because those in sectors or places that are in decline don't have the resources to make the investments needed to move into the sectors of the future. Detroit, Michigan, and Gary, Indiana, my home town, are testimony to what happens when one leaves it to the market. Countries that have helped ordinary citizens and places under stress adjust to the changing economy, such as Sweden, have a more dynamic economy, and a polity that is more open to change.

A globalized economy, **where what happens inside a country often depends on what happens outside its borders.** We've become more interdependent, more exposed to risks, often beyond the ability of most individuals to cope. There is greater need for global collective action, to manage this interdependence, this risk; but economic globalization has outpaced political globalization, the development of institutions to manage economic globalization. The burden remains on the nation-state, but just as the burden on the nation-state is increasing, its capacity to respond is decreasing, and especially with conservatives arguing that it should not respond. Globalization itself has played a role in this decreased capacity to respond: it has provided new opportunities for tax avoidance and evasion, and some (wrongly) have argued that to compete in a globalized world, taxes and government programs have to be cut.

Conclusions

In this chapter, we've described the need for collective action. When we act together and in concert, we can be far better off than when we act alone. People get together to cooperate in a whole variety of ways. They form partnerships and corporations to produce, clubs and social organizations to socialize, voluntary associations and NGOs to work together for causes they believe in. They form unions to engage in collective bargaining, and they engage in class action lawsuits— cooperative actions by a group of people who have been injured, say, by the actions of a corporation, knowing that any one, acting alone, would not be able to get redress.[28] One of the strategies of corporations and the Right has been to preserve the current imbalance of power by making such collective action more difficult, making it more difficult for workers to unionize, making it more difficult for individuals to bring class action suits or to have recourse to public courts.

Government is one of the most important ways we work together. The difference between government and all these other forms of cooperation is the power of compulsion: it can force people and institutions not to do something (like carrying a gun which could lead to the death of your neighbor and impose other harms) or to do something (pay taxes, so that we have an army to defend us). Because in our modern society there are so many ways we can help and harm each other, government is inevitably going to be large and complex. Because of the "free-rider problem"—so many would like to benefit from publicly provided goods and services, from the military, police and fire protections, and the basic knowledge produced by government laboratories, to the protection of our environment, without paying their fair share of the costs—contributions have to be compulsory, that is, there has to be taxation. Decisions of what the government should and should not do, how it should do it, and who should pay for it thus have to be made through a political process.

Political institutions, like market institutions, are complex; they have the power to do good, but also to do harm. They can be used to redistribute up—from the poor and middle classes to the rich; they can be used to enforce, preserve and exacerbate existing power relationships; they can exacerbate social injustices rather than alleviating them. They can be an instrument of exploitation, rather than an instrument to prevent exploitation.

Constructing public institutions to enhance the likelihood that government will be a powerful force for good has been the challenge confronting democracies from the beginning. This is a challenge confronting the US today. The next chapter describes some of the pivotal reforms needed to ensure that our democracy works well for the majority of its citizens, rather than the few at the top. The chapters that follow show how, with this reconstructed democracy, we could reconstruct our economy to make it more competitive, more dynamic, more equal—so that a middle-class life would once again be attainable for most Americans.

PART II
RECONSTRUCTING AMERICAN POLITICS AND ECONOMICS:
The Way Forward

CHAPTER 8

Restoring Democracy

America was constructed as a representative democracy. Of critical importance was the inclusion in the system of strong checks and balances, and the Bill of Rights, to ensure that minority rights were protected by the majority. But the nation has evolved in practice into a country where a minority seems to wield power over the majority. We have a presidential electoral system in which two of the three presidents who took office in this century did so with a distinct minority of votes. Further, we have gerrymandering in the House of Representatives, the one branch of the government that was supposed to closely reflect the population. Thus, in the 2012 elections, Democrats couldn't even gain a majority in the House of Representatives despite getting 1.4 million more votes than Republicans did. And our Senate, deliberately designed to give equal weight to each state has, as the result of population concentration, exacerbated the problem of minority party control, at least when measured from the vantage point of the nation as a whole. We led the world in creating a modern democracy and democratic institutions; now we seem to be lagging. It might have been different if these presidents and legislative bodies had conducted themselves with a modicum of decorum, a modesty reflecting the fact that they did not have the support of the majority of Americans. Instead, they pioneered new extremes of winner-take-all politics. This domination of the majority by the minority is distinctly undemocratic, and has discouraged voters and weakened the legitimacy of American government at home and abroad. Issues like gun control, minimum wage, and tighter financial regulation have had the support of large majorities of Americans but can't be addressed. The book began with a brief discussion of the 2017 tax bill—usually cutting taxes receives overwhelming support. This time, though, voters understood that it was a tax cut for the rich, at the expense of those in the middle and the next generation; it was viewed unfavorably by a majority—the most unfavorably of any tax cuts.[1]

It is becoming clearer that the objective of the Republican Party is a permanent rule of the minority over the majority. This is an imperative for them because the policies for which they had advocated, from regressive taxation (taxing the rich at lower rates than the rest), to cutting back on Social Security and Medicare, and cutting back on government more generally, are anathema to the majority of voters. Republicans have to make sure that the majority doesn't get control. And if the majority does get control, they have to make sure that it can't put in place the policies that it would like, and which would advance the interests of the majority. As Nancy MacLean, professor of history at Duke University, put it[2], they have to put "democracy in chains."

Taking stock of how far this agenda has already progressed provides a stark picture of the political reforms that America needs, which are prerequisites for the lasting economic reforms I'm arguing for in this book. This chapter focuses on three critical areas: ensuring fairness in voting, maintaining an effective system of checks and balances in government, and reducing the power of money in politics.

Voting Reforms and the Political Process

A system intended to protect minority rights has been perverted. In a fair democracy, it is important to protect minority rights. But it is also important to protect majority rights.

The effort to privilege the political will of the minority over the majority begins with controlling the vote.[3] Our divided country's political battle over voting—who is allowed to vote—and representation is not new: in framing the Constitution, representatives from the southern states succeeded in enhancing their own representation by demanding that slaves be counted as three-fifths of a free man, even though the slaves themselves couldn't vote.[4] But with the recent growth in partisanship, this battle has taken another ugly turn. The Republicans have sought to disenfranchise those who they think might not support them. In fact, the country has had a long history of disenfranchisement: one of the most vivid examples of this is not allowing convicted felons to vote, which occurs in many states. Mass incarceration may have had many motives,[5] but clearly one of its effects has been mass disenfranchisement: some 7.4 percent of African Americans—2.2 million in total—were unable to vote in the 2016 election because of these state laws preventing voting.[6]

In some Republican-dominated states,[7] there is also an attempt to control the vote by making it more difficult for working people to register or to make it to the polling booth. Republicans can't impose a poll tax, as states of the segregated South once did; but they can increase the transaction costs of registering and voting, and this can be just as effective a deterrent. Rather than making it as easy as possible to register—to exercise one's basic right as a citizen—say, by registering as one gets one's driver's license, they make it as difficult as they can get away with. They can, for instance, demand hard-to-get identification papers.

Historically, no party had a monopoly on attempts at disenfranchisement: when the Democrats controlled the South, they tried to discourage voting by African Americans and the poor, as we already noted. But one of the divides that has opened up is over views of disenfranchisement: today, unfortunately, disenfranchisement is largely a one-party battle.[8]

And then elections are held in ways that make it more difficult for ordinary working people to vote, in some cases with shorter hours for poll booths (Indiana closes polling stations at 6 p.m.[9]), in other cases by challenging registrations, in still others by having fewer polling booths more inconveniently located. America is one of the few countries not to have voting on Sunday, when most people are not at work.

The electoral system is unfair in other ways. Gerrymandering, for example, makes sure that some votes matter more than others.[10]

Six reforms that could make a difference are (1) voting on Sunday (or by mail or making voting day a holiday), (2) paying individuals to come to the voting booth (or alternatively fining them for not coming, as Australia does), (3) making it easier to register, (4) ending the disenfranchisement of those who have served prison time, (5) ending gerrymandering, and (6) ensuring a path to citizenship for the Dreamers—young people who have grown up in the country and know no other home than the US.

These reforms are based on a simple set of principles: every American citizen should vote, and every vote should count equally. America has a dismally low percentage of citizens who vote.[11] These reforms would change that. They would also diminish the power of money—one of the expensive parts of any campaign is identifying who is likely to support one's candidate and ensuring that these individuals actually vote. More participation has the promise of leading to a more representative government. It is a civic virtue to vote; we know that there is a cost in time to turn out to vote—a cost that is often felt most keenly by ordinary workers. In a society in which incentive payments have become the norm, it seems a small price to pay to incentivize individuals in the exercise of their democratic rights—as opposed to the barriers that have been constructed to disincentivize them.

Taxation without representation was the motto that ignited the American Revolution, and yet we have created a system where large numbers of people can be taxed and never have representation— those who've served prison time, as discussed earlier, and temporary migrants. This is to say nothing of our citizens in the District of Columbia or Puerto Rico.

Drive through California's Central Valley and see the migrant laborers bent in the farm fields: they live in double-wide trailers, drink polluted water, suffer from elevated disease rates, and are politically powerless.[12] Many are from generations of laborers who have shuttled back and forth across the border—there is no path toward political rights for them. To some degree, the picture is reminiscent of the cotton fields of the antebellum South. Worse still, our political and economic systems work together to maintain these extremes of injustice: mass incarceration provides cheap convict labor and ensures that large numbers of people who might vote Democratic are denied the vote; temporary migrant labor, without a path to citizenship, ensures that these workers' grievances can't be aired in the political process, at least not by themselves. These individuals are *temporary* migrants, even though they may come back year after year, and the US is their only source of livelihood, because we have not allowed them to be permanent residents, for that would lead to citizenship and voice. Employers like this arrangement too, for it not only provides a source of cheap and docile labor, but workers' low wages also helps to drive down wages elsewhere.

Preventing Abuses of Political Power: Maintaining Our System of Checks and Balances

Long experience with democracy has shown the importance of systems of checks and balances.[13] Democracy is about ensuring that no individual or no group has excessive power—and indeed, the US Bill of Rights was designed to ensure that not even a majority could take away certain liberties from a minority. It was set up this way because excessive power is so often abused ("Power tends to corrupt, and absolute power corrupts absolutely," as Lord Acton famously put it), and because all individuals and institutions are fallible. A system of checks and balances is central to the prevention of the agglomeration and abuse of power. It has been alarming to watch President Trump undermine our system and our professional bureaucracy, so essential to preventing excessive politicization of public processes. He has, for instance, proposed increasing the discretion to fire government employees, reversing efforts for more than a century to depoliticize the government. Policies, including the rules and regulations that govern our country, are set through a political process, but the execution of the policies should be fair and objective, administered through a nonpolitical bureaucracy. One of the strengths of the United States has been the competency and integrity of its bureaucracy—and Trump is trying to undermine this.[14] The Right has long criticized government incompetency; perhaps these "reforms" are intended to make this a self-fulfilling prophecy, part of the concerted agenda to undermine government, which will lead to a government that is indeed weaker and more politicized.

It goes without saying that a key part of a progressive political agenda is resisting these attempts to weaken our system; indeed, the lesson is that we need to strengthen our systems of checks and balances and the role of our professional civil services and our independent agencies. We need to think more how we can maintain democratic accountability and, at the same time, prevent politicization and enhance the professionalization, efficiency, and efficacy of government.[15] Other countries have shown that it can be done.

The judiciary

Trump's attacks on the judiciary have been particularly vitriolic. When court after court ruled that his travel ban of Muslims was an abuse of power—violating the basic rights of individuals—he, like other presidents who have confronted a ruling with which they disagreed, appealed. But he did more, taking a page from the playbook of despots everywhere: he attacked the courts themselves, undermining confidence in the judiciary and its role as a fair arbiter.[16]

The Supreme Court's loss of status as a fair and wise arbiter did not, however, begin with the Trump presidency. It has instead been a gradual slide, the result of a long-term strategy by the Republicans to pack the Court with judges likely to make decisions based on their ideology and the interests of their establishment elites. The strategy seems to have paid off: the last two decades have seen a string of strongly partisan decisions. Of course, presidents have always wanted a Court supportive of their perspectives; traditionally, however, presidents also realized the importance of having the Court viewed as a fair, balanced, and wise arbiter. President George H. W. Bush should perhaps be given credit for initiating the assault on the Court, with the appointment of a grossly unqualified judge, Clarence Thomas.

The Republicans' brazen attempts to fill the courts with partisan judges have created another problem arising out of the inchoate set of "principles" that underlie their peculiar coalition, bringing together, for instance, libertarians, Trump protectionists, and the corporate establishment.[17] Never is this more so than when the Court rules on issues of politics and the political rules of the game, as when it effectively chose George W. Bush to be president, even though he had a distinct minority of popular votes. Normally, Republicans believe strongly in states' rights. But in *Bush v. Gore*, if the state had had its way, Gore would have been elected. So the Republican justices in the Supreme Court rode roughshod over their normal values to get the political result they wanted.[18] Similarly, when the Court allowed unlimited campaign contributions with the *Citizens United v. Federal Election Commission* opinion, reinforcing the role of money and economic inequality in our political system, it suggested that somehow money had not (yet) corrupted American politics.

The challenge facing "conservative" (partisan Republican) judges was to make seemingly principled and coherent decisions that were simultaneously loyal to their partisan positions. As the Republican Party has become more unprincipled, this task has become harder and harder.[19]

The result has been a Court that is viewed by many as simply another instrument in a wide-ranging partisan battle, rather than as a Solomonic institution whose wisdom is supposed to bring the country closer together; a Court that has widened the country's economic and racial divides, and exacerbated the already deep political and philosophical divides.[20]

It is naïve to think that we could have a Court that rises fully above politics. But we could have a Court that is more balanced, and where this gaming does not occur with such intensity. A simple institutional reform that might move us along in that direction entails converting life tenure to, say, a twenty-year term. This proposal has been around for decades, but has recently gained more urgency, and more supporters, as the Court has become ever more divided.[21] On average, approximately two justices would reach the end of their term in any (four-year) presidency.[22] This reform might also reduce the incentive for the extreme partisanship exhibited at the end of the Obama administration, when Congress refused even to consider Obama's highly qualified nominee, Merrick Garland.[23]

The Constitution does not specify the number of Supreme Court justices. There is much talk that, given that Republicans have violated traditional norms in so many ways, particularly by refusing to even review Garland's nomination, the Democrats should fight back by increasing the size of the Court by at least two should they come to control the presidency and both houses of Congress. As alluring as this might be, it could lead to a further weakening of America's democratic institutions: each side would be tempted to add further judges to the Court when they could, to ensure control of the Court—until the opposing party took power. The Court is already seen to too great an extent as merely another partisan weapon; this act might confirm the perception.

Still, it should not be acceptable for a minority, brazenly using all of the mechanisms we have described, to install themselves in power, and while there, pack the Supreme Court to ensure that were they to lose power, their interests and ideology would continue to prevail through their ideological Court appointees.

Term limits for Supreme Court justices, mentioned above, are probably the best way out of this conundrum. The next Democratic administration should formally propose such an amendment, and as a temporary measure, until the amendment is passed and goes fully into effect, the number of positions in the Court should be increased.

The Power of Money

Perhaps the greatest failing of the American political system is the increasing power of money, so much so that our political system can better be described as one dollar, one vote than one person, one vote. We all know the components of this awful nexus between money and politics: lobbyists, campaign contributions, revolving doors, and a media controlled by the wealthy. Wealthy individuals and rich corporations use their financial power to buy political power and to propagate their ideas, sometimes with truly "fake news." Fox News has become emblematic of this, and its power is now well documented.[24]

Those with money use it to garner even more wealth for themselves through the political system. The oil companies sought and gained access to tracts of government land under which there is oil and other minerals at a fraction of the value of the resources. These corporations were in effect stealing from ordinary Americans—but it was a stealth theft, with few Americans knowing that their pocket was being picked. The Clinton administration tried to force these corporations to pay full value, and the corporations waged a successful campaign to retain their ability to get the country's resources on the cheap.

The flip side of corporations paying too little to the government for public assets is to have the government pay too much for what it purchases from the private sector. The pharmaceutical companies put a little provision in the law providing the elderly with drugs under Medicare: the government, the largest buyer of drugs in the world, was not allowed to bargain on price. This and other provisions were put in at the behest of the drug companies to generate higher prices and profits. It worked. Medicare drugs cost far more than those provided, say, by the other government programs, like Medicaid for the poor or those for veterans. *For the same brand-name drugs, Medicare pays 73 percent more.* The result is that every year, taxpayers fork over tens of billions of additional dollars to the drug companies.[25]

What does it say about our political system when not just the president but some of the largest political contributors, especially to the Republican Party, are those who have made their fortunes from running casinos, notorious for the role they play in money laundering, other illicit activities, and exploiting gambling addiction?[26] They know that their fortunes depend on the good graces of the public. Should the government take too aggressive a stance on money laundering, their fortunes would suffer a reversal. So too, real estate developers knew that a small provision inserted into a tax bill giving them preferential treatment—such as the one passed at the end of 2017, which essentially allowed real estate trusts to get the same 20 percent lower tax rate given to small businesses—could mean fortunes for themselves.[27] And they knew too that a small change in regulations—for example, forcing the disclosure of the true buyers of expensive real estate, which would inhibit if not stop the use of real estate for money laundering[28]—can destroy their entire business model. The examples just given in this paragraph may be among the most distorting and most distasteful forms of rent-seeking; but it should be no surprise that a government run by rent-seekers will be a government *for* rent-seekers; and such a government will be short on growth and social justice.

The Supreme Court increases the power of money in politics

Combating the power of money within our democratic framework, with our strong belief in freedom of the press and freedom of speech, is not easy; but other countries with an equal commitment to democracy and freedom of the press and speech have done better than we have.

To a large extent, our problems are of our own making—or more accurately, of the making of our Supreme Court, which by some narrow five-to-four decisions has taken some extreme positions. *Citizens United* is an example.[29] The Court's decision in the case allowed unlimited contributions by corporations, nonprofit organizations, and unions to PACs (political action committees); only contributions by these entities made directly to campaigns remain restricted. The argument that corporations should be allowed unlimited expenditures because otherwise their "rights" would be abridged is silly. Corporations are not people. People have rights, but corporations are creations of the State, and as such, they can be "endowed" with whatever properties we want. There is no individual abridgment of rights when we restrict corporate contributions; indeed, one might argue the reverse. I buy a stock on the basis of my judgment of the corporation's economic prospects. It weakens the economy to have to conflate those judgments with whether I agree with the CEO's political judgments. The reality is that shareholders have little say in what the corporation does, and when a CEO uses corporate money for politics it's almost as bad as if he used that money to feather his own nest.[30]

The Court ruled that because the money was not given to the candidate, so long as there was no direct coordination with the candidate, the spending does "not give rise to corruption or the appearance of corruption." The latter claim is obviously false. Even the perception of corruption can corrupt confidence in our democratic institutions. One of the reasons that so many Americans think the political system is rigged is that they believe, rightly, that it is being driven by money.[31] There is little doubt that most Americans see what is going on as corruption, plain and simple. If a cigarette company lets it be known that it will spend money in support of candidates who oppose cigarette regulation, it inevitably leads to disproportionate influence[32]; it induces, for instance, candidates to come forward to oppose cigarette regulation. It's a form of corruption that is hardly less crude and just as effective as old-fashioned methods. The five justices who concurred with the *Citizens United* decision seem to be living in a different world than the rest of America—or were doing the best they could to come up with arguments that supported the moneyed interests of the Republican Party.[33]

Even worse was a decision in a case involving Arizona, where the state had attempted to even up contributions or spending when they exceeded a certain level (so that if a rich candidate spent $100 million on his campaign, more than his rival could possibly raise, the state would add to the campaign chest of his rival)[34] to create a more level playing field among candidates. The Court ruled that individuals had a right to create an unlevel playing field through monetary contributions, and what the state was doing was in effect denying them that right.[35]

An Agenda for Reducing the
Power of Money in Politics

There is a broad agenda for reducing the power of money in politics, entailing reducing the need for private financing, promoting greater transparency, and curbing contributions and other sources of moneyed influence.

Enacting better disclosure laws

Disclosure was supposed to curb the power of money: sunlight is the strongest antiseptic, as the saying goes. Members of Congress who voted against tobacco regulations might be embarrassed to do so if it were known that they had received large payments from the tobacco industry. Transparency hasn't proven as effective as had been hoped for two reasons: First, politicians and the interests they serve are more brazen than anyone might have expected. Because the influence of money is so pervasive, the disclosure of one instance or another can easily be shrugged off. "Everybody does it." And second, we have put enough loopholes into our system of transparency to make it ineffective, especially through the notorious secretive PACs.

True and complete transparency would be a step in the right direction. Even if we can't achieve full transparency, we could have much more transparency than we have today, and that would help. There is no reason why the PACs' contributors and actions are not fully disclosed.

Curbing campaign spending

Disclosure by itself is not enough, however. We have to curb campaign spending. And that's where the tension between the principles of free speech and fair elections come into play. The best ways to reconcile the two are to reduce the need for funds, to reduce the advantages that contributions afford, and to make it more difficult for those with wealth and power to make contributions, especially in unlimited amounts through the secretive PACs. The latter is especially important, given the imbalance of wealth and power in the US.

Funding campaigns publicly and requiring public broadcasters (all of whom make use of the public airwaves and the rights-of-way granted publicly to cable) to provide adequate air time to candidates would greatly reduce the need for money. So too would the mandatory voting requirements discussed earlier in the chapter—much campaign spending goes to "getting out the vote" of those who are more likely to agree with the candidate's position.

Public leveling of expenditures (making up for large contributions to one candidate or large expenditures by a wealthy candidate, by providing some public campaign support for those without financial resources) would also reduce the power of money—this too would require a change in the Supreme Court ruling, which in turn would require a change of just one vote.

Corporations are creations of the State, and therefore, as I argued earlier, have just the rights that the State endows them with. Restricting their right to make political contributions is not an abridgment of the individual rights guaranteed in the Constitution. The individuals who own the corporation are allowed to make contributions—subject, of course, to whatever restrictions Congress imposes. These restrictions on individuals make sense—they are a reasonable attempt to curb the power of money. But it makes no sense not to impose even stricter requirements on corporations and the secretive PACs.

In short, *Citizens United*, the Supreme Court case that effectively allows the unlimited spending of money on political campaigns, needs to be reversed.[36] But even without a reversal of *Citizens United*, there is much that can be done. Corporations should only be allowed to make a political contribution with a vote of a supermajority of their shareholders (say, two-thirds)—so it's not just the voice of the CEO that's being heard. If shareholders want to contribute on their own, that's another matter—and that's already well regulated.

Curtailing revolving doors

One of the most invidious ways that influence is exerted is the "revolving door," in which politicians get payoffs, not today but in the future, in the form of good jobs in the private sector when they leave office.[37] The revolving door is pervasive and corrosive. That those in the US Treasury and elsewhere in government quickly go from serving their country to working on Wall Street leads to questions about whether they have been serving Wall Street all along. But the revolving door permeates government, even including the military, where generals and other high officials seem to seamlessly move from serving their country to working for defense contractors.

Various presidential administrations have worked to curb access to the revolving door, to limited avail. Part of the problem is that whatever the rule, individuals find ways of skirting it. Typically, there may be restraints in their dealing *directly* with the agency from which they came. But they can give advice to their corporate colleagues about what to say to whom—and let their presence be felt in a variety of other ways.

This is an arena where what is required above all else is the right norms and ethics. And the greed-is-good ethic of twenty-first-century American capitalism works against creating the right norms. An ex-public official, especially one with further political ambitions, should worry that accepting a large check from Goldman Sachs in exchange for a short speech might look unseemly. And this might be especially so for an ex-secretary of treasury or state or the president. Any official should especially worry about receiving money from a financial institution that benefited from an action the official took while in office. Conscientious officials, especially in this era where there is so much skepticism of government, might worry about the appearance of corruption, even if there was only a whiff of it. But under the norms of twenty-first-century capitalism, an ex-government official who turns down these big paydays is regarded as a fool.

The Need for a New Movement

Pondering the vexing political and economic mire into which the United States has wandered can provoke feelings of hopelessness and paralysis. Our problems are inextricably bound up with one another. It can seem impossible to know where to begin. But begin we must, and not in measured steps but on all fronts. To do this, we will need a new politics. The dysfunction in our systems of voting and representation has amplified the dysfunctions in the way our political system works.

Our political system is supposed to translate our views, beliefs, and opinions into policies. We elect officials who in turn are supposed to adopt legislation and regulations that conform to our beliefs. And central to that process are our political parties. There is, however, widespread disenchantment with our political parties. If not outwardly corrupt, they are viewed as, at best, opportunistic. Moreover, in recent years, extreme elements of the Republican Party such as the Tea Party have been active in the primaries, acting as centrifugal forces, pulling the country apart.[38]

Disenchantment with parties has led some to suggest that we do without them; they are unnecessary in twenty-first-century America. That is wrong, but we do have to reinvent our parties, to ensure that they are grounded first and foremost in America's highest values.[39]

What motivates people, especially younger ones, to participate in politics today are *movements*, committed to one purpose or another. Some may be concerned with gender rights, others with economic opportunity, and still others with housing, the environment, or gun control. While these movements emphasize different things, there is a common thread running through them all: *Current arrangements are unfair, leaving some groups behind, and ignoring some important dimension of well-being.* These movements will be more effective if they work together; if there is a common alliance of these progressive movements: the whole is greater than the sum of the parts. The Democratic Party needs to reinvent itself as the voice of such an alliance.

Movements are important. They can raise consciousness and engender widespread support. But full success will typically require political action, and that requires support from at least one of the two parties. Any movement by itself is unlikely to succeed. And while many issues should have bipartisan support, and a few receive such support, in practice America's Great Divide is reflected in its two parties. In some ways, it's worse than that: I noted earlier that the Republican Party is an uneasy coalition among the religious Right, discontented blue-collar workers, and the ultra-rich. In many ways, these different constituent parts have conflicting interests—discontented blue-collar workers want higher wages, but the corporations and the ultra-rich want lower wages; the bargaining power of corporations vis-à-vis their workers is increased with open markets and higher unemployment, just the opposite of what serves the interests of the discontented workers. The 2017 tax bill showed how this plays out in practice: the billionaires and corporations got large breaks; the middle class got a tax increase.

Among the progressive movements, there is none of this tension. They hold in common a vision of a better society, with greater equality and well-being for all. When there are differences, they are about priorities and strategies. Reducing toxic waste and access to guns are both ways of increasing life expectancy. Our quality of life will increase if we have a better environment and if all children have access to health care and better education.

Nonetheless, sometimes different progressive movements are seen as being in conflict with one another. Some argue, for instance, that a focus on economic empowerment and rights distracts attention from racial and gender empowerment and rights. Martin Luther King Jr. understood that economic and racial justice were inseparable. He called his famous August 1963 demonstration in the nation's capital the March on Washington for Jobs and Freedom. One of the reasons for the persistence of the racial divides in incomes is the growing economic divide in the country.

So too, economic growth that is environmentally unsound is not sustainable; and the effects of a bad environment—toxic waste or lead in paint—are felt most keenly by the poor. Thus, there is a clear complementarity between the environmental justice movements and the social, racial, and economic justice movements. In short, the various progressive movements are complementary and can and must work together.

IN THE PAST, national parties have thought of themselves as bringing people together from all the fifty states. There were differences in views across the states, with some regions being more liberal than others. But in twenty-first-century America, geography offers a different political insight. There are likely to be greater similarities between those living in cities across the country than between the rural and urban within the same state. Those in the cities face one set of problems; those in rural areas, another; those in the suburbs still another. Politics will, of course, still be local; but we need to reconceptualize the national parties along the natural political identities of the twenty-first century, which are far more than local, and are concerned with the big national and international issues of the day.

Curbing the Influence of Wealth in Our Democracy

I believe that no tinkering with a democratic political system can succeed when the economic divide is too large. The reforms I've described in this chapter are necessary, but if the wealth and income divide is too great, the wealthy will win out—in one way or another. Even with public radio and TV and public subsidies to newspapers, a wealthy person like Rupert Murdoch can use his money to dominate in at least a niche of the market, to create a cult with distorted views.

With the well-educated, systems of fact-checking can be very effective—no one in the 65 percent to 70 percent who are not his devoted followers takes a Trump utterance seriously before it is fact-checked, given that so much of what he says are lies, and so much of what remains are half-truths.[40] But Trump and Fox News can create a group of devotees seemingly immune from the truth; at the very least, they have been inoculated against the truth with a very strong vaccine. And besides, if their objective is to undermine confidence in the institutions of the State, they can do that simply by sowing doubt. One might not believe what Trump says, but he views it as a victory if one is skeptical about what his critics say. Just as the cigarette companies considered it a victory when smokers simply came to doubt the science demonstrating that smoking was bad for one's health, so too Trump, Murdoch, and others who would destroy the institutions of the State win if they can simply cast doubt.

Murdoch did transparently what the wealthy have always done in one way or another—used the power of money to help shape society.[41] Inevitably, when there are large wealth disparities, the wealthy will have hugely disproportionate influence. Even with systems of campaign finance that are mostly publicly funded, those who can provide one kind or another of material support to the party are needed, and listened to.

Of course, in any society, some citizens are more articulate, some are smarter, some have a better understanding of what to do. There is never going to be a perfectly level playing field. But very large wealth disparities don't just allow some to have a cushier life than others— they also allow the wealthy to unduly influence the direction of society and politics. In some ways, this is the fundamental perversion of government. It is supposed to help those who cannot help themselves, to protect the vulnerable and to redistribute income from the rich to the poor and to write rules that at least treat ordinary individuals fairly. But in a society with excessive wealth disparity, it may do just the opposite. Ordinary citizens felt this "perversion" strongly in the aftermath of the 2008 crisis. But the response of the Tea Party movement, to disempower government, is the wrong response: without government, the exploitation of the poor by the rich would be even greater. It is the rich and the powerful who win under the law of the jungle.

Thus, if we are to avoid this dystopia, we have to somehow create a more egalitarian society, without dangerous concentrations of power. But here we come to the fundamental quandary of democratic politics in societies with extremes of inequality like the United States. How do we break out of this equilibrium, this vicious circle where economic inequality leads to political inequality that maintains, preserves, and even augments economic inequality?

It can be done, but only if there is a countervailing power—sometimes called "people power." Large numbers of truly engaged individuals, in movements such as those described above, with the movements working in concert with each other, through a political party, can be more important than money. Indeed, the defeat of the well-funded Republican candidates Mitt Romney (in the 2012 general election) and Jeb Bush (in the 2016 Republican primary) was a stark reminder that in politics money isn't everything. But money doesn't have to be everything to distort our economy and our society.

That's why the two sets of reforms discussed here are *both* essential and complementary: we need to do more to curb the influence of money; but we also have to reduce the disparities in wealth. Otherwise, we will never be able to adequately curb the power of money in politics.

CHAPTER 9

Restoring a Dynamic Economy with Jobs and Opportunity for All

P art I focused on the malaise into which the United States and many other advanced countries have fallen—slow growth, low opportunity, increasing anxiety, and a divided society. The divisions are so deep that the politics is seized with paralysis at a time when there should be a united resolve to find a way out of this quagmire. There is a way out: earlier chapters of this book have shown how the challenges of financialization, globalization, and technology can be met in ways that enhance competition and employment and achieve greater shared prosperity. We won't, however, be able to make the economic changes we need if we don't change our politics, as described in the previous chapter.

In this and the next chapter, we flesh out an economic agenda—based on the principles already outlined—that can restore growth and social justice and enable most citizens to have the middle-class life to which they aspire. All of this will only be possible if there is more collective action—a greater role for government. Properly defined, this greater role doesn't constrain society, but rather liberates it and the individuals within it, by allowing them to live up to their potential. Further, by restraining the power of some to harm others, government can free those who would otherwise always have to be on their guard, always having to take protective measures.

Managing markets to make them serve our economy is one part of getting America back on track. The market can produce wonders—but not so for the distorted and misshapen capitalism that has emerged in twenty-first-century America. Earlier chapters have explained how to make markets work as they should.[1] These reforms, including stronger and better-enforced competition laws, and better management of globalization and our financial sector, are necessary, but they are not sufficient. They are part of a progressive economic agenda, but that agenda has many more elements.

This chapter begins with a discussion of growth—how we can restore it not by stripping away the regulations that prevent some in our society from exploiting the rest, but by restoring the true foundations of wealth described in chapter 1. It then goes on to address the challenge of the moment—making the transition from the industrialized economy of the twentieth century to the twenty-first-century service, innovation, and green economy in ways that maintain jobs and opportunity; provide for better social protection; provide better care for our aged, sick, and disabled; and provide better health, education, housing, and financial security for all of our citizens.

The agendas promoting a more dynamic and green economy and promoting social justice, with greater inclusion and security, are inseparable. The previous chapter referred to Martin Luther King Jr.'s belief that one had to simultaneously address economic opportunity and jobs and racial discrimination. We take that argument further, contending that one cannot separate economic security, social protection, and social justice from creating a more dynamic, innovative economy and protecting the environment. Too often economists think in terms of trade-offs: if one wants more of one thing, one has to give up on others. But, at least moving from our current vantage point of a highly unequal society, marked by extensive racial discrimination, with per-

vasive insecurity and massive environmental degradation, all of the
goals set forth are in fact complementary.

Growth and Productivity

Chapter 2 showed how growth had slowed over the past four decades.
Economic growth depends on two factors: growth in the size of the
labor force, and increases in productivity, output per hour. When
either one goes up, so does the output of the economy. Of course,
what matters is not just growth in national output, but in living standards of ordinary Americans,[2] and that requires not just increases in
productivity, but that ordinary citizens get a fair share of that increase.
The trouble in recent decades is that neither labor force participation
nor productivity have been doing well—and the benefits of what gains
have occurred have gone to the top.

Labor force growth and participation

Labor force growth is related in part to demographics about which
government can't do much: the aging of the baby boomers and the
decline in birthrates.[3] But the government can do something about
immigration and labor force participation. Trump is set to lower the
former—thus slowing growth—and has no agenda for the latter even
though there are some attractive options. We could get more women
into the labor force with more family-friendly policies (greater flexibility of hours, better family leave policies, more support for child
care). With active labor market policies, we could get good jobs for
more of those whose skills today are mismatched to the job market.

We have never treated our senior citizens well—for too many, as
they aged and their skills were no longer needed, we said thank you
for their years of service and sent them out to pasture. These "forced"
retirements, when individuals were able and willing to work, were a
waste of human resources; but the cost for the economy as a whole was

manageable when those over fifty were a small fraction of our labor force. This won't be true going forward: unless we do something, a faster pace of innovation may lead to sending off more to an earlier retirement. With an aging population, the costs to our society will be even greater. Just as we need to change our workplace to accommodate families with children, and especially women, we need to change it to accommodate our older workers. It helps that some of the efforts to increase flexibility (for instance, more flexible hours, more scope for part-time work, and more opportunities for working from home, much easier in today's world of the internet) will work for both. Again, unfortunately, these are reforms that the market won't make on its own. The power of corporations over workers is just too great; they don't need to do these things; and they don't care about the greater benefits to our society. That's why government will have to take an active role in pushing these changes.

Our labor force participation would be higher too if we had a healthier population. It's not the climate, and it's not the air we breathe or the water we drink that has led America to have a less healthy population living shorter lives than in other advanced countries, less able and willing to be active participants in the labor force. We need better regulations to protect us from the food industry, which has been doing what it can to ply us with addictive, unhealthful foods. We also need a better health care system, discussed further in the next chapter. Finally, a healthier labor force would be one lifted out of the despair to which a third of a century of bad economic policies has given rise.[4] Even if we didn't care about human suffering, we could make the case for these policies purely from the perspective of economic growth.

Productivity

Productivity, too, is affected by a host of variables. A healthy and happy labor force is a productive labor force, and there are good reasons that those whose income is in the bottom half of the US might be neither happy nor healthy. So too, the pervasive discrimination in US labor markets is obviously not only discouraging and unfair to those who are discriminated against, but it also means that workers are not optimally matched to jobs.

EARLIER CHAPTERS highlighted how market power distorts our economy and undermines both growth and efficiency. Monopolies have less incentives to innovate, and the barriers to entry that they set up actually stifle innovation. Curbing market power is thus part of a growth and jobs agenda, not just part of a power and inequality agenda.

Another important lacunae of recent years is a deficiency in investment in infrastructure. While there *seems* to be consensus on the importance of infrastructure, it's superficial. In terms of priorities, the Republicans have shown it far less important than giving tax cuts to rich corporations. Just weeks after the Republican tax bill passed at the end of 2017, an act of multitrillion-dollar largesse to the rich,[5] a senior Trump administration official said: infrastructure is still our priority, but we don't have money.[6] They should have thought of that earlier. Indeed, the tax bill makes it more difficult for states that have high spending to continue to raise revenues,[7] and this will almost surely lead to a contraction of public infrastructure spending, relative to what it otherwise would be. It is also easy to predict that the massive federal fiscal deficits resulting from the 2017 tax bill will dampen future federal spending on infrastructure.

Creating a learning society

This book began by emphasizing that the true source of a country's wealth—and therefore increases in productivity and living standards—is knowledge, learning, and advances in science and technology. It is this, far more than anything else, that explains why living standards today are so much higher than they were two hundred years ago—not only the increase in our material goods, but also the longer lifespans and better health throughout our lives.

At the center of our knowledge and innovation economy is research. Basic research produces knowledge, a "public good," something from which all could benefit were it made accessible. The essential insight of economists concerning public goods is that on its own the market undersupplies them. In the case of knowledge, moreover, when private firms produce knowledge, they try to keep it secret. This limits the benefits that society can get from the knowledge while simultaneously increasing the risk of market power. That is why it is essential for there to be large *public* investments in research, especially basic research, and in the kind of education system that can support the advance of knowledge.

It's not just that the Trump administration doesn't recognize this; they're actively hostile to it. As with infrastructure, the Trump administration was willing to spend hundreds of billions of dollars for a tax cut for billionaires and rich corporations, while proposing large cutbacks in spending on research.

The new tax bill taxed some of our leading research universities, while it provided tax benefits for real estate speculators. To my knowledge, no country has ever taxed research universities; rather, they recognize the essential role universities play in growth, and so provide public support. While the Trump tax on universities is small, it is a meaningful, and dangerous, expression of values. No large country grew prosperous on the basis of real estate speculation, though a few individuals may do well. Evidently, not recognizing the differences between the wealth of nations and the wealth of individuals, the Republican tax bill encouraged speculation and discouraged research and education.

FURTHER, IT IS important to understand another key mistake behind the 2017 tax bill. The Republican hope is that even with a slowdown

in publicly funded research and the lack of public investment in infrastructure, lower taxes will encourage private firms to pick up the slack
and invest more. Twice before the country tried this experiment. The
hope was that lower taxes would spur growth, savings, and investment. Both times the experiment failed. As has already been noted,
growth after Reagan's tax cut was not only much lower that he had
promised,[8] but lower than it had been in earlier decades. After Bush's
tax cuts, savings fell—the personal savings rate declined to almost
zero. And while investment rebounded, this owed much to investment in real estate, which, to put it lightly, did not end up working
out well.[9] Today, prospects are even worse: with the Fed believing
that we are near full employment, it will raise interest rates faster *than
it otherwise would*, discouraging private investment. (Of course, if the
global uncertainty created by Trump's trade wars helps precipitate a
global slowdown, the Fed might not raise interest rates, or could even
lower them. This is particularly likely if the "sugar high" from the
tax cut wears off quickly and the tax cuts' adverse effects set in—its
distortions and the huge increase in the fiscal deficit.)

Broadening our knowledge base means we also have to remain
an open society—open to ideas and people from elsewhere. In some
ways, the flow of knowledge across borders is the most important
aspect of globalization. We don't have a monopoly on the production
of knowledge; and if we close ourselves off from others, both we and
they will suffer.[10] With private and public investment curtailed, and
the allocation of investment distorted, with Trump's shutting down
our borders to the best and brightest from abroad, it's hard to see how
his policies could increase productivity and growth.

If we want to increase productivity, this is really where we have to
begin: encouraging more research, both through our tax code and by
government spending, by providing more support to our higher education institutions, and by keeping the country open—including open to
ideas and people from abroad. Further, we need to go beyond revers-

ing the tax bill: we need to increase taxes on corporations that don't invest in the US and create jobs, and spend some of the tax revenue on increased infrastructure and investments in technology and science.

Facilitating the Transition to a Postindustrial World

The US, like most countries in Europe, has been struggling to adapt to deindustrialization, globalization, and the other major shifts in its economy and society. This is another area where markets need the help of the government. Facilitating transition after the fact is extraordinarily costly and problematic. We should have done more to help those who were losing their jobs to globalization and advances in technology, but Republican ideology said no, let them fend for themselves. Government must anticipate the broad strokes of future structural shifts. Adapting our economy to climate change and to the changing demography are just two of many challenges of "transition" facing our economy and society in coming years. New technologies discussed in chapter 6—including robotization and artificial intelligence— represent further challenges.

Recent and earlier episodes of such changes have generated one important lesson: the market on its own is not up to the task. There is a simple reason already explained: those most affected, for instance, those who are losing their jobs, are least able to fend for themselves. The changes often imply that their skills are less valuable. They may have to move to where the jobs are being created—and house prices in the growing parts of the country are often far higher. Even if, after training, their job prospects might be good, they don't have the resources for retraining, and financial markets will typically only advance them the money at usurious interest rates. They lend at normal interest rates only to those who have good jobs, a good credit history, and good equity in their home—in other words, to those who don't need the money.

Thus, there is an essential role for government to facilitate the transition, through what have been called active labor market policies. Such policies help retrain individuals for the new jobs and help them find new employment. Another tool for government is referred to as industrial policies, which help restructure the economy into the directions of the future and assist the creation and expansion of firms, especially small and medium-sized enterprises in these new sectors.[11] Some countries, like those in Scandinavia, have demonstrated that well-designed active labor market and industrial policies can create jobs as fast as jobs get destroyed and can move people from the old jobs to the new. There have been failures, but that is because sufficient attention has not been paid to what makes for successful policies.[12]

Place-based policies

As government pursues labor market and industrial policies, it needs to be sensitive to questions of location. Too often economists ignore the social and other capital that is built into a particular place. When jobs leave a place and move elsewhere, economists sometimes suggest that people should move too. But for many Americans, with ties to families and friends, this is not so easy; and especially so since with the high costs of child care, many people depend on their parents so they can go to work. Research in recent years has highlighted the importance of social bonds, of community, in individuals' well-being.[13]

More generally, decisions about where to locate are not efficient. Too many people may want to crowd into the big urban centers, causing congestion and putting strains on local infrastructure.[14] Among the reasons that factories moved to rural areas in the Midwest and South was that wages were low, public education ensured that workers had enough skills nonetheless to be highly productive, and our infrastructure was sufficiently good that it was easy to get raw materials into the factories and the finished goods out. But some of the same forces that had led to low wages are now contributing to the problem of deindustrialization. Wages were low in part because of lack of mobility—with perfect mobility, wages (skill-adjusted) would be the same everywhere. But this lack of mobility is key to understanding why deindustrialization is so painful.

In short, we need policies focusing on particular *places* (cities or regions going through stress), in what are called place-based policies, to help restore and revitalize communities. Some countries have managed such policies extraordinarily well: Manchester, England, the textile capital of the world in the nineteenth century, has reinvented itself—with help from the UK government—as an educational and cultural center. It still may not be as relatively prosperous as it was in its heyday, but it is instructive to compare Manchester with Detroit, which the United States simply let go bankrupt.

Government played a central role in the transition from agriculture to a manufacturing economy; it now needs to play a similar role in the transition to the new economy of the twenty-first century.[15]

Social Protection

One of most important detractors from individual well-being is a sense of insecurity. Insecurity can also affect growth and productivity: individuals, worrying about whether they will be thrown out of their house or lose their job and only source of income, can't focus on the tasks at work in the way they should. Those who feel more secure can undertake riskier activities, often with higher payoffs. In our complex society, we are constantly confronting risks. New technologies may take away jobs, even if they also provide new ones. Climate change itself presents untold new risks, as we have recently experienced with hurricanes and fires. Again, large risks like these and ones associated with unemployment, health, and retirement, are risks that markets do not handle well.[16] In some cases, like unemployment and health insurance for the aged, markets simply do not provide insurance; in other cases, like retirement, they provide annuities only at high costs, and even then, without important provisions—such as adjustments for inflation. That is why almost all advanced countries provide social insurance to cover at least many of these risks. Governments have become fairly proficient in providing this insurance—transaction costs for the US Social Security system are a fraction of those associated with comparable private insurance. We need to recognize, however, that there are large gaps in our system of social insurance, with many important risks still not being covered either by markets or by government.

Unemployment insurance

One of the biggest gaps in our system of social protection is that our unemployment insurance program covers a relatively small risk—being unemployed for twenty-six weeks—but leaves the much more serious risk of long-term unemployment unaddressed. A simple reform would be a vastly strengthened unemployment insurance scheme, with better payments for longer periods and with more people covered. A more complex reform would be to make some of the benefits take the form of income-contingent loans, that is, the repayment of the loans depends on individuals' future income. A small bout of unemployment leaves an individual's lifetime income little changed; the real "market failure" is that the unemployed individual can't borrow against this future income to sustain his family's living standard today. We could change this.[17]

Of course, we want workers who lose their jobs to make a quick transition to new jobs, and the active labor market policies described earlier can be a big help. So too might programs that encourage individuals who have lost a job to take another one, even if it doesn't pay as well. Individuals often have unrealistic expectations of what wages they *should* get, and underestimate the value of having a job—not just the income, but the social connections, with important consequences for well-being—and the cost of not having a job for future employability.[18]

Any time we consider unemployment insurance programs, it is essential to recall that they have a further macroeconomic benefit; they act as automatic stabilizers—when the economy is weak and jobs aren't being created fast enough, they automatically kick in, and the income they provide helps the economy maintain an even keel.[19] Having in place programs ready to deal with a deep downturn, such as the one the country went through after the 2008 crisis, makes good sense: Such protections cost us little in times when the labor market is tight, and despite the expense, save us a great deal during recessions. Without them, the slowing or shrinking of the economy would be much worse. The relative weakness of the American social safety net is part of what accounted for the severity of the 2008 Great Recession, much worse than in Germany and other Northern European countries, some of which were initially hit even worse.

Universal basic income

Some, especially in the hi-tech community, have put forward the intriguing suggestion of a universal basic income (UBI) as a supplement to our existing social safety nets. Some have even suggested that such a program should replace the myriad other social support programs. A UBI would essentially be a financial stipend for all citizens. Everybody would get a check from the government, say on the first of the month. Of course, those with good jobs would be sending back in taxes to the government far more than they receive. The UBI would serve as a safety net for everyone, but without the administrative costs associated with targeted programs like unemployment insurance and food stamps.[20]

Its supporters specifically cite its usefulness to dampen the negative effects of an economy with increasing automation, where wealth may be generated at a quick pace even as traditional job opportunities become more scarce.

There are some distinct advantages of a UBI. A UBI could increase equality and provide a backstop for those who fail to get jobs. It could eliminate the bureaucratic processes entailed in getting access to each of the multiple safety net and social protection programs, like food stamps and Medicaid. [21]

But I don't believe simply providing income is the right approach: for most people work is an important part of life. That doesn't mean it has to be forty hours a week; the labor force survived—more than survived, prospered—when the work week shortened from sixty hours to forty hours, and we can survive if it gets shortened again to, say, twenty-five hours. Shorter hours actually led to more productivity, and many found productive ways to use the additional leisure, though many did not.

There is much work that needs to be done—and much that won't be able to be accomplished by robots for some time. Our cities could be beautified, our more frail elderly and sick need to be taken better care of, our young better educated. With people who want to work and work that needs to be done, and the market not being able to bring the two together, there is a responsibility for government to take action—the jobs program described in the next section.

Many in the younger generation tell me that this focus on work is simply twentieth-century thinking, and that a minimal UBI would enable them to pursue a spiritual life, or a life helping others, without formal employment. The idea should not be dismissed—but I remain unconvinced that it solves the inherent economic problems, the deficits to dignity of widespread unemployment. Jobs remain the backbone of a healthy economy, and we need a broad-based agenda of the kind I discuss below to support a strong labor market.

But before turning to that, we should note one more limitation of UBI: it is simply unlikely that, given the stinginess of America's fiscal policy, any UBI system would be generous enough to provide support at anywhere near a subsistence level. The cost of doing so would require substantial increases in taxes.

Decent Jobs with Good Working Conditions

At the core of the angst in the United States and Western Europe—
and central to restoring a dynamic economy—is jobs, good jobs, plain
and simple. Those with jobs worry that migrants will take away their
jobs and drive down wages. They worry that globalization will move
jobs abroad. They see as largely a fairy tale the standard economists'
argument that as old jobs get destroyed new and better jobs are created. Even if such creative destruction works for some, it obviously
isn't working for many.

Most are struggling to maintain a reasonable work–life balance.
Women want to progress in their careers, but they also want to have
a happy family. Men want to do their part, but often worry too about
the trade-offs between advancing in their jobs and other dimensions of their lives, most importantly, spending more time at home.
Many men and women feel uncomfortable working for firms that
are despoiling our environment, or just not playing the positive role
they could.

Markets on their own won't ensure full employment, and "markets"
do even more poorly in ensuring that jobs will be well paid. Markets
do a still poorer job of addressing these issues of work–life balance.

If our economy is richer as a result of either globalization or the
march of technology, it should be obvious that we could use the fruits
of that progress to make at least the vast majority better off. It isn't
inevitable, it isn't necessary, and it isn't a good thing that so much
of the benefits go to the 1 percent—in some recent years, an overwhelming majority of the increment in GDP. Given that we are so
much richer than we were, surely we could run our economic system
in a way that didn't exert such a toll on so many families—this in an
economy that pays homage to "family values." I explain here what
government can do to create the economy we should have.

Ensuring full employment

No policy is more important for equality, growth, and efficiency than maintaining full employment. And the most important ingredient in a middle-class life style is having a decent job. That in turn requires that there be jobs—a macroeconomic framework that ensures full employment. In spite of the fact that many conservative economists believe that markets always work efficiently, it should be obvious: there have been long periods of time in which the market, on its own, has failed to achieve full employment. Massive unemployment is a great waste of resources. Many economists believe that monetary policy—lowering interest rates—is the instrument that should primarily be relied upon. Whether that argument is correct or not, it is clear that there are times—such as the past decade—when monetary policy by itself does not suffice to restore the country to full employment.[22] At such times, there need to be strong fiscal policies—increases in government spending or reductions in taxes; and this is so even if it results in deficits.

It took a decade, but ten years after the onset of the Great Recession the US was finally near full employment. (In September 2018, only 3.7 percent of the labor force was without jobs.) These statistics, though, give too rosy a picture: only 70 percent of the working-age population has jobs, far lower than in other countries, such as Switzerland and Iceland, where it is 80 and 86 percent, respectively.[23] And many in the United States—some 3 percent—are working part-time involuntarily because they can't get a full-time job. America's unemployment rate might be still higher if it were not that so many people were in jail—almost 1 percent of the working-age population, far larger than in any other country.[24] A reflection of the weakness in the labor market is that real wages have been increasing slowly—even after years of stagnation during the Great Recession, in 2017 they increased only 1.2 percent for full-time workers over sixteen, and even then, they were still below their 2006 level.[25]

Fiscal policy

Even when monetary policy fails, fiscal policy can stimulate the economy. Increasing spending on high-multiplier activities (activities that provide a large stimulus to the economy per dollar spent—like spending more to get better teachers) at the expense of those that don't (like paying foreign contractors to fight in a foreign war)[26] can provide a big boost to the economy when there is a shortage of demand, as there was in the years after the 2008 financial crisis. So too can shifting the burden of taxes from the poor and middle to those better able to pay taxes, because those at the bottom spend so much more of their income than do those at the top. This is, of course, just the opposite of the tax bill enacted in December 2017. America's regressive tax system—where those at the top pay a lower percentage of their income in taxes than those who are less well-off—is not only unfair but also weakens the macro economy, destroying jobs. So too for the myriad of loopholes, tax dodges used by the super-rich: they not only increase inequality, but also distort and weaken the economy.

Some taxes prove beneficial to the economy—some can even stimulate the economy. Imposing a tax on carbon emissions would encourage firms to make investments in emission-reducing technologies; firms would have to retrofit themselves to reflect the end of the massive carbon subsidy that they have, in effect, been receiving.[27] And the economy would receive a triple benefit: a better environment, with revenues that could be used to address some of the country's long-term needs, and increasing demand leading to more jobs and higher growth.[28]

Even when there are fiscal constraints arising from worries about the deficit and the national debt, appropriately designed fiscal policy can be used to stimulate the economy. The *balanced budget principle* says that an increase in taxes with a corresponding increase in spending stimulates the economy; and if the taxes and spending are chosen carefully, the boost to the economy—and thus, to the job market—can be very large.[29]

An area where fiscal policy can have a particularly profound benefit is investing in infrastructure. For years, there has been underinvestment in infrastructure, implying there are huge investment needs and large returns to further investment. Improvements in infrastructure can increase private investment, as businesses benefit from better access to markets. Thus, public spending will encourage private spending. Another benefit is resource savings. Huge amounts of *private* resources are wasted as a result of congested airports and roads.

There can be further benefits of a well-designed infrastructure investment. Individuals have to be able to get to the jobs that exist—and often public transportation systems are inadequate or simply absent. A part of the new infrastructure program should be good public transit that connects people with jobs.

Another area where targeted fiscal policy can make a difference is in research—the private sector thrives off of the advances in science and technology funded by the public. Indeed, a large fraction of the key advances of the last three-quarters of a century have been largely publicly funded, from the internet, to the browser, to radar—the list goes on.[30]

These measures that increase aggregate demand and thus growth when there is a deficiency in demand are simultaneously supply-side measures, increasing the economy's potential output. Unlike the failed Reagan-style approach to stimulate the supply-side (lowering taxes, deregulation), they actually work.

Other countries, most notably Europe, have found it useful to have a national infrastructure investment bank to help provide finance for these various investments. The European Investment Bank, for instance, invests more than $94 billion a year in projects that have contributed to Europe's growth and increased the living standards of its people, with fast trains connecting major cities, a reliable electricity grid, and a good road network.[31] America will have to spend a great deal to meet the infrastructure needs of our growing economy, and a similar bank would help provide the necessary financial resources.[32]

A guaranteed job for all who are willing to work

Most of the time, the measures described so far will enable the economy to achieve full employment. Still, it is far from certain that that will be the case in the economy we are moving toward. So strong has been the influence of "market ideology" in our thinking that most economists believe that full employment should and can be achieved relying largely on the *private* sector, if only the government exercises fiscal and monetary policy correctly. But what happens if that is not so?

There is an alternative: government hiring workers. In twenty-first-century America, we should recognize a new right—the right of every person able and willing to work to have a job. And if the market fails, and if our fiscal and monetary policies fail, the government needs to step into the breach. People care about economic security, and the increase in security that this backstop would provide would be of inestimable value. Besides, there is much work that needs doing. Many of our schools are dilapidated, in need of repair, or at least of painting. Our cities could be cleaned up and beautified.[33] As we saw earlier, it is a shame that there is work that needs to be done and people wanting to do that work, and yet our economic and financial system is failing both our society and these individuals.

India has provided such a guarantee (of one hundred days of work) to its rural citizens willing to do unskilled manual labor, and some fifty million Indians a year have taken advantage of the scheme. If a poor country like India can afford it, so can the United States. There, it's had a further advantage—it has helped drive up rural wages, reducing extreme poverty; there's a good chance that it would help drive up wages at the bottom in the US, and that would in turn help reduce inequality.[34]

Better jobs, restoring work–life balance, and reducing exploitation

The world of work and the nature of families have changed since World War II: then, it was standard to have only one wage earner in a family (the man), with one individual (almost always the woman) remaining at home; now, in a very large fraction of households, both adults are in the labor force. That means that there is the need for a kind of flexibility that wasn't there in the past. There is a need, for instance, for family leave policies, and firms have to provide more flexible hours. And there is a need for government assistance in helping with childcare.[35] Most importantly, we have to stop the abuses of market power associated with on–call scheduling and split scheduling described in chapter 3.

It would be nice if we could achieve all of this by simply cajoling employers. But that hasn't worked in the past and isn't likely to do so in the future. Changes described earlier in rebalancing the power between workers and their employers are essential. So too would having a tighter labor market. But these are unlikely to suffice. We need regulations and incentives, rewards and punishments. These changes will not only have economic benefits for the family, but also for the economy as a whole, and benefits for society that go well beyond any increase in GDP: they will promote inclusion and reduce the persistent gender gap in wages and incomes.

Restoring Opportunity and Social Justice

Even the most avid advocates of markets realize that markets on their own won't ensure social justice and opportunity, especially in places marked by discrimination and in a society like that in the US where nearly a fifth of the children grow up in poverty. In competitive labor markets (and I have emphasized, they are seldom competitive) wages are determined by supply and demand. The interaction of market forces may leave low-skilled individuals with a wage too low to survive, let alone have a meaningful life. There is a major role for government in promoting social justice, ensuring that everyone has a livable income; that young people have the skills they need to thrive, and access to good job opportunities commensurate with their skills, regardless of the income, education, social standing, or other circumstances of their parents; and that some individuals or firms do not use their market power to walk off with a disproportionate share of the national pie.[36]

As we move toward a more dynamic economy, the broader societal goals of opportunity and social justice should be part of the plan. We first need to make the distribution of market income more equal (this is sometimes called pre-distribution). But try as we may, inequality in market income will almost surely be too high. We have to then use more progressive taxation, transfer, and public expenditure programs to equalize standards of living further.[37] If we succeed in making market incomes more equal, there is less of a burden on redistribution. This emphasis on *pre-distribution* is important. It highlights that getting a fairer distribution of income is not just a matter of *redistribution*, of taxing the rich to give to the more needy.

Inequities are created in the very process by which incomes get generated, as firms exercise monopoly and monopsony power or as they exploit others (as described in earlier chapters) or as they discriminate against the vulnerable or those of particular races or ethnic groups. Inequality is also created when CEOs take advantage of deficiencies in corporate governance to pay themselves exorbitant salaries, leaving less to pay workers or to invest in the firm. Prohibiting these practices, reforming corporate governance laws, passing better labor laws, strengthening and enforcing discrimination and competition laws—all of these are easy steps (politics aside) in creating a fairer distribution of income. As we've said, markets don't exist in a vacuum; they have to be structured, through rules, regulations and policies. Some countries have done a better job in structuring them, leading to greater efficiency and equality in market incomes.

Inequality is created not just by the rules that affect the incomes individuals receive,[38] but also by those that govern how corporations can engage in exploitation. Our financial system is designed to increase inequality: those at the bottom pay high interest when they borrow but get low interest rates when they put their money in the bank. "Reforms" in the financial sector—such as the abolition of limits on interest rates charged—have only made matters worse. Too much of the increasingly limited competition that remains in this sector is directed at how to exploit the unwary.[39]

There are many reforms that could lead to greater equality. For instance, other policies to help those at the bottom are increasing minimum wages, and providing wage subsidies and an earned income tax credit, topping up what the private sector pays to the level of a livable wage.[40]

The role of intergenerational transmission of advantage and disadvantage

Even if the higher incomes of the well-off are not derived from exploiting those down below, we might judge their advantage as unfair if it came not from their own efforts, but from their inheritances. Thus, we come to the key issue of the intergenerational transmission of advantage and disadvantage. It is inevitable, of course, that those with more income and wealth and higher education do what they can to advantage their children; and the greater the inequalities in income and wealth and education in one generation, the greater they will be in the next. That's why the agenda of reducing inequalities *today* is part and parcel of an agenda for ensuring greater equality of opportunity tomorrow.[41]

It is unconscionable that a child born to a poor parent is destined not to live up to his or her potential. No humane society can condemn a child because of the misfortunes or poor choices of parents. In a country where one out of five children grows up in poverty, this is not a theoretical question; it's a matter of pressing practical relevance. That's why childhood nutrition and health programs and programs advancing educational opportunity, from pre-K to university, are so important.

High-quality free public education can be a major force for bringing society together. Fifty years ago, discrimination against women foreclosed many opportunities, and thus jobs in education could attract talented women at low pay. As some aspects of gender discrimination weakened and women entered other sectors, this reduced the pool of highly qualified women who could be hired at relatively low pay to be teachers. To maintain the same quality of education with this new labor dynamic, we needed to have increased educator salaries (and thus educational expenditures) far more than we have.

And because the country has become more economically segregated, with poor children increasingly living in neighborhoods with other poor children, our local education system results in large and increasing disparities in education.[42] The children in rich communities are thus able to get a better education than those in poor communities. That pattern continues at colleges and universities, as tuition has increased far faster than incomes of those in the middle and bottom of the income ladder. The only way that children from poorer families can get a college education often entails crushing debt. They face an unpleasant choice: forego a college education, condemning themselves to a life of low wages; or get a college education, bringing with it a debt burden that will last a lifetime.

Good, *public* education for all is thus at the center of any agenda of equality and equality of opportunity. This will require increased national spending. How can we expect education to attract good teachers when the gap between their pay and those in banking and elsewhere in our society is so large, and how can we expect a high quality of education everywhere when the gaps between local communities' resource base is so large? It's not a matter of incentivizing teachers through performance pay—giving them a pittance, even a couple of thousand dollars more if their students perform better, hardly makes a dent in the pay disparity between teachers and, say, bankers. Besides, teachers are professionals, and incentive pay denigrates their professionalism. A heart surgeon would be offended if told, "To incentivize you, I'll pay you more if the operation is a success." The surgeon gives everything in every surgery. So too for large fractions of our teachers. We would get better performance if we showed more respect (instead of the constant bashing of teachers and their unions, which has become fashionable among certain educational reform circles), recruited better teachers by paying them better wages (ending the legacy of gender discrimination that has long plagued the profession), and provided better working conditions, including, in many cases, smaller classes.[43]

Discrimination

One of the real cancers on American society is its racial, ethnic, and gender discrimination. We are just waking up to its pervasiveness and its persistence, shown most recently in the graphic evidence of police brutality and the statistics on mass incarceration. Discrimination is a moral issue, but it has economic consequences. Like any cancer, it undermines our vitality. Those who suffer from discrimination often never are able to live up to their potential, and this constitutes a waste of the country's most important economic resource, our citizens.

As was noted in chapter 2, progress in reducing racial discrimination over the past half century has been slow and halting—after a few years in which the impact of civil rights legislation was felt and segregation reduced, the courts stymied further progress, until finally in 2013, the Supreme Court gutted key provisions of the Voting Rights Act of 1965.[44] Chapter 2 documented how the American dream had become a myth for those born in the bottom of the income pyramid, and especially members of minority groups. Racial, ethnic, and gender discrimination is part and parcel of the increase in economic inequality, the lack of opportunity, and economic and social segregation.

The many forms of discrimination

Discrimination in America takes on many forms. Discrimination in finance, housing, and employment is often subtle—though not in our systems of police enforcement and justice, in which it is all too evident. Nothing defines America as much, for itself as well as for others, as its commitment to the rule of law and justice. The Pledge of Allegiance with which many American children begin the school day contains the ringing words ". . . . with liberty and justice for all." But like the American dream, this too is a myth. A more accurate description would be " . . . with justice for all who can afford it" and should include a proviso " . . . especially if they are white." America has become famous around the world as the country that has put more people in prison (relative to its population) than any other country. Amazingly, the United States has 25 percent of the world's prisoners, though it has but 5 percent of the world's population, and these prisoners are disproportionately African American.[45] This system of mass incarceration[46] is beginning to be recognized for what it is, not only grossly unfair and discriminatory, but also grossly inefficient.[47]

What to do?

Legacies that are as long-standing as racial and gender discrimination won't end on their own. We have to understand the deep-seated institutional bases of racism and other forms of discrimination and root them out.[48] This means that racial, ethnic, and gender equality won't be achieved unless we more strongly enforce our antidiscrimination laws, in every aspect of our economy. But we have to go beyond that. We also need a new generation of civil rights legislation.

WE NEED affirmative action and economic programs to promote equality of opportunity. There are multiple poverty traps in our country—groups of individuals, whether in particular places, like Appalachia, or of particular backgrounds, like Native Americans and African Americans, who need help in finding a way up.[49] We've come to understand the mechanisms by which advantages, and disadvantages, can be passed on from generation to generation. We need to apply these lessons to breaking up these poverty traps, wherever they occur and on whatever basis.

ACCESS TO EDUCATION, nutrition, and health are necessary (but not sufficient). Recognizing that our locally financed and locally based educational system has become a mechanism for the perpetuation of economic inequality, we need a massive increase in federal funds. Recognizing that the disadvantageous position of poor children begins even before they enter school, we also need national programs of preschool education.

RACIAL JUSTICE and economic justice are inextricably linked. If we reduce inequalities overall, if we ensure that families at the bottom can give their children the same opportunities as families at the top, then we will be able to make strides in enhancing racial, economic, and social justice, and in creating a more dynamic economy.

Restoring Justice across Generations

There is one dimension of fairness to which politicians often pay lip service, but little more than that: the well-being of future generations. The 2017 tax bill will produce huge government deficits, and thus raise the government debt. Ironically, Republicans in Congress argued against excessive debt—it would burden future generations—until they had an opportunity to enrich corporations and billionaires. There are three aspects of intergenerational justice that have been given short shrift, and which a progressive agenda needs to correct.

First, what really burdens future generations is a lack of investment, both public and private. Best estimates suggest that America's capital stock hasn't even been keeping up with the growth of income. If we don't provide our young with adequate education, they won't be able to live up to their potential. And if we don't invest in infrastructure and technology, the world that they inherit will not be able to sustain the kinds of living standards that we have had.

Second, our planet is irreplaceable. If things don't work out well here, there's not another place we can go. Yet we are despoiling our world, most dangerously with climate change. Every year, in a way that is now predictable, the damage mounts. Even the way the government thinks about the environment and goes about making decisions is unfair to our children. Recall from chapter 7 that whenever the government considers a regulation, it has to do a cost-benefit analysis. Part of a cost-benefit analysis entails comparing, say, the cost of an environmental regulation *today* with the benefits that will be received not just today but also in the future. If we restrict, for instance, dirty coal-burning electric power plants, costs may go up today, but the benefits in better health and reduced climate change stretch out for years into the future. The key issue in conducting these cost-benefit analyses is: How do we compare a dollar of future benefits with a dollar in today's costs? Under Trump administration procedures, a ("real") dollar in 50 years, when our children are reaching their prime, is worth just 3 cents. In substance, it simply shortchanges the future. Unless the benefit of an environmental regulation to our children is more than thirty times larger than today's cost, the administration's view is that it shouldn't be adopted. With this calculus, which gives our children short shrift, no wonder there is no interest in doing something about climate change.[50]

Third, for a variety of reasons large fractions of young people don't have the opportunities that, say, I had when I was starting out. Millions are saddled with burdensome student debt, which impedes their ability to choose a career freely—they're constantly thinking of the payments due—or even start a family or own a home. Meanwhile, house prices, relative to incomes, have soared as a result of easy money, a poorly designed tax code, and financial deregulation. *Our* generation got the capital gains. The next generation has to figure out how to get affordable housing. This divide in well-being across generations is one of the most troubling. Parents who made a killing in real estate may share that wealth with their children, who, in turn, may hand it down to their children. But parents who don't own any real estate have little or nothing to pass on to their children and grandchildren, and that leaves their descendants scrambling. Inequalities in this generation may thus be amplified in the next. Changes in tax policy described later in this chapter and mortgage and student loan programs in the next provide a way out.

Taxation

A progressive, fair, and efficient tax system should be an important part of a dynamic and just society. We've described the important activities that government needs to undertake, including public education, health, research, and infrastructure; running a good judicial system; and providing a modicum of social protection. All of this requires resources, meaning taxes. It is only fair that those who have a greater capacity to pay—and who typically gain more from our economy—contribute more. But as was noted in chapter 2, those at the very top actually pay a lower tax rate than those with lower incomes. In these and other ways, matters have only grown worse in the last three decades—with the 2017 tax bill, with its increase in taxes on a majority of those in the middle to finance tax cuts for corporations and billionaires, standing out as perhaps the worst piece of tax legislation ever.

Simply asking corporations and rich individuals to pay their fair share of taxes—a modest change from our current regressive system—could by itself generate a couple of trillion dollars over ten years.[51] This entails not just raising rates but eliminating the myriad loopholes that the lobbyists for special interests have helped to put into our tax code.[52] Instead of taxing real estate at preferential rates (as the 2017 bill did), the returns to land should be taxed at a higher rate. When workers are taxed, they might not work as hard; when capital is taxed, it might go elsewhere or people might not save as much.[53] Not so for land. It's there, whether taxed or not. Indeed, the great nineteenth-century economist Henry George argued that returns to land—rents—should be taxed at 100 percent.[54] Taxing rents can lead to a more productive economy. Now, a large fraction of savings goes into land rather than into productive assets (investments in research, plants, and equipment). Taxing the capital gains on land and rents would encourage more savings to be directed toward productive capital.[55]

There are other taxes that can simultaneously increase economic performance and raise revenue. For instance, a tax on carbon emissions reminds households and firms that we must reduce our carbon emissions.[56] In the absence of such taxes, individuals don't take into account the social cost of their carbon-emitting activities. Such taxes would also incentivize investments and innovation that reduce carbon emissions, and could play a central role in achieving important goals set forth in international meetings in Paris (2015) and Copenhagen (2009) limiting global warming.[57] Without such a tax, it will be hard for these goals to be reached; and the costs of not reaching them are enormous—already in 2017 the world experienced a record number of losses from weather-related natural disasters, including a $245 billion loss resulting from hurricanes Harvey, Irma, and Maria, a manifestation of the predicted increase in weather variability associated with global warming.[58] The increase in sea level will also have enormous costs on coastal states; much of Florida and Louisiana will be under water or suffer from much more frequent tidal flooding. Wall Street too will be inundated, though some might say that is a good thing.

There is a general principle: whenever there is an economic activity for which the private return exceeds the social return, a tax will enhance welfare. Another example of a needed tax: short-term financial trading is largely socially unproductive. Typically in these trades, one person hopes to get the advantage of another because of superior information. Both people may even believe that they've got the advantage. In many ways, the stock market is just a rich person's casino. And while gambling may afford some short-term pleasure, money simply moves from one person's pocket to another. The gambling—and short-term trading—doesn't make the country richer or more productive, and often it ends in bitter tears on the part of one party or the other. Excessive trading, especially associated with high-frequency trade, performs no social function.[59] A well-designed financial transactions tax will not only raise money, it would improve the efficiency and stability of the economy.

OF COURSE, special interests will line up against each of these taxes. I don't want to pretend that it will be politically easy. But, politics aside, there should be no shortage of funds to ensure that America will no longer be a rich country with poor people—that a middle-class life can be and should be attained by all Americans.

Conclusions

The changes covered in this chapter, combined with the reforms discussed earlier in the book, are necessary to achieve a more dynamic economy, growing faster, an economy that serves people, and not the other way around. Many of the policies are hardly novel—as was noted earlier in this book, variants of these policies have worked successfully in other countries. It's not the economics that are difficult. It's the politics.

Even if we get the politics right and succeed in achieving the reforms described here, attaining a middle-class life may still be difficult: even families with reasonable jobs may not be able to have an adequate retirement or afford to send their children to college. Just as, traditionally, farmers helped each other raise a new barn, and just as families pull together in times of need, our society works best when everyone works together. The positive agenda of restoring growth for all is part of the broader ambition of making a middle-class life accessible to all. The next chapter explains how this can be done.

CHAPTER 10

A Decent Life for All

A combination of markets, civil society, and government regulations and programs like free public education created the middle-class life with middle-class jobs of the last century—making life for workers far better than the abject state they were in a century earlier. But over the past forty years, we seem to have taken our middle-class life for granted and grown complacent. The result is that large fractions of citizens are struggling to maintain that lifestyle, and for significant numbers, it's become unattainable. When wages for very large parts of the country stagnate or decline over a period of a half a century in the most prosperous large country in the world, it is clear that something has gone wrong. The reforms discussed in the previous chapter would go a long way toward ensuring that the take-home pay of every worker is at least a livable wage in twenty-first-century America. They also hold the prospect of restoring sustainable growth. But they won't suffice to enable many Americans to have a decent, middle-class life.

Over recent decades, markets have not done a good job of ensuring the basic requisites of a decent life for all. Some of these failures are by now well understood: markets would prefer to insure only the healthy, and they devote enormous resources to differentiating between the healthy and others. But a society where only the healthy can get insurance will not be a productive or healthy society. So too, markets can do a good job at providing education for children of the rich, but a society where only the children of the rich get a good education is neither fair nor efficient.

Sometimes, conservatives say, these aspirations to correct market failures and to overcome their limitations are well and good but they cost money. It's something we can't afford now, especially with our massive public debt. This is sheer nonsense. Countries much poorer than the US do a better job than we do in meeting these aspirations of their citizens to health care and education for all and the other prerequisites of a decent life.[1]

In fact, the United States did a better job some sixty years ago. At the end of World War II, we were much more indebted, and we were much poorer, with a per capita income just a quarter of what it is today.[2] Yet in the years after World War II, we could afford to provide free education at the best schools to all those who fought in the war under the GI Bill, which meant essentially to all young men and many women—except African Americans, who were denied many of the benefits of the GI bill.[3] So too under President Eisenhower, we expanded our national road network and enacted the National Defense Education Act, beginning a massive program of advancing science and technology. Under President Johnson we enacted the Medicare Program and under President Nixon we expanded Social Security. If we could afford these things then, we can afford them now. It is a matter of choice—and we have been making the wrong choices.

A central idea in the proposals below is *the public option*.[4] Government has proven itself more efficient than the private sector in many arenas. Administrative costs of government retirement programs are a fraction of those in the private sector. Countries with public health care systems have lower costs with better outcomes than America's profit-driven system. Still, Americans value choice. With a public option, the government creates an alternative, basic program to provide products like health insurance, retirement annuities, or mortgages. Competition between the public and private sectors will break the back of market power. It will enhance citizens' choice, alleviating some of the sense of powerlessness they feel today when their choices are so limited and they are so often abused by the private sector.[5] It will make them better off, with a feeling of better control over their lives.

Over the long run, in some markets, public and private programs may coexist (as they do today for providing income in retirement). In some cases, the private sector may be able to tailor a program to better meet the needs of particular individuals. In other cases, I suspect, except for certain niches directed at the very wealthy, the private sector will wither away. It won't prove competitive. In still other cases, a majority of citizens will turn to the private sector. But in all cases the public option will provide for competition between the private and the public sector, enriching choice, and will encourage the private sector to be more efficient, more competitive, and more responsive, with lower prices and better service.

Unfortunately, the country has been moving in the wrong direction. President Obama had proposed a public option within the Affordable Care Act. The private sector, not wanting competition, successfully suppressed it.[6]

America has prided itself on "American exceptionalism," meaning America is special and stands out from other countries because of its unique history. More recently, this exceptionalism has taken on a sinister overtone: greater inequality and inequality of opportunity, more prisoners, and a lower—and declining—life expectancy by far than in countries with similar income levels. America's private health insurance system is far more costly with far poorer results than the public programs in Europe. At the very least, all of this suggests that we should be paying more attention to what is done elsewhere. America should get over the attitude that there is nothing to learn from other nations. They have paid close attention to what we've done, and, when they saw something that worked, and seemed likely to work for them, they've imitated and adapted. We should do similarly.

Access to Health Care for All

The Affordable Care Act ("Obamacare") made an important start in ensuring that all Americans have access to health care. There is obviously room for improvement, especially given the refusal of some states to participate in the expanded Medicaid program (providing health care to the poor). But in some dimensions, matters are becoming worse, particularly after the passage of the 2017 tax bill, which eliminated the mandate that all individuals purchase insurance. The elimination of the mandate, in combination with rules forbidding discrimination against preexisting conditions, creates a death spiral for private insurance: healthy individuals drop out until they need insurance, forcing premiums to increase as only those who are sick or about to need health insurance buy; but this induces more relatively healthy people to drop out, leading to further increases in premiums.[7] If one wants to have an insurance system covering everybody—and there are good economic and social reasons for that—then one has to have public provision of insurance, along the lines of the European single-payer systems, or one has to have a mandate requiring individuals to purchase insurance privately, along the lines of Obamacare, or one has to give large public subsidies to insurance firms.[8] In a society in which there is little social solidarity—each person for him- or herself—the notion that the healthy are subsidizing the unhealthy might seem objectionable, until we remember: eventually almost all individuals are going to be "unhealthy." Even among the very healthy, as we march toward death, only those who die suddenly, without warning, never draw upon the health care system.

The reason that Trump and the Republicans didn't come up with an alternative to Obamacare ("Repeal and Replace") is that there aren't other solutions. Obama and the Democrats worked hard to create a system in which all individuals who were already covered could keep their insurance, but that also ensured that everyone else would be covered. It was an imperfect system, but it was a framework which could be improved over time.

A critical missing part couldn't get through Congress—the public option. This option would have made Medicare available to all who wanted it, for a price. This would have meant that no one would be left without insurance, should all the private insurance companies decide not to provide it in some locale, and would have simultaneously provided competition, restraining the abuse of market power in a sector in which the limited number of firms in most geographic regions makes that likely.

Trump and the Republicans, by removing the individual mandate, may well have succeeded in breaking Obamacare, a program which has turned out to be enormously popular. If this happens, millions more Americans will be left without health insurance, especially those with preexisting conditions. Millions more will find themselves facing increasing premiums, particularly painful as one gets older and less healthy—when insurance is most needed but one cannot easily afford it. There are but two directions—restoring the mandate and public subsidies, but this time with the public option; or the single payer, where the government (the "single payer") provides basic health insurance for all. As the system in the United Kingdom demonstrates, one can have a robust private market with supplementary insurance and single payer insurance sitting side by side.

Retirement

After working hard for their entire lives, workers deserve a decent retirement. In their waning years, they shouldn't have to worry about whether they will be able to make ends meet, whether they will become dependent on some charitable agency or their children or have to take a part-time minimum wage job at McDonald's, a big step down from where they thought they would be at this stage of their life. Of course, as we argued in the last chapter, government should ensure that older people who are able and want to work can find meaningful employment, using the skills and education that they have acquired over a lifetime.

On the Right, there are efforts to cut back Social Security, a key part of retirement funding for most Americans. In describing Social Security, they use the derogatory term "entitlement," trying to reframe the program as a gift rather than something that's been earned: individuals have made contributions to Social Security for their entire working lives, just as if they had purchased a retirement annuity. There are some critical differences: the private sector is less efficient, with higher transaction costs; tries to skim off large amounts as profits; and provides less comprehensive coverage of risks; but has a tighter link between contributions and benefits.

President George W. Bush tried to privatize Social Security, to leave individuals to be exploited by private markets and rely on the vicissitudes of the stock market—possibly to be devastated by economic forces beyond their control, as a stock market crash wipes out their retirement savings. It is particularly painful to think about this now through the historic lens of the Great Recession, brought on by America's major banks, the very financial institutions that individuals were supposed to rely on for their retirement security in this myth. Those whose savings were not wiped out by the financial crisis then faced a new problem, this time from the Federal Reserve, as it valiantly tried to resuscitate the economy in the face of intransigence from Republicans in Congress refusing to provide the fiscal stimulus the economy needed. As the Fed lowered its interest rates toward zero, those who had prudently put their money into government bonds saw their retirement income disappear—a devastation no less bad than that which could have been brought about by rampant inflation or by a market crash.

In other countries, even before the Great Recession, those who were forced to rely on private retirement accounts found their retirement benefits decreased by the fees imposed by the firms handling their accounts, in some cases by as much as 30 to 40 percent.[9] The reason that the private sector wants to manage these retirement accounts is, of course, the fees—what is going on in privatization is a simple transfer from the pockets of retirees to the pockets of the bankers. There is no evidence that bankers generate higher or safer returns; quite the contrary.

Making matters worse, many Americans have fallen victim to financial predators, looking for those whom they can take advantage of, again through outsized and often hidden fees.[10]

The lesson is clear: Americans cannot be asked to rely on markets for their retirement. The fluctuations in market values and the incomes generated are too great and the bankers are too avaricious. They need an alternative—not the cutbacks in Social Security that the Right is demanding, but the revitalization of Social Security, making sure that it is on sound financial footing, and providing a *public option*. The easiest way to provide the public retirement option would be to allow any individual to put additional funds into his Social Security account with a commensurate increase in retirement benefits.

The public option would provide effective competition to the private sector, and might be able to induce banks and insurance companies to produce better financial products, at lower costs and fees—the public option may, in fact, be a better instrument for encouraging good behavior even than government regulation. Of course, those in the financial sector are adamantly opposed to such a public option. They talk a big game about believing in competition, but when push comes to shove, they like their cozy arrangements.

Part of the revitalization of Social Security would involve expanding the instruments in which it can invest, away from low-yielding US government bonds. One possibility would be to invest money in a broad-based equity fund or in bonds to be issued by a newly created Infrastructure Investment Bank discussed earlier (an American version of the European Investment Bank). The returns to our economy from such infrastructure investments are large. And providing a modest fraction of those returns to bondholders—at, say, 5 percent—would simultaneously put the Social Security Trust Fund on a sounder footing.

Home Ownership

Just as the 2008 financial crisis showed the deficiency in our retirement system, so too for our system of housing finance. Millions of Americans lost their homes, many as a result of predatory and fraudulent practices of America's financial system. Our mortgage system[11] remains broken, with the federal government continuing to underwrite the vast majority of mortgages.[12] America's financial institutions have made it clear that they are unwilling to accept any "reform" that leaves them responsible for the risks of the mortgages that they write. In effect, they say they can't take responsibility for the financial products they create! A decade after the crisis, there seems no consensus on the way forward. There is a simple answer, recognizing that changes in modern technology and information systems enable the creation of a twenty-first-century mortgage system. Among the central problems of any mortgage finance system are screening (ascertaining whether a particular home is appropriate for a particular family, and that there is adequate equity in the home) and the enforcement of the terms of the mortgage, in particular the collection of payments.

For the former, the critical database is the history of family income—and that database already comprehensively resides in the public sector, at the Social Security Administration and in the Internal Revenue Service (IRS). It is inefficient to have this information copied down onto paper, transmitted, verified, and then re-entered into a new corporate database. A second critical database is that concerning housing transactions, enabling the lender to assess the value of the collateral. Here again, since all sales are publicly registered, there is a complete database, on the basis of which one can construct the most accurate estimate of the current value of any property.[13]

Other data is, of course, relevant for issuing a mortgage—whether this is the individual's primary home or whether the individual plans to rent the house out. Most of this data, too, is part of what is reported on tax forms—individuals can take interest deductions for a primary home and declare the income derived from renting property on a separate income tax schedule. And while in the run up to the 2008 crisis there was massive fraud (lying) in the process of securitization (where mortgages are pooled together into "securities," which in turn were sold on to investors),[14] there is likely to be much less of this when such information is reported to the IRS, partly because the consequences can be more severe.

These factors point to the possibility that we could use the IRS as a mortgage payments vehicle. Moreover, there are significant savings in doing so.[15]

These information and transaction costs economies would enable large reductions in the costs of issuing and managing a mortgage. A thirty-year mortgage with a 20 percent down payment could be provided at an interest rate little above the thirty-year rate at which government can borrow from the market, and the government could still make a profit. [16] And with a focus on helping American families manage the risk of home ownership, new mortgage products could be created, for instance, those which enabled reductions in payments when family income is reduced significantly, with a corresponding increase in the duration of the mortgage. These would not only reduce the risk of costly foreclosures, but would also reduce the anxiety individuals feel when they face an adverse shock, such as the loss of a job or a serious illness.

The fact of the matter is that our private markets have not been doing a good job of helping their clients manage risk. Our bankers have been more focused on exploiting individuals to the extent they can—and in increasing their fees. In doing that, they created toxic mortgages, mortgages that *increased* the risks that individuals face. That's why millions of Americans lost their homes, including many who had already had full ownership, had lived in their homes for years and years but were persuaded by the bankers to "cash in" on the large increases in housing prices through home equity loans. They couldn't lose (so they were told)—and why wait until they are near death to enjoy the gift that the housing boom had brought? But of course, they did lose.

The government-headed mortgage system we have now is a public–private partnership, where the private side takes the gain in the form of high fees and the public takes the losses. This is not the kind of efficient capitalism depicted in textbooks or by the advocates of free and unfettered markets. It is, however, the ersatz American-style capitalism that has evolved in practice. This is not the kind of market economy to which we should aspire, not the kind of market economy which results in rising standards of living.

We need, in short, to have a mortgage market with the kind of innovative public option suggested above. Such a market would not only enable more Americans to own homes; it would also enable more Americans to keep their homes, their most important asset.

Education

All Americans want their children to live up to their potential, and that requires providing them with the best education that fits their talents, needs, and desires. Unfortunately, our education system has not kept up with the times. The nine-month calendar and short school day may have been appropriate in a nineteenth- or early twentieth-century agrarian economy and in a world with stay-at-home mothers, but it doesn't work for today's world. Nor does the structure of education match the advances in technology, where individuals can obtain instant access to more information than was available only in the best of libraries not that long ago.

Most importantly, our education system has become an important part of our growing inequality: there is a high correlation between the education and income of a parent and the educational attainment of the child; and between education, in turn, and future income.[17] Thus, deficiencies in our education system exacerbate the intergenerational transmission of advantage—rather than, as public education once did, acting as the most important leveling force in our society.

Equalizing educational opportunity requires a comprehensive agenda—from the availability of pre-K education for all to access to colleges and universities for all—without burdensome student debt. We now know that there are large gaps even as children enter school, which pre-K programs can help ameliorate.[18]

There are many ways of ensuring the universal access to higher education—lower tuition and publicly provided income-contingent loans, where the amount repaid depends on one's income. These can be calibrated so that student debt is never the threat that it is today. This is a system that has worked very well in Australia, and could work here.[19] My point here is not to evaluate the merits of these alternatives, but simply to argue not only that can we afford to ensure universal access but also that we cannot afford *not* to make these investments. And making sure that there is access for all at affordable terms should be a central part of an agenda ensuring a decent life for all Americans.

The country has a legacy problem: we've left millions of young people burdened by student debts beyond their ability to pay—some $1.5 trillion. It's ruining their lives, forcing them to delay getting married, buying a home, or even accepting the job they would like, as all their energies are devoted to paying back this onerous debt. It's also hurting our economy.

To make matters worse, the financial sector used its lobbying power to make it virtually impossible to discharge these debts through bankruptcy. This has to be reversed: Why should someone who has borrowed money to invest in himself be treated worse than someone who has borrowed money to buy a yacht?

Further, there should be a public option, publicly provided student loans. For those already burdened with student debt, there has to be a way to convert private loans into public ones.[20] Government loans should, in turn, all be transformed into income-contingent loans, with interest rates just slightly higher than the government borrowing rate: we shouldn't be making a profit out of young people trying to get ahead in life.

Moreover, a K–12 education system that relies as heavily on local taxation as ours does means that those in poor communities will get a worse education than those in rich communities. Unfortunately, this problem has been getting worse. But it is a problem we can address.[21] The federal government should provide incentives for states to engage in more equalization of funding between rich and poor communities, and should itself provide more funds to help equalize opportunities among the states. Further, because those at the bottom need help to catch up, there should be even more special assistance from the federal government to districts with large numbers of poor individuals.

Conclusions

There are just a few things that are at the core of a decent life: people care about jobs with fair pay and a modicum of security both before and after retirement, about education for their children, about owning a home, and about access to good health care. In each of these areas capitalism American-style has failed large swaths of our population. We can do better. The program outlined above is a beginning. It cannot fully address some of the deep-seated problems that have been festering since the era of Reagan. We should have done something to help those who were losing their jobs and whose skills were not up to the new technologies. But we didn't. We should have had better health care and education systems. But we didn't. We should have helped those cities that were facing deindustrialization and the destruction of their community. But we didn't. We are now paying the price for these failures. We can't redo history, and we shouldn't try to go back to the past. We have to do the best we can, given the hand we've dealt ourselves.

The agenda I've laid out can be achieved within the financial constraints facing the country today, making our families' lives better and our economy stronger. To those who say we can't afford it, I reply: we, as a rich country, can't afford not to ensure that this middle-class life is within the grasp of more of our citizens.

Another world is possible, and this progressive agenda can help us create it.

CHAPTER 11

Reclaiming America

"Give me your tired, your poor,
Your huddled masses yearning to breathe free,
The wretched refuse of your teeming shore.
Send these, the homeless, tempest-tost to me,
I lift my lamp beside the golden door!"

—INSCRIPTION ON THE STATUE OF LIBERTY. FROM
"THE NEW COLOSSUS," A SONNET BY EMMA LAZARUS

Our polity has slid so far that we are now compelled to turn to fundamental issues in order to cure what ails us. Minor tweaks of current arrangements won't get us to where we need to be.

For one, what do we believe in, as Americans? My conviction is that, despite the moment in which we find ourselves and the image we are now presenting to the world, we are still at essence a country that believes in fairness, in equality of opportunity, and in what the Statue of Liberty represents, with its epic inscription. We are still a country of people who care about their neighbors and the less advantaged. We also care about the truth, about knowledge, and our community: we are more than rugged individualists roaming the Western ranges.

Restoring our politics—and in turn, our economics—to embody and uphold those values must begin with an examination of our values themselves—and an acknowledgment that our political class has dangerously failed to express them in policy.

The Disparity between Our Values and Social Reality

What are American values? Ask a politician and he'll tell you one thing. Observe his actions and you'll infer another. The question may seem soft at the edges, but it is at the heart of fixing what afflicts us as a country. And I do not mean "values" in the sense that those on the religious Right often mean it: values as expressed in our *personal* choices and in our family life. No, what I am referring to are the values that inform our *public* policies, programs, and economic perspectives.[1]

One of the contradictions of the economics discipline is that we model individuals simplistically, as if we were just selfish and materialistic. But even upon reflection, we know humans are more than that. We strive for money, and yet we find nothing admirable in excesses of greed and materialism, or the moral depravity by which some succeed in acquiring their fortunes. Some strive for attention, while others prefer more anonymity; yet few find anything admirable in Trump, who has achieved attention through constant prevarications and narcissism.

We admire too those who give of themselves for others. Most of us, I suspect, want our children to be caring and giving, not selfish and self-serving. We are, in short, far more complicated than, and far different from, the *homo economicus* so well studied by economists, those selfish individuals constantly striving for their own gratification. Yet if we make no effort to acknowledge our more admirable impulses, and to incorporate them into our models and policies, the less noble motives—avarice and indifference to the well-being of others—will fill the vacuum. The vessel of the country will veer into dark seas, where the most vulnerable are left to fend for themselves, rule-breakers are rewarded, regulators are effectively "captured" by those they are supposed to regulate, watchdogs are cowed, economic gains accrue mainly to those who are already rich, the result of exploitation rather than wealth creation, and ideas like truth, facts, liberty, empathy, and rights are mere rhetorical devices, employed when politically convenient.

Look around, and it is plain that our country, in the age of Trump, is steaming headlong into these darker waters. Nevertheless, there are also signs that we can still find our way out. The revulsion we feel for the conduct of our political and business leaders is a good sign—it means that we are not yet a perfect mirror of the economic system based on self-interest and greed that we have created. If the nation's course is left unchecked, however, we will become increasingly so.

Myths mask our failings

A society creates myths, stories, and narratives that reflect its values and shape its culture, especially its youth. At their best, myths can reinforce shared values and motivate. Ours are of rugged individualism, the self-made man, the entrepreneur as job creator, and the American dream. The myth of the American dream is important in reinforcing the idea that America is the land of opportunity. It serves to distinguish us from other countries, from "old Europe," from which so many Americans came so long ago, in search of opportunity.

The poor, hard-working American who prospers is a national archetype.[2] We tell ourselves that anyone who works hard enough can make it. And yet, as we have already seen in this book, the statistics overwhelmingly show otherwise. Many who are working hard are not making it, and many who are making it are doing so not through hard work but through shady business practices and by dint of having the right parents.

We are so in love with our mythologized self-image that we insist upon its reality even when the facts scream otherwise. For instance, many continue to believe that opportunity is an immutable quality of the country, even though statistics tell us the opposite. Ironically, our attachment to our mythological self-image leads us to embrace policies that actually undermine the expression of our values—making it ever less likely that the American dream becomes a reality. If everyone simply by dint of hard work can pull themselves up by their own boot-straps, we don't need financial aid programs for the poor—somehow, they'll get a job and work their way through college—and we don't really need affirmative action programs to level the playing field for those facing a legacy of discrimination—those with grit and determi-nation will overcome this, making them better people for it. We've seen the statistics though: even with the admittedly limited assistance we provide, those from poor families and from discriminated-against groups simply aren't making it.[3] The odds are overwhelmingly against it, so much so that one has to label the American dream as fiction. A moment's honest reflection by anyone who has made it from upper-middle-income white families should make them doubt whether they could have done so if they had been born otherwise.

The myth, though, shapes news coverage: when our media discov-ers someone who has made it from the bottom to the top, they give the story airtime and ink, and this in turn reinforces our preconcep-tion of ourselves. Psychologists call this confirmatory bias: we give weight to the evidence that is consistent with our prior beliefs—our sustaining myths. We discount evidence to the contrary—the obvi-ous evidence of self-perpetuating elites at the top and the poverty and inequality traps that characterize the bottom.

Or take the myth of "rugged individualism." Businesses know that rugged individualism rarely works: a company succeeds only through teamwork, through cooperation. Companies often construct inter-nal teams, enhancing solidarity, cohesion, and cooperation. They sometimes try to take advantage of employees' competitive spirit, by encouraging healthy rivalries among teams within the company. Sometimes, to encourage competition, compensation will be based in part on team performance, a strategy that is at odds with traditional economic theory. That theory says that teamwork won't succeed because team members will try to free ride on their teammates. Most of us know that the reality is otherwise. We all want the approval of our peers, and we won't get that if we are seen as free-riding. This is just one of the many ways in which standard economics has wrongly modeled behavior and human nature, but, in doing so, it has led to an economy that has actually been shaping Americans and their behavior in ways that are often inconsistent with higher values.[4]

Tension between embracing change and deep conservatism

Another one of the national myths and narratives is that we are a country that embraces change. Indeed, some seem to embrace change for change's sake. But a closer look at America shows a strong countercurrent, a deep-seated conservatism in some parts of the country.[5] Some are constantly looking in the rearview mirror, and thinking that what was in the past is better than what the future holds for us.

In matters of social and economic policy, going back in time is not a viable option, nor is it something that we would want if we could have it. Would we want shorter lifespans? Poorer health? A much lower per capita income? It should be obvious what the consequences would be if Trump succeeded in leading the country backward in the way he wishes, restoring our manufacturing economy, for instance, to the greatness it had in the mid-twentieth century: going back in time would have its price—a lower standard of living for the vast majority, even if the coal miners' jobs were restored.

Internationally, the risks of looking backward are greater. We can't pretend that our position is the same as it was three-quarters of a century ago. The reality is that America no longer dominates the world as it did in the years after World War II. The attempt to reassert such domination will inevitably fail, our position in the global economy and, more broadly, our global influence, will wane still more.

The problem with the economic changes of the past four decades, and a central theme of this book, is that while we as a country are so much richer today than we were then (at least as measured conventionally, say, by GDP), many have not shared in that prosperity. Some have seen their prospects diminish not just relatively, but absolutely. Many have felt a middle-class life gradually eluding their grasp.

The right response to change is to evaluate each possible change, accept those things that really cannot be altered, and design policy so that, to the degree possible, change reflects our values, and individuals, especially the vulnerable, are not harmed.

Since the 1980s, the United States has been unable to achieve such a balanced response. For instance, there are those who tell us we should blindly accept the march of globalization, as it is currently taking place, while others cling to an imagined past and attempt to reject everything that is new and different—and not just trends in manufacturing and automation, but the global flow of goods and people. Chapter 4 showed that neither of these is the way forward.

The United States is certainly capable of not just accepting but managing economic change. We have done it time and again. The economy and society of the twenty-first century is markedly different from that of three-quarters of a century ago, let alone that of the late eighteenth century. Social constructs and institutions like racism, slavery, and gender discrimination are no longer acceptable to the vast majority of Americans, or so I believe and hope.

When the Constitution was written we were an agrarian society, with more than 70 percent of the population directly or indirectly dependent on agriculture. By the 1950s, we were a manufacturing/industrial society. Today, we are a postindustrial society, with manufacturing comprising less than 10 percent of our labor force.

These changing economic circumstances necessitate a changing role for government. Not only what the government does has had to change, but also how it does it. The reason that regulations and public expenditures increased is not a power grab by politicians, but because we had to, if we were to have a dynamic, well-functioning twenty-first-century innovative, urban, postindustrial economy.

None of our successes in managing these issues arose from each individual going it alone. All involve cooperation—and in time, that cooperation has expanded from the folkloric American image of the community getting together to raise a barn, to more systemic ways of working together, including agreeing to certain rules, regulations, and compromises of unbridled personal liberty. Still, the kinds and extent of cooperation that our twenty-first-century economy requires are new and unprecedented. There is no comparison between the level of collective action required now and what was needed in the late eighteenth century, the time that the Constitution was written and to which some look back to with such fondness.

Our Values

Previous paragraphs have described the many myths that have distorted our reasoning about who we are as a nation and what needs to be done. For all the divisions that have marked the country in recent years, there remain many shared values. We (or at least most of us) believe in equality, not complete equality, but far more than that characterized by today's economy. We especially believe in equality of opportunity and justice, and in democracy—not the one dollar one vote system that we have become but the one person one vote system that we learned about in school. We believe in tolerance, letting others do as they please as long as they don't harm others. We believe in science and technology, and the scientific method—keys to understanding the universe and the increase in our standards of living.

We believe that we can use reason and deliberation, too, to figure out how to better arrange the affairs of society, to create better social and economic institutions that, in turn, have not only increased our material well-being, but created a society in which diverse individuals are better able to work together, to achieve far more than they could working alone. This is true even though we are not fully rational and, thank goodness, we are not fully selfish. Adam Smith emphasized the importance of our *moral sentiments*[6]; these moral values constitute an important aspect of who we are.

The Constitution was a product of that kind of reasoning and argumentation. Such reasoning made the Founders realize that humans were fallible, as were all human institutions. Institutions could be improved upon. The Constitution itself reflected this—it provided for a process of amendments. It employed checks and balances. It even provided for the removal of the president; no one was above the rule of law.

We agree, too, about those basic principles that have to be embedded in any functioning market economy, such as the rule of law. And most of us believe that rule of law should be especially attentive to protecting the rights of ordinary individuals against the powerful.

Though it may not be so commonplace, most who understand the distinction I have made between the wealth of nations and the wealth of individuals would, too, agree with it; they would want to reward those who add to the national pie by their creativity and hard work; but there should be no accolades for those who become wealthy by exploiting others, by stealing from them openly or furtively, the rent-seekers who abound today. Most (apart from the rent-seekers themselves) would agree that we should tilt the economy to encourage wealth creation at the expense of rent-seeking.

Fundamental to the Founders' conception of the role of government was an understanding of the limits of majority rule. The framers of the Constitution realized government had to be constructed to ensure individual liberties, but to balance them against the collective interest. The government could, for instance, take an individual's property for public purpose, but only with appropriate compensation.

By and large, over more than two centuries, our government, based on these shared values and beliefs, has worked well.[7] However, the system can, as now, also result in dysfunction, when one part fails to perform the role it is supposed to, and gridlock, when there are pervasive disagreements. This is part of the reason that, over the years, a country founded on many noble ideals has often taken an excessively long time to make seemingly basic moral choices. We are now, again, in one of these moments when our system seems to be failing us.

Today's Anxieties

We now rightly worry about the fragility of our democratic norms and institutions. When our economic and political systems fail to deliver for large fractions of the population, many will look elsewhere; they become easy prey for demagogues and their false promises. These demagogues blame others for society's travails, and will heap further blame on these outsiders as their own promises come to naught.

Today's problems go well beyond gridlock and a failure of our politics to keep up with the times. A system designed to protect the majority from the minority has been turned topsy-turvy. The majority now worries about how it can be protected from abuses by a minority that has attained power and is now using that power to perpetuate its control.

The worry is that the rules of the game are being written disproportionately by this minority, which was described earlier as a coalition of the very rich, evangelical conservatives, and the disaffected working families, with an economic agenda set largely by the moneyed elites, even when it went against the interests of the rest. In a sense, this inchoate coalition is even worse for the country than if it were being run only by and for the 1 percent. This is because to keep the coalition together, the elites have to throw occasional sops to the coalition partners, dangerous protectionism at one moment, making access to abortions for the poor more difficult at another.

As bad as things are, they could be much worse—and Trump is pulling us in that direction. I haven't spent much time in this book criticizing particular policies that he's put forward. Even when enacted, they don't represent the real danger, for they can be reversed. I worry more about things that are harder to reverse—the attacks against our institutions, our understanding of what makes for a good society and how we come to discover that, the growing divides not only in income and wealth but in beliefs, and the waning sense of trust that is necessary for a diverse society to function.

Undermining public institutions

Trump, taking a page from Andrew Jackson, is attempting to undermine both our regulatory system and our professional civil service. As part of a new and expanded creed of winner-take-all politics, he has asked for new discretion to fire government officials so he can hire his friends and corporate lobbyists who support him.

In a sense, he has simply carried to an extreme the long-standing attack of modern-day Republicans on faceless bureaucrats. But most of those in the government are actually efficiently and fairly managing the things we love and need: sending us our Social Security checks, making sure that we get health benefits through Medicare and Medicaid, defending us against threats from abroad (our military) and disorder from within (the FBI), preserving our natural heritage and managing the national parks (our National Park Service).

We've come to rely on government for our systems of social protection—Social Security, unemployment insurance, Medicare. We have them because people want and need them. The market failed to provide them, and government filled the gap.[8]

So too, like Republicans before him, Trump has accused these government employees of being inefficient. While everyone has encountered examples of inefficiency in government, the same is true in the private sector—I can easily recall innumerable examples as I think about my encounters with airlines, my telephone company, internet provider, and insurance company. We noted earlier that the transaction costs associated with Social Security are a fraction of those of private-sector providers of annuities. Looking around the world, America's private health care system delivers less health for far more money. Overall, government employment today is approximately the same in *absolute* numbers as it was a half century ago, even as the numbers government employees serve have increased by more than one hundred million, and the range of duties they have to perform has greatly expanded.[9]

Standard conservative discussions of public expenditures beyond Social Security and Medicare contend that they are basically a waste. This ignores the enormous benefits we get from government expenditures on education and infrastructure. The returns on these investments are in fact greater than the returns achieved by most private investments, reinforcing a broad consensus—we are starving our public investments.

Even higher returns are achieved by government investments in research and development—advances that this book has put front and center as the source of increases in our standard of living. Imagine where our society and our economy—even our lives—would have been had it not been for government-sponsored research: We would be dying younger. We would not have the internet, the smart phone, the browser, or social media.

Trump has raised the howling against regulations and our bureaucrats to new levels, describing the regulatory process as run by unaccountable officials. As we have seen, his description was totally wrong, another lie: regulations and the regulatory process are themselves extensively regulated. There is a strong system of checks and balances and extensive accountability, both through the courts and through Congress. Thank goodness for this: these checks on the regulatory process mean that the regulations themselves cannot be easily and capriciously undone. Otherwise, Trump and his team would have been able to short-circuit all democratic processes and rewrite the rules to favor large corporations, leaving ordinary citizens, our environment, and our economy unprotected from their whims and relentless search for profits.

Imagine what life would be like if every time we bought a financial product we had to worry that the bank was out to cheat us; if every time we bought a toy, we worried whether the paint was poisonous or there were parts that might break off and choke our child; if every time we got in a car, we worried whether it was safe.[10] We forget about the course we were on fifty years ago: a country where the air was unbreathable and the water undrinkable. We can see in New Delhi and Beijing how things might have evolved, had it not been for strong and strongly enforced environmental regulations.

The attack against our system of governance and our knowledge institutions

I've argued in this book that there are two pillars to the increases in our standards of living over the past 250 years: better understanding of how to organize society (checks and balances, rule of law); and better understanding of nature—the advances in science and technology. We've seen how Trump and his team have tried to undermine both—again, at least in some instances, carrying a more quiet Republican assault to new extremes.

Our politics have degraded to the point that what were once taken for granted—for instance, the rule of law and a system of checks and balances—are now being challenged on a daily basis.[11]

We've described, for instance, the attacks on the judiciary and on the media. While our systems of checks and balances have, by and large, worked, some key regulations are being changed.[12] But Trump and his ilk now see that our very system of checks and balances is constraining them from pursuing their agenda of restructuring our economy and society to serve even more their cadre of rent-seekers. And so they have heightened their attack on these institutions. It is clear that constant vigilance is required if we are to maintain our democratic institutions.

THERE IS an attempt to despoil even truth and science by political leaders who have no self-imposed limits and no compunctions about what they will do to cement their power by manipulating the worst instincts of the electorate. As has been emphasized, perhaps the most dangerous aspect of the Trump administration in the long run is its attack on epistemology—on our beliefs about what it true and how we ascertain the truth.

The hardest task will be to heal the deep divide in our body politic. The growing economic divides are exacerbating all the other divisions. Most importantly, we explained how the kinds of societal checks and balances that are needed if our country is to function well together require limiting wealth and income inequality: extremes of inequality, of the kind that we have today lead to inequalities in power, including political power. While market power in any area is of concern, it is especially so in media. We already have evidence of how market power in that sector can help shape (or manipulate) political outcomes.

IN SHORT, the damage that is being done to our economic and political institutions is palpable. It won't be undone overnight: there will be a legacy long after Trump is gone.

Some silver linings

By carrying a long-standing debate over the role of government to an extreme, Trump has succeeded in generating a renewed understanding of the need for government and good governance, with strong systems of checks and balances and accountability.

In Europe, some leaders are describing a silver lining in Trump: he has brought Europe closer together. They now see more clearly what they stand for—and what they stand against; and they understand better the threat posed by the appeal to bigotry by the far Right. They stand, for instance, for an international rules-based system— just as they stand for a rule of law at home. An international rule of law—even in limited form—is as important for the functioning of the international economy and polity as the domestic rule of law is for the domestic economy and polity. By walking away from agreements signed by his predecessors, he has undermined international agreements and law. Going forward, recognizing that one can't rely on good faith, more careful attention will be paid to what happens when a signatory leaves.

Even darker clouds on the horizon

Today's dark moment is so different from that of thirty years ago, when democracy and markets seemed triumphant as the iron curtain fell. Free global markets would, so it was believed, be the torch that would eventually bring democratic ideals to all corners of the earth.

For anyone who might have forgotten about the fascism of the 1930s, and who has held on to any Pollyannaish notions that people and the world are basically good, Trump and Putin have reminded us that there are, in fact, some really bad actors out there; there is a fight between good and evil, and in that struggle, unfortunately, evil sometimes wins out, especially in the short run. These experiences have warned us of the damage to society that a few bad leaders can bring about. But, so far at least, *eventually* the decency of the vast majority of humankind triumphs. Our task today is to ensure that this happens once again.

America has always prided itself on its soft power, on the influence for the good that we have exerted around the world. We were, of course, never quite as good as we claimed—there are many dark episodes during the Cold War—but overall, the US did promote democracy, human rights, and economic development. But now, we are seeing the flip side of this coin: Trump is providing a role model that others around the world are following, a model of racism, misogyny, and the undermining of the rule of law. We have institutions that (so far) have protected us. In some of these other countries where illiberal democracies have sprung up, like Hungary and the Philippines, this may not be the case.

With this generation of unscrupulous leaders at the helm challenging the ideal of truth, the world and the country are at risk of a much graver disintegration—one in which it will eventually not be safe even to voice the sort of peaceful calls for action found in this book. One shudders to think of what sort of economic contraction, war, or security crisis could nudge us into the abyss.

Trump's Sugar High

Some looked at the success of the US economy in the years following Trump's election and the rise in the stock market as testimony to the wisdom of his policies. By now, it should be clear that I believe that Trump's economic agenda will fail (along with those in other countries pushing similar nativist and populist programs). The sugar high from the enormous increase in the deficit, following the tax cut and expenditure increases, will be short lived—but even while it was enjoying its sugar high, US performance was only a little better than the average of the advanced countries.[13] The stock market boom itself was short lived, petering out before the end of his second year in office. The deeper problems in our economy are unsolved or aggravated—weak real wages, growing inequality, poor health, declining life expectancy, weak long-term investment. His economic policies, including the 2017 tax bill, especially when fully implemented, will worsen inequality and result in less health care coverage.

The tax bill will move the country further away from the dynamic and innovative knowledge-based economy that is the only path for sustained growth. It made a mockery too of the principles of fiscal responsibility which had seemed to be the bedrock of the Republican Party and the business establishment, exposing these beliefs as nothing but instrumental: convenient, for instance, as arguments against increasing programs for poor or middle-class Americans, but easily dispensed with when it came to a tax cut for the rich and corporations. It is a miracle that Americans haven't become more cynical.

Widening the economic, racial, and ethnic divides is obviously bad for society and for democracy, but it's also bad for the economy. It distorts the labor market, with large fractions of the population not living up to their potential. Immigration barriers mean that we won't be able to draw upon some of the most talented people in the world and won't be able to fill some important gaps in our labor market.

A well-functioning society and economy requires trust and stability; Trump has been sowing distrust and his capricious policies, including a trade war with no clear strategy and no clear attainable objectives, have led to great uncertainty. The manner in which the 2017 tax bill was rushed through, without committee hearings, with the initial version voted on by the Senate containing illegible changes so that the senators didn't even know what it was they were voting for, not only made a mockery of democratic procedures, but also means that it was filled with mistakes, inconsistencies, and loopholes that one special interest or another put in when no one was looking. Without widespread popular support, and not a single Democratic vote, almost surely, much of it will be reversed as the political winds shift. The corporate largesse was supposed to promote investment. So too for Trump's protectionist policies. They haven't, partly because investment requires stability, and Trumpian policies have fostered uncertainty.

But let's be clear: even if the sugar high lasted long enough to get

Trump elected to a second term, the long-term damage Trump will have done to our economy and society may be deep. We've described how Trump has attacked the very pillars of our civilization, those that have in fact made us great, and are the basis of the remarkable advances in standards of living.

How We Arrived at This Juncture

The narrative for how we got here is well known: Globalization, financialization, and new technologies proceeded in ways that have left many workers behind, and the way they proceeded was largely shaped by economic policies.[14] Even during the bullish turn the business cycle took in 2018, the economy failed to deliver improvements to the well-being of too many, to restore them to where they had been a decade earlier, before the onslaught of the financial crisis. Inequality of wealth is now far worse than it was before the Great Recession of 2008, when it was bad enough already; and with the 2017 tax law and the mania for deregulation in the current administration, it is likely to get both more extreme and more painful.

Both Republicans like George H. W. Bush and Democrats like Bill Clinton promised that neoliberal policies of liberalization and globalization would bring prosperity to all. Now, these promises are seen for what they are, just self-serving platitudes (or lies): it is no wonder that disillusionment with the elites and their "system" should grow.

Combine these disappointments with advances in marketing and behavioral economics (and a dose of Russian intervention), and it is understandable how close to half the country could be sold Trumpian snake oil.[15] With our elites failing us, manipulation took hold.

We didn't get into our present perilous position overnight. There were warnings that things were not going well for large parts of the country, and that if these failings were not addressed, our situation could easily give rise to a demagogue.[16] We may not have known what shape the challenge would take, but the risk was there. We chose to ignore these warnings and in this sense, our current predicament is of our own making: we got the economics, the politics, and the values wrong.

We got the economics wrong: we thought unfettered markets—including lower taxes and deregulation—were the solution to every economic problem; we thought finance and globalization and advances in technology would, on their own, bring prosperity to all. We thought that markets were, on their own, always competitive—and so we didn't understand the dangers of market power. We thought the blind pursuit of profits would lead to societal well-being.

We got our politics wrong: too many thought that just having elections was all that democracy was about. We didn't understand the dangers of money in politics, its power; we didn't understand how concentrated money corrupts democracy and how the elites can use money to shape both the economy and our politics to generate ever more concentration of economic and political power. Nor did we understand how easily we could slide into a system best described as one dollar one vote, or how easily disillusionment with our democracy could set in, with large fractions of the population believing the system is rigged.

We got our values wrong. We forgot that the economy is supposed to serve our citizens, not the other way around. We confused ends and means: globalization was supposed to create a stronger economy to better serve our citizens; but then we told our people, because of the globalization *that we had created*, they had to have cutbacks in wages and public programs. Finance too became an end in itself, leading to a more unstable economy, growing more slowly, with more inequality, preying on ordinary citizens. Its pursuit of profits did not lead to their betterment.

A distorted economy and a distorted politics was supported by and exacerbated distorted values. We have become a more selfish society—selfish in the way that the economic models said we were supposed to be but not like the better selves to which we aspire. We let the wrong models of human nature drive us to become like the models themselves. We became more materialistic, less other-regarding, less altruistic, at first amoral—morals was something reserved for our religious leaders and for Sunday; but then immoral, with the moral turpitude that was the hallmark of finance being evidenced in sector after sector, until we elected a president who was himself the paragon of this new anti-ethics.

We didn't understand the true foundations of our well-being—the increases in our standard of living as well as the fulfillment of our highest ideals—rested on the foundations of science, rational enquiry, and discourse, and the social institutions derived from them, including the rule of law based on democratic processes.

The internationalism and free markets of neoliberalism with its false promises are now being replaced with primitive protectionism and nativism, whose promise of restoring the United States to prosperity is even less likely to be fulfilled. For an economist, it is easy to attack the market fundamentalism/neoliberalism that came to dominate in the years after Reagan. It was based on a set of refutable (and refuted) hypotheses. But at least one could have a rational discussion about neoliberalism, ascertaining whether there is a grain of truth in some of the arguments and empirical hypotheses. Not so for Trump, partly because the underlying ideas (if they can be dignified with that term) are inchoate. While in domestic policy he champions the virtues of the market economy—even America's rent-seeking variant—in international trade he takes the opposite stance: he doesn't believe in unfettered competitive markets, but rather in power-based managed trade, going back to discredited mercantilist ideas.

Putting Today's Despair in Historical Perspective

Reviewing other dangerous episodes of American and world history can give us some hope and inspiration for moving forward. Trump is not the first president to abuse his power. And this is not the first time we have been confronted with obscene inequality and that our economy has been distorted by excesses of market power. In each case, we contained the abuses and we corrected our course.

Andrew Jackson reportedly said of a Supreme Court decision of which he disapproved: "John Marshall has made his decision; now let him enforce it!"[17] He knew that in our political system, the president was supposed to enforce the laws—they controlled all the agencies responsible for doing so. The courts did not have their own enforcement capacity. Jackson presided over another time of great division, in a younger Republic.

Over the course of the Republic, our institutions have been refined and rethought. Disastrous experiences with Andrew Jackson's "spoils" system eventually led to the creation of a professional civil service.

This is also not the first era in which politicians have tried to take advantage of baser instincts to get political advantage. After the Civil War, Reconstruction and the decades of Jim Crow that followed provide more examples of persistent crisis and injustice that must have seemed at least as intractable and hopeless to people of the day— especially to the victims of racism. The problems then were not just the prejudices, but also a persistently exploitative economic system.[18] The current American situation, with Trump stirring up bigotry to direct the anger of white working-class voters toward immigrants, has echoes of these earlier situations.[19]

These battles for racial justice had their counterpoint in the fight for economic justice. Inequality and the agglomeration of market and political power reached new heights in the Gilded Age at the end of the nineteenth century. Then progressive legislation, including laws intended to ensure competition, brought us back from the precipice. After economic inequalities again reached new heights in the 1920s, the social and economic legislation of the New Deal opened up a new era in which Americans benefited from the economic security provided by Social Security and unemployment insurance, and economic powers were rebalanced through legislation curbing the financial sector and giving new life to the labor movement.[20]

Promoting the General Welfare

In this book, I have presented an alternative agenda—one might call it the progressive agenda. It takes at its heart one part of the Preamble of the Constitution, to "promote the General Welfare." The General Welfare means not just the welfare of the 1 percent, but the welfare of all. I have outlined a platform that I believe can serve as a consensus for a renewed Democratic Party. It can show that the party is united not just in opposition to Trump and what he stands for, but in support of the kind of values that I described briefly earlier in the chapter. There is a vision of where we are, where we can go, what we can be, and how to get there; and a new twenty-first-century social contract to bring it about and sustain it. It is a vision based on a sense of history and a deep understanding of economics and the social forces that shape the economy and are shaped by it. This vision speaks the language of technocrats but reflects our highest moral aspirations and is willing to use the language of morals and values.

We need to begin with a clarity of purpose—not the platitudinous reiteration that we have values, but an understanding of what those values are and that economics is a means to an end. We have to have a sense about what those ends are: the success of the economy is to be measured not just by GDP but by the well-being of citizens. In President Clinton's phrase: we have to put people first. The new social contract includes the preservation of the environment for future generations,[21] and restoring political and economic power to ordinary people.

This twenty-first-century agenda is committed to ensuring the fruits of progress are shared with a modicum of equity and security, with everyone having a chance at a middle-class life without the blight of discrimination, bigotry, and exclusion. We as a country can prosper only if there is shared prosperity: this is both an economic reality and an expression of deeply held values. This new social contract should include a commitment that every individual has the opportunity to live up fully to his or her potential, and that every person's voice is heard in our democracy. Thus, among the key terms of this new social contract would be those that provide for justice and opportunity for all, rich and poor, black and white: making the American dream a reality.

An agenda focused on fostering progress has to be based on a deep understanding of the sources of the wealth of the nation; and it has to be committed to ensuring that the advances in technology and globalization are both shaped and managed in ways that can benefit all: the current controversies over both are unnecessarily divisive. This book has tried to lay out both the foundations of this progress and the policies which can bring it about.

In this progressive agenda, government plays a central role, both in ensuring that markets work as they are supposed to, and in promoting the general welfare in ways that individuals on their own, or markets on their own, can't. If this program is to be accepted, though, we must disabuse ourselves of the idea that government is always and everywhere inefficient and obtrusive, and replace it with the notion that, like all human institutions, including markets, government is fallible and can be improved. The view that government is the problem, not the solution, is simply wrong. To the contrary, many if not most of our society's problems, from excesses of pollution to financial instability and economic inequality, have been created by markets and the private sector. In short, markets alone won't solve our problems. Only government can protect the environment, ensure social and economic justice, and promote a dynamic learning society through investments in basic research and technology that are the foundation of continued progress.

Libertarians on the Right see government as interfering with their freedom. Corporations on the Right see government as imposing regulations and taxes that decrease their profits. The 1 percent worry about the potential of a strong government using its powers to take money away from them and redistribute it to the needy. All of these actors have an incentive to portray government as inefficient and contributing to the country's ills. But the underlying hypotheses of each are badly flawed. Today, the 1 percent is actually paying less than their fair share in taxes, giving a lower share of their income to support the public well-being, including defense. Meanwhile they appropriate, largely in "rents," more than a proportionate share of the nation's income and wealth.

The book has described how, moreover, they've succeeded at shaping the rules of the game to favor themselves at the expense of the vast majority. It is not "natural" economic forces that have resulted in near stagnation in incomes of the majority while those of the 1 percent have soared. It is not the laws of nature but the laws of man that have resulted in these unnatural outcomes.

The reality is that markets have to be structured, and over the last four decades we've restructured them in ways that have led to slower growth and more inequality. There are many forms of market economies, but we have "chosen" one that ill-serves large portions of our population. We now have to once again rewrite the rules, so that our economy serves our society better. We must, for instance, make markets act, once again, like markets are supposed to, by ensuring that there is competition, and taming outsize market power.

America also has a richer set of institutions than "market funda-mentalists" are willing to admit. Not only do we have multiple effec-tive and efficient government institutions, but we also have a strong and vibrant set of nongovernmental institutions and foundations. At the center of much of our progress has been our universities, and all of our leading universities are either public institutions or not-for-profits. We have cooperatively owned firms. The one part of our financial system that did not evidence moral turpitude in the 2008 crisis was the credit unions, those member-owned cooperative banks often tied to specific firms and industries.[22] Cooperatives have played an impor-tant role in many sectors in many parts of the country.[23] Cooperatives and firms with greater worker participation in decision-making and ownership performed better during the crisis.

America is capable of strengthening this rich ecology of different kinds of institutions. Each has a niche, and they are complementary to one another. The private sector, for instance, thrives on the infra-structure provided by the government and the knowledge produced by our universities and research institutes, often with public support. Our private sector has, in fact, accomplished much, but it is not the font of all wisdom, nor the source of all solutions to our society's problems. The private sector's gains have been built on foundations provided by the government and our not-for-profit research universi-ties and research centers.

Thus, a central plank in this twenty-first-century agenda calls for creating a better balance in our society and our economy, among the various parts of our society, government, private, and civil soci-ety. There are other elements in this restored balance: it must curb the extremes of materialism and moral turpitude that have been in evidence in recent decades; give a place to both individual and col-lective initiative and well-being;[24] and exhort individuals and society generally to behave in a way that reflects our higher values and aspi-rations. Among those values are the respect for knowledge and truth, for democracy and the rule of law, and for the institutions of liberal democracy and knowledge: it is only with these that the progress that we have seen over the past 250 years can continue.

Is there hope?

America's history gives us hope. But any student of the dark history of authoritarianism and fascism in other countries knows this brighter future is not inevitable.[25]

As we've noted, America twice before pulled back from extremes of inequality—after the Gilded Age and the Roaring 20s. The challenge today, though, may be even greater than then: there is perhaps even more inequality now, and with recent Supreme Court decisions, money has more power in politics. And modern technology can more effectively translate disparities in money into disparities in political power.

Ultimately, today, the only countervailing power is people power, the power of the voting booth. But the greater the inequality of wealth and income, the harder it is for this countervailing power to be exercised effectively. That is why achieving greater equality is not just a matter of morals or good economics; it is a matter of the survival of our democracy.

With the agenda I've proposed, all Americans *can* attain the life to which they aspire—in ways that are consonant with our values of choice, individual responsibility and liberty. The agenda is ambitious and yet necessary: as bad as things are today, there is a good chance that, with the advances of technology that are already on the horizon, they may get much worse—if we continue on our current course. We may wind up with even more inequality and an even more divided society, with even more discontent. Incrementalist policies—a little more education here, a little more assistance there—as important as they are as components of an overall strategy, are not up to the challenges America faces today. We need the dramatic change in direction that this book's progressive agenda calls for.

We have set in motion an unhealthy dynamic. Left on its own, one can only shudder to think where it might lead. This book has been written in the hope and faith that an alternative world is possible, and that there are enough Americans who believe this, that working together we can reverse this dire trajectory: These include young people who have not yet lost their idealism, those in older generations who still cling to ideals of equality of opportunity and shared prosperity, and those who recall the struggle for civil rights in which so many joined with their hearts and souls—and for a moment glimpsed some progress, only to see this darker cloud come over the country. This alternative world is not based on reconstructing an imagined past but constructing a realistic future, using our knowledge of economics and politics, including what we have learned from these failures of recent decades. Properly designed, well-regulated markets, working together with governments and a broad array of civil society institutions, are the only way forward.

This alternative vision of the future, this twenty-first-century new social contract that I've described, is markedly different from what the Trump administration and the Republican Party offer America today—too often with considerable support from the business community. Our failures of the past are the prologue to our future: unless we manage technological advances better, we could well be moving to a dystopia with ever more inequality, an ever more divided polity, with individuals and a society that are ever more distant from what we would like.

It is still not too late to save capitalism from itself.

ACKNOWLEDGMENTS

As I noted in the preface, this book builds on and brings together insights from my earlier books, including four on globalization (*Globalization and Its Discontents* [2002], *Fair Trade for All*, with Andrew Charlton [2005],* *Making Globalization Work* [2006], and *Globalization and Its Discontents Revisited: Anti-Globalization in the Era of Trump* [2017]); three on inequality (*The Price of Inequality: How Today's Divided Society Endangers Our Future* [2012], *The Great Divide: Unequal Societies and What We Can Do about Them* [2015], and *Rewriting the Rules of the American Economy: An Agenda for Growth and Shared Prosperity*, with Nell Abernathy, Adam Hersh, Susan Holmberg, and Mike Konczal [2015]); a treatise on the true sources of economic growth, *Creating a Learning Society: A New Approach to Growth, Development, and Social Progress*, with Bruce C. Greenwald (2014, 2015)**; and two books on economic policy and finance (*The Roaring Nineties* [2003] and *Freefall* [2010]). These, in turn, were based on a large number of academic papers. Over the years, I have thus accumulated a vast store of debts, and especially to

* New York: Oxford University Press
** New York: Columbia University Press

my many coauthors and my colleagues, including those at Columbia University, the Roosevelt Institute, INET (Institute for New Economic Thinking), the World Bank, and in the Clinton administration.

I have benefited too from the ideas of a large number of scholars who've been thinking about questions related to those posed here. While I cite many throughout the book, I would especially like to note a few:

I have drawn extensively on the data and insights of the growing group of scholars on inequality, including François Bourguignon, Sir Angus Deaton, Ravi Kanbur, Branko Milonović, Thomas Piketty, Emmanuel Saez, Raj Chetty, Gabriel Zucman, James Galbraith, and my dear friend and coauthor, the late Tony Atkinson. I also want to acknowledge the influence and important work of Lawrence Mishel at the Economic Policy Institute, of Winnie Byanyima at Oxfam International, and of Janet Gornick, formerly director of LIS, the Luxembourg Income Study (a cross-national data center focusing on inequality).

The notion that market power and rent-seeking are major sources of today's inequality, which I articulated many years ago in *The Price of Inequality*, has now become mainstream, and I have benefited greatly from conversations with many of the contributors to the growing literature on market power and what can be done about it, including Steven Salop, Michael Katz, Carl Shapiro, Mike Konczal, Tim Wu, Eleanor Fox, and Emmanuel Farhi. I have been involved in a number of antitrust suits, trying to preserve competition in the American economy, and the insights of Keith Leffler, Michael Cragg, David Hutchings, and Andrew Abere have been invaluable. My understanding of the role these market imperfections have in labor markets has been enhanced by Mark Stelzner and Alan Krueger.

The discussions of new technologies have been particularly influenced by my coauthor Anton Korinek; on artificial intelligence, by Erik Brynjolfsson, Shane Legg of DeepMind, Mark Sagar of Soul

Machines, and a dinner on AI at the Royal Society after my lecture there on the subject of work and AI. Yochai Benkler, Julia Angwin, and Zeynep Tüfekçi have contributed to my understanding of the special issues posed by disinformation.

As I return to the issues of globalization, I need to thank Dani Rodrik as well as Danny Quah, Rohinton Medhora, and Mari Pangestu; and on the role of globalization in tax avoidance, Mark Pieth and the Independent Commission for Reform of International Corporate Taxation, chaired by José Antonio Ocampo, on which I serve.

Daniel Kahneman, Richard Thaler, and especially Karla Hoff have greatly influenced my thinking on the role of culture, our society, and our economy in shaping individuals, and other aspects of behavioral economics.

As I've thought about how to respond to the challenges of globalization, financialization, and new technologies, I need to acknowledge my indebtedness to Akbar Noman, Giovanni Dosi, Justin Yifu Lin, and Mario Cimoli for insights about industrial policy; and to Karl Ove Moene, Leif Pagrotsky, Isabel Ortiz, and other members of the Initiative for Policy Dialogue/Roosevelt project on revisiting the welfare state, for insights on the welfare state, including the Scandinavian model.

My thinking about climate change has been influenced by Nicholas Stern and John Roome, and my understanding of the legal implications of the deprivation of the rights of children, by Julia Olson and Philip Gregory.

I've had invaluable conversations with John Attanasio on chapter 8, on reforms in our political system, especially the legal challenges in reducing the influence of money in our politics.

Thanks are also due to Martin Wolff, Rana Foroohar, Edmund Phelps, George Soros, George Akerlof, Janet Yellen, Adair Turner, Michael Spence, Andrew Sheng, Kaushik Basu, Winnie Byanyima, and Peter Bofinger (the latter six who together with Rob Johnson,

Rodrik, Quah, Medhora, and Pangestu are among the members of the Commission on Global Economic Transformation, sponsored by INET, which I cochair with Spence).

In thinking about how to respond to the 2008 global financial crisis, strong intellectual bonds were formed, including with Elizabeth Warren and Damon Silvers (who served on the Congressional Oversight Panel of the Troubled Asset Relief Program), and with the members of the Commission of Experts of the President of the United Nations General Assembly on Reforms of the International Monetary and Financial System, appointed by the President of the General Assembly of the United Nations that I chaired in 2009.

Another commission that I chaired that helped shape my views on many of the topics under consideration is the International Commission on the Measurement of Economic Performance and Social Progress, cochaired with Jean-Paul Fitoussi, with Amartya Sen; and its successor, the High-Level Expert Group on the Measurement of Economic Performance and Social Progress, cochaired with Martine Durand. These played an important role in broadening my thinking about what constitutes well-being. I want to acknowledge the contribution of all the members of the commission.

For two decades, since he first came to work with me at the Council of Economic Advisers, Jason Furman has been an invaluable colleague, with insights into reforms that would make the American economy perform better for all.

Over a span of almost twenty years, I have been spending a week most summers discussing the future of social democracy with a group of progressives brought together by George Papandreou, called the Symi Symposium, and the many ideas bandied around have undoubtedly infiltrated much that is here. I wish to thank George and other participants in the symposium, including Kemal Derviş, Misha Glenny, Yanis Varoufakis, and Matts Carlsson.

Once again, I need to thank Columbia University for providing, for almost two decades, an intellectual home in which I have been able to flourish, and the influence of my long-term coauthor and Columbia colleague, Bruce Greenwald.

I am also gratefully indebted to The Rockefeller Foundation Bellagio Center, where I worked on early drafts of this book in beautiful and peaceful surroundings. The camaraderie and lively conversation I found there provided the perfect setting for undertaking this ambitious project.

The Roosevelt Institute, the think tank established "to carry forward the legacy and values of Franklin and Eleanor Roosevelt by developing progressive ideas and bold leadership in the service of restoring America's promise of opportunity for all," where I serve as chief economist, has provided an active venue for debate and discussion on how to realize the progressive agenda that I describe in this book. I wish to thank Felicia Wong, its president, and Nell Abernathy, its vice-president for research and policy. Their "rewriting the rules" project was especially important to me. Its success was picked up by FEPS (Foundation for European Progressive Studies, an alliance of social democratic think tanks in Europe); I want to thank Ernst Stetter, secretary general of FEPS, Carter Dougherty, who shepherded *Rewriting the Rules of Europe* to completion, and the team of scholars from throughout Europe who worked on it. Park Won-soon, mayor of Seoul, spearheaded a similar effort in Korea.

IN THIS BOOK, I go beyond economics to politics. Given the moment, it's hard not to. I've long argued that a central determinant of the success of an economy are its rules, and these are set by politics. As I've delved into this area, Edward (Jed) Stiglitz has provided enormous insights, for which I am greatly indebted.

Robert Kuttner, Jeff Madrick, Felicia Wong, Rob Johnson, Martin Guzman, and Leif Pagrotsky read earlier versions of this book, and provided invaluable comments.

My postdoctoral students and Martin Guzman, the senior researcher in charge of our postdoctoral program, have provided insights into various issues discussed here: Mayuri Chaturvedi and Ignacio Gonzales into market power, rent-seeking, inequality, and growth; Juan Montecino into certain aspects of globalization; Michael Poyker on convict labor and mass incarceration; and Levent Altinoglu on financial markets. I am especially indebted to Martin, an invaluable colleague in discussing all the issues raised here.

My research assistants, Matthieu Teachout, Haaris Mateen, Naman Garg, and Anastasia Burya, went well beyond the call of duty, as did the editors in my office, Debarati Ghosh and Andrea Gurwitt, who brought the manuscript to completion.

I also need to acknowledge the invaluable help of the other members of my office, not only in this project but also in ensuring that I have the time to devote to a project such as this: Gabriela Plump, Caleb Oldham, Susanna De Martino, and Sarah Thomas.

As always, Stuart Proffitt at Penguin/Alan Lane, my UK publishers, provided insightful and detailed comments.

This book grew out of discussions with Drake McFeely, my longtime editor at Norton, and he provided the kind of hands-on editing that seems to have become a lost art. Brendan Curry provided invaluable suggestions in an earlier draft, and Nathaniel Dennett managed the manuscript to the end. Charlotte Kelchner deftly copyedited the manuscript, Lynne Cannon Menges proofread it with an eagle eye, and project editor Dassi Zeidel and production manager Lauren Abbate were invaluable to the process.

I owe an especial debt to Eamon Kircher-Allen, my longtime in-house editor, who immersed himself in the early stages of this project and was a full partner for much of it.

Finally, my wife Anya, as always. With my first popular book, *Globalization and Its Discontents*, she taught me to write. With this book, her role is, if anything, greater. Not just editing, but inspiring: I hope every reader feels the passion we both have for understanding what has gone wrong and what to do about it, and for the importance of knowledge and for keeping our truth-institutions strong.

A note on the dedication: in 1965, I went to Cambridge, England, as a Fulbright scholar and studied under great teachers like James Meade, Joan Robinson, Nicholas Kaldor, Frank Hahn, and David Champernowne, all of whom were passionate about issues of inequality and the nature of our capitalist system. Among the many lifelong friends I met there were Anthony Atkinson, one of my first students, and James Mirrlees, then a young lecturer and researcher.

NOTES

PREFACE

1. I described my many battles during those years in my 2003 book
    *The Roaring Nineties: A New History of the World's Most Prosperous
    Decade* (New York: W.W. Norton, 2003).
2. As inequality grew, I returned to the subject that had originally
    brought me into economics. In *The Price of Inequality: How Today's
    Divided Society Endangers Our Future* (New York: W. W. Norton,
    2012) and *The Great Divide: Unequal Societies and What We Can Do
    About Them* (New York: W. W. Norton, 2015), I warned about
    the startling inequality that has become a defining feature of the
    American economy. I emphasized that a failure to head off Ameri-
    can inequality would have far-reaching consequences that would
    spread well beyond economic indicators: disparities would ulti-
    mately infect our society with mistrust and corrupt our politics. It
    would be very bad for everyone, even the 1 percent. In *Rewriting
    the Rules of the American Economy: An Agenda for Growth and Shared
    Prosperity*, with Nell Abernathy, Adam Hersh, Susan Holmberg,
    and Mike Konczal (New York: W. W. Norton, 2015), I explain
    how the rewriting of the basic rules of the economy, especially dur-
    ing and after the Reagan administration, led to lower growth and
    more inequality, and how these adverse trends could be reversed if
    we once again rewrite the rules.
3. The title of my May 2011 *Vanity Fair* article, paraphrasing the

famous lines of the Gettysburg Address (reprinted in *The Great Divide*).

4. When the bill is fully implemented, taxes will increase for a majority of those in the second, third, and fourth deciles.

5. He also served as secretary of labor under Nixon.

6. Private equity firms manage funds that are typically invested in enterprises that are not publicly listed; they themselves are not publicly listed. They may, for instance, buy other companies, restructure them, and then sell them off for a profit. The managers of these funds are doing little different from a manager of any other company, who would have to pay ordinary income taxes on their pay. There is no justification for the favorable tax treatment—that they receive such treatment simply demonstrates their political power. Worse, these funds have a much-criticized record of restructuring in ways that lead to large job losses and heavy debt, with the restructured firms often going into bankruptcy not long after the private equity firms sell them off.

   The reduced tax rate that private equity funds manage to pay, due to the so-called carried-interest loophole, was something Trump railed against in the campaign but never insisted on its repeal—if he mentioned it at all—as the tax bill wended its way through Congress on the way to his signature. Confronted with the broken promise, his advisers blamed Congress. See Louis Jacobson, "Despite Repeated Pledges to Get Rid of Carried Interest Tax Break, It Remains on the Books," *Politifact*, Dec. 20, 2017.

7. Over the ten-year period 2018–2028, the tax cut alone (with interest) is expected to add $1.9 trillion to the deficit. If the temporary tax cuts were made permanent, then the addition to the deficit would be $3.2 trillion.

8. "Transcript of the Press Conference on the Release of the October 2017 World Economic Outlook" (Washington, DC: International Monetary Fund, Oct. 13, 2017); and Christine Lagarde, "2018 Article IV Consultation for the United States Opening Remarks" (Washington, DC: International Monetary Fund, June 14, 2018).

9. This was a central insight of Nobel Prize winner Simon Kuznets, and the fact that it always seemed so, as he wrote in the middle of the twentieth century, led it to be called Kuznets's Law.

10. This book builds on my earlier work on globalization, financialization, inequality, and innovation, weaving these threads together, showing their interrelation in a tapestry that, I hope, is a convincing depiction of the sources of progress and the pitfalls that we've

encountered along the way. At several key points, it advances the argument further.

My earliest critiques of globalization, written after I left the World Bank, where I saw how badly it was being managed from the perspectives of the developing countries and workers everywhere, are contained in *Globalization and Its Discontents* (New York: W. W. Norton, 2002). In *Fair Trade for All* (New York: Oxford University Press, 2005), written with Andrew Charlton, I focused on how the global trade regime disadvantaged the poor. In *Making Globalization Work* (New York: W. W. Norton, 2006), I set forth a set of reforms that would, I thought, at least make globalization work better than it had been. In *Globalization and its Discontents Revisited: Anti-Globalization in the Era of Trump* (New York: W. W. Norton, 2017), I showed the progress that had been made in reforming globalization, until Trump arrived, and how he has, perhaps irreparably, set back the agenda. The first of my two books focusing on financialization is *The Roaring Nineties*, written after I left the Clinton administration, arguing that the deregulation undertaken during, before, and after were setting the stage for a financial crisis. In the years following, as the imbalances in our financial system grew and with them the risk of a major financial and economic calamity, I lectured and wrote about the threat of an impending crisis. Unfortunately, I was all too prescient: the global financial crisis soon rocked the world economy. In 2010, in *Freefall: America, Free Markets, and the Sinking of the World Economy* (New York: W. W. Norton), I analyzed the unfolding Great Recession, giving recommendations for how serious, extended economic underperformance could be avoided, and how the financial sector could be reformed to prevent such bubbles and their bursting in the future.

CHAPTER 1: INTRODUCTION

1. The full title of Fukuyama's 1992 book is *The End of History and the Last Man* (New York: Free Press). After the election of Trump, his views changed: "Twenty five years ago, I didn't have a sense or a theory about how democracies can go backward. And I think they clearly can." Ishaan Tharoor, "The Man Who Declared the 'End of History' Fears for Democracy's Future," *Washington Post*, Feb. 9, 2017.

2. This is the thesis of a recent book by Adam Tooze of Columbia

University, *Crashed: How a Decade of Financial Crises Changed the World* (New York: Viking, 2018).

3. New York: Harper, 2016.

4. New York: The New Press, 2016.

5. See also Jennifer Sherman, *Those Who Work, Those Who Don't: Poverty, Morality, and Family in Rural America* (Minneapolis: University of Minnesota Press, 2009); Joan C. Williams, *White Working Class: Overcoming Class Cluelessness in America* (Boston: Harvard Business Review Press, 2007); Katherine J. Cramer, *The Politics of Resentment: Rural Consciousness in Wisconsin and the Rise of Scott Walker* (Chicago: University of Chicago Press, 2016); Amy Goldstein, *Janesville: An American Story* (New York: Simon and Schuster, 2017); and Michèle Lamont, *The Dignity of Working Men: Morality and the Boundaries of Race, Class, and Immigration* (Cambridge, MA: Harvard University Press, 2000). My own more limited forays into these territories led to perspectives that were consistent with these in-depth studies.

6. This paralleled studies conducted by the World Bank when I was its chief economist. In *The Voices of the Poor*, they expressed concerns about a lack of voice in the decisions that affected them. Deepa Narayan with Raj Patel, Kai Schafft, Anne Rademacher, and Sarah Koch-Schulte, *Voices of the Poor: Can Anyone Hear Us?* (New York: Oxford University Press, 2000). This is the first of three volumes in a series under the *Voices of the Poor* title; each volume had different editors.

7. See, for instance, my discussion of these issues in my books *Freefall* and *The Great Divide*.

8. The reason that I had focused my *Vanity Fair* article, "Of the 1%, by the 1%, and for the 1%" (May 2011) on the 1 percent was to emphasize that the old class divisions (a small upper class, a vast middle class, and a medium-sized group of poor) were no longer relevant.

9. Bankrate, in its 2017 annual Financial Security Index survey, found that 61 percent of Americans could not meet a $1000 emergency without going into debt. Taylor Tepper. "Most Americans Don't Have Enough Savings to Cover a $1K Emergency," *Bankrate.com*, Jan. 18, 2018, https://www.bankrate.com/banking/savings/financial-security-0118/.

　　Similarly, the Federal Reserve Board, in its *Report on the Economic Well-Being of U.S. Households in 2017*, based on the fifth annual Survey of Household Economics and Decisionmaking, found that

"Four in 10 adults, if faced with an unexpected expense of $400, would either not be able to cover it or would cover it by selling something or borrowing money. . . . an improvement from half of adults in 2013 being ill-prepared for such an expense." It also found that "Over one-fifth of adults are not able to pay all of their current month's bills in full" and that "Over one-fourth of adults skipped necessary medical care in 2017 due to being unable to afford the cost." Both of these results are consistent with the finding of another survey, that 15 percent of Americans have no savings, and 58 percent have less than $1000 in savings. See Board of Governors of the Federal Reserve System, "Report on the Economic Well-Being of U.S. Households in 2017," Federal Reserve Board, May 2018, https://www.federalreserve.gov/publications/files/2017 -report-economic-well-being-us-households-201805.pdf; and Cameron Huddleston, "More than Half of Americans Have Less than $1,000 in Savings in 2017," GOBankingRates, Sept. 12, 2017.

10. Oxfam, *Reward Work, Not Wealth*, Oxfam Briefing Paper, Jan. 2018.

11. Warren Buffet quote from Ben Stein, "In Class Warfare, Guess Which Class Is Winning," *New York Times*, November 26, 2006.

12. There were further constraints imposed by long-standing legal doctrines that the US inherited from the UK, such as the Public Trust doctrine, which holds that the State (the "sovereign") is trustee for certain natural resources on behalf of future generations, so cannot fully privatize them or allow them to be despoiled.

13. *New York Times* reports 59.2 percent of votes were for Democratic senators. See election results available at "U.S. Senate Election Results 2018," Jan. 28, 2019, https://www.nytimes.com/ interactive/2018/11/06/us/elections/results-senate-elections.html ?action=click&module=Spotlight&pgtype=Homepage.

14. One might question whether the causation actually works in the other direction—whether selfish and shortsighted individuals are the cause of an economy with those traits. But selfishness and shortsightedness are, to some degree, qualities of all humans. The rules that govern an economy and how the economy functions play a large role in determining whether those qualities are expressed to a greater degree than, say, altruism, empathy, and care for the community.

15. His classic example was of a pin factory. It was clear that what he was thinking about was a far cry from a modern innovation economy.

16. See Kenneth. J. Arrow, "Economic Welfare and the Allocation of Resources to Invention," in *The Rate and Direction of Inventive Activ-*

ity: Economic and Social Factors, ed. Universities-National Bureau Committee for Economic Research and the Committee on Economic Growth of the Social Science Research Council (Princeton: Princeton University Press, 1962), 467–92; Kenneth J. Arrow, "The Economic Implications of Learning by Doing," *The Review of Economic Studies* 29, no. 3 (June 1962): 155–73; and Joseph E. Stiglitz and Bruce Greenwald, *Creating a Learning Society, A New Approach to Growth, Development and Social Progress* (New York: Columbia University Press, 2014; reader's edition published 2015).

17. Workers' wages went up slightly during the Black Plague, with the resulting scarcity in labor—demonstrating that there was something in economists' law of supply and demand—but then fell. See Stephen Broadberry, Bruce Campbell, Alexander Klein, Mark Overton, and Bas van Leeuwen, *British Economic Growth, 1270–1870* (Cambridge: Cambridge University Press, 2015).

18. A critical aspect of the scientific process entails repeated verification of the results, and clarity about the scientific precision and certainty with which various results have been established. Science itself is thus a social enterprise: we know and believe what we do because of the collective efforts of thousands of individuals, all operating within the discipline provided by the scientific method.

19. Each of these concepts is complex and subtle, and the terms are often abused. Feudal lords might claim to invoke a rule of law as they abused the serfs that worked for them; so too for slave owners in the South, who used the "law" to force the return of escaped slaves. (See Eric Foner, *Gateway to Freedom: The Hidden History of the Underground Railroad* [Oxford: Oxford University Press, 2015]). America's justice system—with its mass incarceration or homeowners losing their homes in the Great Recession even when they owed no money in the mass robosigning scandal (see Stiglitz, *Freefall* and *The Great Divide*, 170–3)—provided "justice for all," so long as they were rich and white. Some of the later discussion in this book will make it clearer what I have in mind.

    Later chapters will also elaborate on these ideas in other ways, for instance, that one person's liberty may have to be circumscribed when it interferes with that of others.

20. Scientists emphasize that we do not know anything for certain, but only with a reasonable degree of certainty. In some cases, we can't be sure what is the right decision—there are too many different views; but we can ascertain whether the process for making the decision is fair and whether everybody's voice is heard. Each

individual in making a judgment is fallible: as Shakespeare put it, "to err is human." But when we make judgments collectively, we reduce the chance of error. Thus, in our criminal justice system, with its presumption of innocence until proven guilty, the unanimous decision of twelve jurors of guilt is not a guarantee of the right decision, even if the trial process was conducted in a fair way; but it makes it likely that that is so—or at least so we thought until still further research discovered implicit biases (e.g., involving deep discrimination) were so prevalent.

Over time, there have been further advances in organizational design, addressing, for instance, the question of how to take into account human fallibility in the process of the selection of projects, balancing out the risks associated with rejecting good projects and accepting bad projects. See, for instance, Raaj Sah and Joseph E. Stiglitz, "Human Fallibility and Economic Organization," *American Economic Review* 75, no. 2 (1985): 292–96; and Raaj Sah and Joseph E. Stiglitz, "The Architecture of Economic Systems: Hierarchies and Polyarchies," *American Economic Review* 76, no. 4 (1986): 716–27.

21. An important set of associated institutions are our educational institutions, which train individuals in how to discover and assess the truth.

22. Robert Solow of MIT showed that the overwhelming fraction of increases in standards of living arises from advances in science and technology, work for which he received the Nobel Memorial Prize in Economics in 1987. His two classic papers were "A Contribution to the Theory of Economic Growth," *Quarterly Journal of Economics* 70, no. 1 (1956): 65–94; and "Technical Change and the Aggregate Production Function," *Review of Economics and Statistics* 39, no. 3 (1957): 312–20. His work spurred an enormous amount of research trying to parse out the role of technological change. The other major contributor to increases in productivity are investments in plant and equipment. Still other sources relate to shorter hours of work, better education, and improved allocation of resources.

Earlier, Joseph Schumpeter in his 1943 book *Capitalism, Socialism and Democracy* had emphasized the importance of innovation, stressing that it was much more important than those things on which economists had conventionally focused. But he did not attempt to quantify the relative role of innovation in the way that Solow did. (For a discussion relating Schumpeter's work and modern growth and innovation theory, see my introduction to the 2010 Routledge edition of *Capitalism, Socialism and Democracy*.)

23. As Bruce Greenwald and I put it in the beginning of our book
    Creating a Learning Society: "From Roman times, when the first
    data on per-capita output are available, until 1800, average human
    standards of living increased only imperceptibly if at all. . . . Con-
    sumption for the great majority of human beings consisted pre-
    dominantly of food, and food was largely limited to staples. . . .
    Housing entailed barnlike living conditions with no privacy. . . .
    Clothing was utilitarian and rarely involved more than single out-
    fits with the seasonal addition of overclothes. Medical care was
    almost nonexistent. . . . Recreation was self-generated and primi-
    tive. Only a small aristocratic minority enjoyed what we would
    consider today an appropriate human standard of living. . . .
    Beginning in 1800 and accelerating markedly after the mid-to-
    late nineteenth century, that privileged standard of living began to
    diffuse throughout Europe, North America, and Australia."

24. The ideas set forth here are elaborated in Stiglitz and Greenwald,
    Creating a Learning Society. The distinguished economic historian
    Joel Mokyr of Northwestern University has developed these ideas
    from a historian's perspective in *A Culture of Growth: The Origins of
    the Modern Economy* (Princeton: Princeton University Press, 2016).
    Later in this book, we will argue that one of the impediments to
    our growth today is the growth of rents, such as those associated
    with monopoly profits. This is consistent with Mokyr's historical
    findings. We, Mokyr, and others often trace these increases in stan-
    dards of living more particularly to what are called the Enlight-
    enment institutions, the educational and research institutions
    (including, most importantly, our universities) and the political and
    economic institutions to which we referred earlier, such as the rule
    of law. More recently, Stephen Pinker has written an influential
    book also tracing current standards of living back to the Enlight-
    enment: *Enlightenment Now: The Case for Reason, Science, Humanism
    and Progress* (New York: Penguin, 2018).

    Of course, economic forces were also at play: even before the
    industrial revolution, England had become a high-wage/low-
    energy-cost economy, and this helped induce the labor saving/
    energy using innovations of the industrial revolution. In the after-
    math of the Black Plague, wages had also been relatively high,
    but this had not triggered the advances that were to come some
    centuries later. The Enlightenment created the context in which
    the high wages/low energy prices led to the Industrial Revolu-
    tion. See Robert C. Allen, *The British Revolution in Global Perspec-*

tive (Cambridge: Cambridge University Press, 2009). (There is a well-developed theory of "induced" innovation dating back to the 1960s.)

There were, of course, other episodes of marked advances in learning and technology. For instance, some historians believe the first industrial revolution was in Flanders with water mills in the 1100s. What distinguished the eighteenth-century advances was not only the increase in the extent of the market (emphasized by Allen), but also the development of science, which enabled *sustained* increases.

25. Keynes, in his famous essay, "Economic Possibilities for Our Grandchildren" (in *Essays in Persuasion* [London: MacMillan, 1931], 321–2) explored the implications of the enormous increases in productivity. See also Joseph E. Stiglitz, "Toward a General Theory of Consumerism: Reflections on Keynes' Economic Possibilities for Our Grandchildren," in *Revisiting Keynes: Economic Possibilities for Our Grandchildren*, eds. Lorenzo Pecchi and Gustavo Piga (Cambridge, MA: MIT Press, 1987), 41–87.

26. As we'll explain in greater detail below, because of exclusionary labor market practices and discrimination, especially against women and people of color, large groups within society did not share in this progress.

27. Thomas Hobbes, *Leviathan*, 1651.

28. There were similar responses in Europe, in some cases earlier than in the US, in some cases later. (Germany, under Chancellor Otto von Bismarck, was the first nation to adopt public retirement insurance in 1889.)

29. The *Washington Post* has been quantifying his lies, and found that he made 8,158 "false or misleading claims" during his first two years in office. See Glenn Kessler, Salvador Rizzo, and Meg Kelly, "President Trump Made 8,158 False or Misleading Claims in His First Two Years," *Washington Post*, Jan. 21, 2019.

30. See Patt Morrison, "Patt Morrison Asks: Robert O. Paxton Talks Fascism and Donald Trump," *Los Angeles Times*, Mar. 9, 2016. Paxton's book *The Anatomy of Fascism* (New York: Knopf, 2004) is a definitive work on the subject. What is remarkable about the book is that, while written fifteen years ago, it feels as if it is directed at today's events.

31. Adam Bluestein, "The Most Entrepreneurial Group in America Wasn't Born in America," *Inc.*, Feb. 2015.

32. Rose Leadem, "The Immigrant Entrepreneurs behind Major

American Companies (Infographic)," *Entrepreneur*, Feb. 4, 2017. Elon Musk (Tesla and SpaceX) spent two years at Queen's University in Canada and then transferred to the University of Pennsylvania, where he received Bachelor of Science degrees in physics and economics. Hamdi Ulukaya, the founder of Chobani, the yogurt company, immigrated to the United States to study English at Adelphi University.

33. Fortunately, Congress has not paid much attention: the 2018 budget actually provided for an increase in science spending of 12 percent, in contrast to the 17 percent reduction that he had asked for.

34. Our media is often rightly criticized for trying to have a false balance in coverage. Even though 99.9 percent of all scientists are convinced about climate change, some outlets try to give almost equal voice to the one dissident, giving legitimacy to the climate deniers.

35. Some historians trace the use of the term to Hitler himself, rather than his chief propagandist. In *Mein Kampf* Hitler wrote, "in the big lie there is always a certain force of credibility; . . . they more readily fall victims to the big lie than the small lie, since they themselves often tell small lies in little matters but would be ashamed to resort to large-scale falsehoods. It would never come into their heads to fabricate colossal untruths, and they would not believe that others could have the impudence to distort the truth so infamously. Even though the facts which prove this to be so may be brought clearly to their minds, they will still doubt and waver and will continue to think that there may be some other explanation. For the grossly impudent lie always leaves traces behind it, even after it has been nailed down, a fact which is known to all expert liars in this world and to all who conspire together in the art of lying." (*Mein Kampf*, trans. James Murphy, London: Hurst and Blackett, 1939.) But Hitler accused Jews of using the Big Lie. Goebbels made the Big Lie an instrument of policy, though even then he attributed it to others, to the British: "The English follow the principle that when one lies, one should lie big, and stick to it. They keep up their lies, even at the risk of looking ridiculous." Joseph Goebbels, Jan. 12, 1941 ("Aus Churchills Lügenfabrik," *Die Zeit ohne Beispiel*. Munich: Zentralverlag der NSDAP, 1941, 364–69; translation available at the German Propaganda Archive, Calvin College, accessed July 17, 2018, http://research.calvin.edu/german-propaganda-archive/goeb29.htm).

36. While in the US, only a fraction of the rich live in these gated

communities, they still face insecurity. I described in *The Great Divide* a dinner party populated with the ultra-rich where a recurring theme was "remember the guillotine"—a call for all of them to circumscribe their unbridled greed.

37. This was a central thesis of my earlier article in *Vanity Fair*, "Of the 1 percent, for the 1 percent and by the 1 percent," and my book *The Price of Inequality*. See also the references cited there and the discussion below.

38. In October 2017, Trump's administration barred scientists who receive grants from the Environmental Protection Agency (EPA) from serving on the EPA's science advisory panels, citing concerns about "conflict of interest." The administration raised no similar concern about panel members who receive grants from industries that the EPA regulates, such as, say, oil and gas. See Warren Cornwall, "Trump's EPA Has Blocked Agency Grantees from Serving on Science Advisory Panels. Here Is What It Means," *Science*, Oct. 31, 2017.

39. And there were, of course, some academics who became handmaidens to these ideologies, acting as cheerleaders for globalization and financial deregulation. In chapter 4, I explain how, in standard economic analysis, trade integration with developing countries and emerging markets results in a lower demand for unskilled labor in the US, at any wage, implying that even if we succeed in maintaining full employment, real wages of unskilled workers will fall, even though GDP has increased. During my years in the Clinton administration—one seemingly concerned about the plight of blue-collar workers—it was hard, nonetheless, to find an economist who was worried about the impact of globalization on unskilled real wages. (Labor Secretary Robert Reich was a notable exception.) Seemingly, even good economists *wanted* to believe globalization was good for all—even if we didn't introduce compensatory policies. Trickle-down economics, even by then, had become deeply ingrained.

40. That is, whether it was a delusion with trickle-down economics referred to in the previous note, or a delusion that, while recognizing that workers were actually worse off, the setback was only temporary.

41. An argument often put forward for regressive tax measures (which benefit the rich more than the poor), is that such measures give money to the rich, who are the job creators, and their job creation benefits all. But this theory is predicated on three false assump-

tions: that there are only a few of these highly talented individuals; that they are only motivated by material incentives, not by the excitement of creating a new business or the satisfaction of providing services that our society wants or needs; and that all that is necessary for their success is low taxes and low regulations.

The real source of job creation is not so much our entrepreneurial class but simply *demand*. When aggregate demand is high, jobs get created. Of course, entrepreneurship is necessary, but there is an ample supply of those able and willing to be entrepreneurs, if only there is demand and if only they could get finance. It is the role of the government to ensure that there is adequate demand and finance.

42. I need to emphasize that when the economy is at less than full employment, the government should run a deficit, that is, expenditures should exceed taxes. German Chancellor Angela Merkel wrongly likened the economy to a "Swabian housewife" who had to balance the household's accounts. The critical difference is that when there is high unemployment, spending more at the national level creates jobs, increasing income, and the increase in aggregate demand then creates still more jobs in a virtuous circle.

43. The reason is that lower tax rates at the top can provide greater incentives for "rent-seeking," i.e., for actions that do not increase the size of the national pie, but increase only the income of, say, those running the corporations. See Thomas Piketty, Emmanuel Saez, and Stefanie Stantcheva, "Optimal Taxation of Top Labor Incomes: A Tale of Three Elasticities," *American Economic Journal: Economic Policy* 6, no. 1 (2014): 230–71.

44. The failures of the Bush tax cuts are set forth in Emily Horton, "The Legacy of the 2001 and 2003 'Bush' Tax Cuts," Center on Budget and Policy Priorities, Oct. 23, 2017. With Anton Korinek, I showed that there was some presumption that investment would even be slowed as a result of the Bush tax cuts. "Dividend Taxation and Intertemporal Tax Arbitrage," *Journal of Public Economics* 93 (2009), 142–59. For some interesting commentary, see William G. Gale, "Five Myths about the Bush Tax Cuts," *Washington Post*, Aug. 1, 2010. For a more detailed analysis, see a series of articles by William G. Gale and Peter R. Orszag on various aspects of "Tax Policy in the Bush Administration" in *Tax Notes* in 2004: "Introduction and Background," 104, no. 12: 1291–1300; "Distributional Effects," 104, no. 14: 1559–66; "Revenue and Budget Effects," 105, no. 1, 105–18; "Effects on Long-Term Growth," 105, no. 3, 415–23;

"Short-term Stimulus," 105, no. 6, 747–56; "Down Payment on Tax Reform?," 105, no. 7, 879–84; and "Starving the Beast?," 105, no. 8, 999–1002.

See also Danny Yagan, "Capital Tax Reform and the Real Economy: The Effects of the 2003 Dividend Tax Cut," *American Economic Review* 105, no. 12 (2015): 3531–63, for evidence of no effect of the tax cut on corporate investment and employee compensation. As Yagan also shows, though, the tax cut didn't affect investment and wages, it increased the wealth of shareholders who got higher dividend payouts. See also Raj Chetty and Emmanuel Saez, "Dividend Taxes and Corporate Behavior: Evidence from the 2003 Dividend Tax Cut," *The Quarterly Journal of Economics* 120, no. 3 (2005): 791–833.

There is also both empirical evidence and good theoretical reasons to expect that lower corporate tax rates would not lead to more investment. President Reagan had, for instance, cut the corporation tax rate from 46 percent to 34 percent. Subsequently, the effective corporate income tax has fallen even more, as corporations succeeded in putting loopholes into tax bills and learned better how to exploit them, so that the effective tax rate before Trump lowered taxes even more was only 18 percent. But the promised increase in investment didn't happen. With tax deductibility of interest, and with most investment financed by borrowing at the margin, the tax rate affects both the return to investment and the cost of capital in an identical way, so lowering tax rates was predicted to have little effect on investment. See Joseph E. Stiglitz, "Taxation, Corporate Financial Policy and the Cost of Capital," *Journal of Public Economics*, no. 2 (Feb. 1973), 1–34. The experience with the Trump tax bill, described in greater detail later in the book, confirms this.

45. It is worth noting that Sweden has much higher tax rates than the US, and yet its household savings rate is systematically almost twice that of the US. US labor force participation rate (the fraction of working-age citizens who either have or are looking for a job) is also much lower than that of many other countries with much higher tax rates.

46. Nancy MacLean, a distinguished historian at Duke University, has put these arguments into historical context in her book *Democracy in Chains: The Deep History of the Radical Right's Stealth Plan for America* (New York: Penguin, 2017).

47. Including our rules-based competitive market economy and our

democracy with its system of checks and balances to which we referred earlier, and upon which we will elaborate below.

48. Inaugural address, Jan. 20, 1961.

49. As we noted earlier, Francis Fukuyama referred to this as the "end of history." All the world would now converge to this economic and political system.

50. Alain Cohn, Ernst Fehr, and Michel André Maréchal, "Business Culture and Dishonesty in the Banking Industry," *Nature* 516, no. 7592 (2014): 86–89.

51. Yoram Bauman and Elaina Rose, "Selection or Indoctrination: Why Do Economics Students Donate Less than the Rest?," *Journal of Economic Behavior and Organization* 79, no. 3 (2011): 318–27. See further references there, in what is a rich body of literature.

52. Especially in his *Theory of Moral Sentiments* (1759), which opens with the famous lines: "How selfish soever man may be supposed, there are evidently some principles in his nature, which interest him in the fortunes of others, and render their happiness necessary to him, though he derives nothing from it, except the pleasure of seeing it."

53. See Karla Hoff and Joseph E. Stiglitz, "Striving for Balance in Economics: Towards a Theory of the Social Determination of Behavior," *Journal of Economic Behavior and Organization* 126 (2016): 25–57.

CHAPTER 2: TOWARD A MORE DISMAL ECONOMY

1. The president of the American Economic Association, Nobel Memorial Prize winner Robert Lucas, in his presidential lecture shortly before the Great Recession declared the death of serious economic fluctuations. He said, in part, "macroeconomics . . . has succeeded: Its central problem of depression prevention has been solved, for all practical purposes, and has in fact been solved for many decades." The address was published as Robert E. Lucas Jr., "Macroeconomic Priorities," *American Economic Review* 93, no. 1 (2003): 1–14; the quote appears on p. 1.

2. As Robert E. Lucas Jr. put it, "Of the tendencies that are harmful to sound economics, the most seductive, and in my opinion the most poisonous, is to focus on questions of distribution." "The Industrial Revolution: Past and Future," Annual Report, Federal Reserve Bank of Minneapolis, May 2004.

3. Sometimes, the two are mixed together, as when an inventor uses the patent system to create a monopoly, and then, through a variety

of mechanisms, some of which will be described below, extends that market power and makes it more durable, with much of the subsequent wealth based on the exploitation of market power.

Much of America, of course, was built on a quite different kind of exploitation: slavery, which played a central role in the development of the American South, was not a market institution—though slaves were bought and sold, slavery was based on coercion. And even after slavery ended, the coercion of Jim Crow kept African Americans down, which resulted in low wages and higher profits for Southern employers. At the time of the Civil War, the market value of slaves represented a significant fraction of the wealth of the South.

4. Preliminary data for 2018 suggests a somewhat better performance, the result of a massive fiscal stimulus (the large increase in the deficit). Such a stimulus would predictably temporarily increase growth, but only temporarily. Given the size of the stimulus, the increase is less than one might have hoped for, partly because the tax bill was very poorly designed.

Between 2010 and 2016 the average ratio of gross investment to GDP was almost 9 percent lower than the average of all OECD countries (the Organization of Economic Cooperation and Development is the "club" of advanced countries) and more than 20 percent lower than the better performing ones—such as Canada. (Gross investment is that part of a country's output that is spent on new plant and equipment and housing, thought of as the productive assets of an economy. It does not include inventory accumulation, nor does it take account of depreciation, the decrease in productive assets as a result of use or time. It doesn't include land purchases either.) The official series in the system of national accounts is referred to as the Gross Fixed Capital Formation.

5. Some of the difference, but only some, is a result of a slower growth rate of population. Per capita income growth slowed from 2.3 percent to 1.7 percent. There are also other factors that may have contributed to slowing growth—for instance, the change in the structure of the economy from a manufacturing to a service-sector economy. It may be more difficult to eke out increases in productivity in the service sector. It could also be just bad luck—fewer important productivity enhancing discoveries happen to occur today than in earlier decades. I believe, however, that more than these structural changes and bad luck are at play.

Most of the data in this chapter comes from standard sources:

FRED, US Census, IMF WEO (their annual World Economic Outlook Report), OECD, and the World Income Database. FRED is used for GDP measures in the US. The US Census is used for data on median real wages. OECD is used when comparing variables across OECD countries. The World Income Database is used for data on average income and income shares of various groups in the income distribution (top 1 percent, top 0.1 percent, bottom 50 percent.). For all these sources, the most recent versions and the most recent data points available when the book went to press were used.

6. Source: United Nations, for the latest year available, 2017. Based on IMF and World Bank data, the United States ranks 7th in per capita income. These compare incomes using market exchange rates. Using purchasing power parity, the US ranking, according to the IMF and World Bank, slips to 11th.

7. World Bank Human Capital Index, available at https://www .worldbank.org/en/data/interactive/2018/10/18/human–capital –index–and–components–2018.

8. Source: PISA (Program for International Student Assessment) tests for the year 2015, the latest year available. The differences are quantitatively large. Someone with only a 10th-grade education in the best performers (Shanghai, China) has an equivalent education to a 12th grader in the best-performing US state, Massachusetts.

9. Source: OECD data for the year 2016.

10. "Hours Worked," OECD, 2017 or latest available, available at https://data.oecd.org/emp/hours-worked.htm.

11. US total growth in productivity over the period was 2.3 percent, while the average for the OECD was 4.9 percent. Source: OECD, available at https://data.oecd.org/lprdty/gdp-per-hour-worked .htm#indicator-chart.

12. In terms of purchasing power parity (PPP). This measure takes into account that different goods cost different amounts in different countries. China's GDP overtook that of the US in 2015. Comparisons are also often done on the basis of current exchange rates, which can fluctuate a great deal. In these terms, China's GDP is still below that of the US. However, in terms of the standard metrics, China is still a developing country, with a per capita income roughly a fifth that of the US.

13. Not surprisingly, because developing countries have to catch up, they have higher growth rates—in 2016, the latest year for which data is available, America ranked 139th.

14. World Bank data for this and the numbers moved out of poverty cited below.

15. World Inequality Database, www.wid.world. Of course, this growth has not been equally shared in China, with the proportion of total income going to the middle and the bottom declining, but this transformation is nonetheless impressive.

16. Presidents try to exaggerate the importance of their policies in contributing to growth. Trump traces the surge in growth in the US to the date of his election—as if just the realization that he would be at the helm would change the course of the economy. In fact, even as Trump championed US 2017 performance during his first year in office, he didn't mention that the US growth rate was actually lower than the average of the advanced countries. Even the difference in the US growth rate between 2017 and 2016, 0.76 percent, was barely greater than that of the average of the OECD (0.64 percent), and far less than half of that of America's neighbor to the North, Canada (1.55 percent). Indeed, in 2016, Canada's growth was little different from that of the US. If anyone had cause to trumpet their success, it was Canada's Prime Minister Justin Trudeau, not Trump. In 2018, America experienced a "sugar high" as a result of a massive increase in the fiscal deficit, resulting in real GDP growth of around 3 percent. But the spurt was not anticipated to be sustainable; 2019 growth is expected to be markedly lower.

17. And almost since the time the country was founded, many American leaders have considered the struggle against inequality essential for creating a thriving democracy. Sean Wilentz has written the definitive history of inequality and politics in the US. See his book *The Politicians and the Egalitarians: The Hidden History of American Politics* (New York: W. W. Norton, 2017).

18. See Olivier Giovannoni, "What Do We Know about the Labor Share and the Profit Share? Part III: Measures and Structural Factors" (working paper 805, Levy Economics Institute, 2014).

19. As measured from 1977 to 2017, the latest year for which data is available. Thomas Piketty and Emmanuel Saez, "Income Inequality in the United States, 1913–1998," *Quarterly Journal of Economics* 118, no. 1 (2003): 1–39. Tables and figures updated to 2017 and available on Emmanuel Saez's website: https://eml.berkeley.edu/~saez/.

20. Table A-4 in the Census Bureau Income and Poverty Report, available at https://www.census.gov/content/dam/Census/library/publications/2017/demo/P60-259.pdf.

21. FRED economic data. It used to be thought that increasing minimum wages would inevitably lead to significant increases in unemployment. But since the path-breaking work of David Card and Alan B. Krueger ("Minimum Wages and Employment: A Case Study of the Fast-Food Industry in New Jersey and Pennsylvania," *American Economic Review* 84, no. 4 [1994]: 772–93), there is a growing consensus that that is not the case, partly because of the prevalence of market power in labor markets (discussed in chapter 4). (See "The Effects of a Minimum-Wage Increase on Employment and Family Income" [CBO, Feb. 18, 2014].) Indeed, increasing the minimum wage may even have positive employment effects.

22. More accurately, compensation, which includes fringe benefits. Economic Policy Institute, based on their analysis of Bureau of Labor Statistics and Bureau of Economic Analysis data, accessed July 17, 2018, available at https://www.epi.org/productivity -pay-gap/.

23. The subject of wage disparities has recently received extensive attention. For instance, Song and his colleagues, using a massive data set, show that increases in differences of compensation within a firm play an important role in growing wage inequality, but not as much as the increases in differences between firms, though those are largely accounted for by changes in the skill composition of firms. Others studies emphasize that differences in wages across firms seem related to differences in firm profitability, though with the data we have, in most cases it is impossible to distinguish between firms whose profitability derives from greater productivity and those with more market power. Evidence cited elsewhere in this book on increasing market concentration highlights the increased importance of disparities between firms with and without market power. Still, there are large and often persistent differences in productivities across firms. Greenwald and I wrote about these in *Creating a Learning Society*. The existence of the disparities is a part of our critique of standard economics, which assumes that knowledge disseminates quickly and costlessly through the economy. Advances in learning and learning technologies have actually worked to reduce these disparities, though there may be forces (such as the increased paced of innovation in certain areas) working in the other direction. See Jae Song, David J. Price, Fatih Guvenen, Nicholas Bloom, and Till Von Wachter, "Firming Up Inequality," *Quarterly Journal of Economics* 134, no. 1 (2018): 1–50;

David Card, Ana Rute Cardoso, Jörg Heining, and Patrick Kline, "Firms and Labor Market Inequality: Evidence and Some Theory," *Journal of Labor Economics* 36, no. S1 (2018): S13–S70; Jason Furman and Peter R. Orszag, "A Firm-Level Perspective on the Role of Rents in the Rise in Inequality" in *Toward a Just Society: Joseph Stiglitz and Twenty-first Century Economics*, ed. Martin Guzman (New York: Columbia University Press, 2018), 10–47; Hernan Winkler, "Inequality among Firms Drives Wage Inequality in Europe," Brookings, Mar. 21, 2017, https://www.brookings.edu/blog/future-development/2017/03/21/inequality-among-firms-drives-wage-inequality-in-europe/; Giuseppe Berlingieri, Patrick Blanchenay, and Chiara Criscuolo, "The Great Divergence(s)," (OECD Science, Technology and Industry Policy Papers no. 39, 2017); and Julián Messina, Oskar Nordström Skans, and Mikael Carlsson, "Firms' Productivity and Workers' Wages: Swedish Evidence" (Vox CEPR Policy Portal, Oct. 23, 2016).

24. I wrote two books on the subject spelling out how inequality was not only weakening our economy but also undermining our democracy and dividing our society (*The Price of Inequality* and *The Great Divide.*) Most Americans seemed unaware either of the magnitude of this growing inequality or its consequences, and to remedy this, I helped curate a *New York Times* series on the topic that ran in 2013 and 2014 and included Judith Warner, Jacob Soll, Andrea Levere, David L. Kirp, Corey Robin, Alice Goffman, Robert Balfanz, Maria Konnikova, and Barbara Dafoe Whitehead. I addressed the issues in every forum I could, from *Vanity Fair* to the *Nation* and *Politico*, and in my monthly Project Syndicate column, published in newspapers around the world.

25. A coauthor of mine in many of my early works on optimal redistributive taxation.

26. Barack Obama, in a speech at the Center for American Progress (Washington, DC, Dec. 2013). He also said: "So let me repeat: The combined trends of increased inequality and decreasing mobility pose a fundamental threat to the American dream, our way of life, and what we stand for around the globe. And it is not simply a moral claim that I'm making here. There are practical consequences to rising inequality and reduced mobility." Earlier, in a speech at Osawatomie High School, Kansas, December 6, 2011, he had said, "When middle-class families can no longer afford to buy the goods and services that businesses are selling, when people are slipping out of the middle class, it drags down the entire

economy from top to bottom. America was built on the idea of broad-based prosperity, of strong consumers all across the country. That's why a CEO like Henry Ford made it his mission to pay his workers enough so that they could buy the cars he made. It's also why a recent study showed that countries with less inequality tend to have stronger and steadier economic growth over the long run." That, of course, was the central point of my book *The Price of Inequality.*

27. *The Kerner Report: The 1968 Report of the National Advisory Commission on Civil Disorders* (New York: Pantheon, 1988).

28. *The Kerner Report.* I was asked to assess how things had changed in the subsequent half century. The dismal findings are reported in "Economic Justice in America: Fifty Years after the Kerner Report," in *Everybody Does Better When Everybody Does Better: The Kerner Report at Fifty/A Blueprint for America's Future*, eds. Fred Harris and Alan Curtis (Philadelphia: Temple University Press, 2017). Most depressing was testimony to the Kerner Commission by a distinguished scholar, Dr. Kenneth B. Clark, who wrote, "I read that report . . . of the 1919 riot in Chicago, and it is as if I were reading the report of the investigating committee of the Harlem riot of '35, the report of the investigating committee on the Harlem riot of '43, the report of the McCone Commission of the Watts riot [of '65]. I must again in candor say to you members of this Commission—it is a kind of Alice in Wonderland—with the same moving pictures re-shown over and over again, the same analysis, the same recommendations and the same inaction."

29. Eileen Patten, "Racial, Gender Wage Gaps Persist in U.S. Despite Some Progress" (Pew Research Center, July 2016). Refined statistics, of course, enable us to ascertain the relative role played by differences in education, employment experience, and discrimination.

30. Among the countries that do better than the US are Japan, Norway, Sweden, Australia, Iceland, Canada, New Zealand, Netherlands, Austria, and Denmark. In 2015 (latest available comparable data) all had life expectancies well over 80, with Japan topping the list at 83.9; the United States was at 78.8, in between Chile and the Czech Republic. OECD data.

31. The most recent data at the time of publication was for 2017.

32. The mortality rate is just the fraction of a given age cohort (say, those between 50 and 55) that die in a year, or in a five-year span. Lower mortality rates are associated with higher life expectancy.

33. "The Growing Life-Expectancy Gap between Rich and Poor,"

Brookings Institution, Feb. 22, 2016, accessed Nov. 24, 2018, available at https://www.brookings.edu/opinions/the-growing-life-expectancy-gap-between-rich-and-poor/.

34. Anne Case and Angus Deaton, "Rising Morbidity and Mortality in Midlife among White Non-Hispanic Americans in the 21st Century," *Proceedings of the National Academy of Sciences* 112, no. 49 (2015): 15,078–83, and see Ann Case and Angus Deaton, "Mortality and Morbidity in the 21st Century," *Brookings Papers on Economic Activity*, (Spring 2017): 397-476. Mortality rates in recent years have been increasing for all whites, in contrast to decreases in the rest of the world. At the same time, it is worth noting that mortality rates for African Americans remain higher than for whites. Adverse economics is bad for health, regardless of race.

35. I had earlier noted these disturbing trends, especially in the 2013 paperback edition of *The Price of Inequality*, including similarly disturbing statistics for women who were not college graduates. The works described earlier by Jennifer Sherman, Joan Williams, Katherine J. Cramer, Michèle Lamont, Arlie Hochschild, J. D. Vance, and Amy Goldstein speak to the societal changes that created the conditions for these increases in "deaths of despair."

36. Reflecting the importance of work, he also reports that they have "low levels of emotional well-being" and "derive relatively little meaning from their daily activities." See Alan B. Krueger, "Where Have All the Workers Gone? An Inquiry into the Decline of the U.S. Labor Force Participation Rate," *Brookings Papers on Economic Activity* 48, no. 2 (2017): 1–87.

37. Abuse of corporate power, the subject of the next chapter, plays a direct role in the story of the opioid epidemic: the drugs were pushed by Purdue Pharma. See Beth Macy, *Dopesick: Dealers, Doctors, and the Drug Company that Addicted America* (Boston: Little, Brown, 2018). It also plays a role in the obesity epidemic. The Centers for Disease Control and Prevention notes that almost 40 percent of Americans are obese. For Hispanics and non-Hispanic blacks, the numbers were even higher (approximately 47 percent); it was less prevalent in men and women with college degrees; and more prevalent in the South and Midwest than elsewhere in the country. Most disturbing was the rapid rise in the percentage of children and adolescents affected by obesity—nearly 1 in 5—which more than tripled since the 1970s. Obesity is greatly affected by diet. The sugary drinks pushed by Coca-Cola and other soft drink companies and the sweet and salty foods that are designed to be

addictive are examples of corporations taking advantage of the unwary. See, for instance, David A. Kessler, M.D., *The End of Overeating: Taking Control of the Insatiable American Appetite* (New York: Rodale Books, 2009). Kessler served as Commissioner of the Food and Drug Administration from 1990 to 1997. (For data on US obesity, see https://www.cdc.gov/obesity/index.html. For role of diet in obesity, see https://www.hsph.harvard.edu/obesity -prevention-source/obesity-causes/diet-and-weight/. For an example of an academic study linking sugary drinks and weight, see Lenny R. Vartanian, Marlene B. Schwartz, and Kelly D. Brownell, "Effects of Soft Drink Consumption on Nutrition and Health: A Systematic Review and Meta-Analysis," *American Journal of Public Health* 97 [2007]: 667–75.)

38. Perhaps the best website for data on inequality is that of *inequality.org*.

    There is some controversy both about the sources of wealth inequality and its future evolution. Thomas Piketty, in his justly praised 2014 book *Capital in the 21st Century* (Cambridge, MA: The Belknap Press of Harvard University Press) has argued, for instance, that the passing on of inheritances from one generation to the next leads to ever-increasing inequality. The recent surge of inequality, he writes, is a reflection of this time-honored process that had been temporarily interrupted by World War II and the surge of social solidarity that it brought about. My own perspective, which I first wrote about in the 1960s, is somewhat different, though not wholly contradictory. I argue that, while the intergenerational transmission of advantage is important, there are offsetting centrifugal and centripetal forces, the former pulling the economy apart, the latter bringing it together, and that over the long run, these normally balance out. What had happened since the mid-1970s was an upsetting of the balance, a strengthening of the centrifugal and a weakening of the centripetal forces. We are witnessing the economy moving toward a new equilibrium, with much more inequality than the old. (See Stiglitz, "Distribution of Income and Wealth Among Individuals," *Econometrica* 37, no. 3 [1969]: 382–97; and "New Theoretical Perspectives on the Distribution of Income and Wealth Among Individuals: Parts I-IV" [NBER Working Papers 21, 21189–21192, 2015].)

39. Just a year before, the figure was 43, and the year before, 61. Billionaire wealth has risen by an annual average rate of 13 percent since 2010; 82 percent of all global wealth created in 2017 went to

the top 1 percent, while none went to the bottom 50 percent. See *Private Wealth or Public Good*, Oxfam, Jan. 2019, and *Reward Work, Not Wealth*, Oxfam, Jan. 2018.

40. These two families' vast wealth (reportedly almost $175 billion for the Waltons, and $120 for Charles and David Koch in 2018) is as large as the total wealth of a staggeringly large proportion of Americans—as of 2016, the most recent year for which a reliable comparison could be made, the Waltons and the Kochs held as much as the total wealth of the bottom 50 percent. Data for wealth distribution is based on the Federal Reserve's Survey of Consumer Finances 2016, removing consumer durables. Wealth data for the Waltons and Kochs comes from *Forbes* magazine. Jane Mayer's bestselling book *Dark Money: The Hidden History of the Billionaires behind the Rise of the Radical Right* (New York: Doubleday, 2016) documents the outsized influence of the Koch brothers on American politics.

41. See Raj Chetty, Nathaniel Hendren, Patrick Kline, and Emmanuel Saez, "Where Is the Land of Opportunity? The Geography of Intergenerational Mobility in the United States," *Quarterly Journal of Economics* 129, no. 4 (2014): 1553–623; Chetty, Hendren, and Lawrence F. Katz, "The Long-Term Effects of Exposure to Better Neighborhoods: New Evidence from the Moving to Opportunity Experiment" (working paper, Harvard University, 2015); and Chetty and Hendren, "The Impacts of Neighborhoods on Intergenerational Mobility Childhood Exposure Effects and County-Level Estimates" (working paper, Harvard University, Apr. 2015). Americans live in increasingly economically segregated communities, so that neighborhood effects contribute importantly to the intergenerational transmission of advantage. See Kendra Bischoff and Sean F. Reardon, "Residential Segregation by Income, 1970–2009," in *Diversity and Disparities: America Enters a New Century*, ed. John Logan (New York: Russell Sage, 2014): 208–33.

42. The data is striking: As the Pew Mobility Project notes, "Forty-three percent of Americans raised in the bottom quintile remain stuck in the bottom as adults," while "Forty percent raised in the top quintile remain at the top as adults." In terms of wealth, matters are worse, with almost two-thirds of those raised in the bottom of the wealth ladder remaining on the bottom two rungs themselves, and a similar percent of those raised in the top of the wealth ladder remaining on the top two rungs. Matters are even worse for blacks, with "over half of blacks (53 percent) raised in the

bottom of the family income ladder remain[ing] stuck in the bottom as adults." They show the critical role of education in upward mobility; those with less education are more likely to get stuck in the bottom. "Pursuing the American Dream: Economic Mobility Across Generations," Pew Mobility Project, July 2012.

43. The Equality of Opportunity Project, accessed July 18, 2018, available at http://www.equality-of-opportunity.org/.

44. "Pursuing the American Dream," Pew Mobility Project.

CHAPTER 3: EXPLOITATION AND MARKET POWER

1. There has also been an increase in our understandings of the limitations of the competitive equilibrium model. It is not robust—slight changes in assumptions (the presence of small fixed sunk costs, or small search costs or small information costs combined with small amounts of information imperfections) lead to large changes in results, e.g., the persistence of large amounts of market power. Even small market power in multiple industries can add up to having large effects. Information economics, game theory, and behavioral economics have all had profound effects on how we think about the economy.

   The irony was that the critique of standard competitive model was in full force just as the model's influence expanded in the eras of Carter, Reagan, and succeeding presidents, showing the importance of lags in knowledge—and perhaps of ideology and interests.

2. Peter Thiel, "Competition Is for Losers," *Wall Street Journal*, Sept. 14, 2014.

3. A commission established by Congress to investigate the causes of the 2008 financial crisis.

4. Interview with the Financial Crisis Inquiry Commission, May 26, 2010. Buffett was a major shareholder in Moody's, one of the three dominant credit rating agencies. Reported by David Dayen, "America's Favorite Monopolist: The Shameful Truth behind Warren Buffett's Billions," *The Nation*, Mar. 12, 2018, p. 16. The credit rating agencies played a central role in the crisis, as the commission noted in its final report, writing that the agencies "were key enablers of the financial meltdown."

5. Address before 2000 annual Berkshire Hathaway (Buffett's main investment vehicle) meeting. See Dayen, "America's Favorite Monopolist." (Buffett had used the "moat" analogy for decades before this quote was reported.)

6. For instance, according to the International Telecommunication Union, the UN's specialized agency for information and communication technologies, report "Measuring the Information Society 2015," US Telecom prices (prepaid, broadband, mobile, 500 mb) were more than twenty times those of India, and almost twenty times that of Estonia. Harvard law professor and telecoms expert Susan Crawford points out that Comcast and Time Warner dominate 66 percent of all broadband internet, and they often don't compete in the same market. See Susan Crawford, *Captive America: The Telecom Industry and Monopoly Power in the New Gilded Age* (New Haven: Yale University Press, 2013).

7. Not just the growth of the market power of corporations and the CEOs who run them, but also the lack of market power of workers. As the discussion below and in the ensuing chapters will make clear, there are many factors contributing to this imbalance of market power, and market power is not the *only* factor contributing to the growth of inequality. For instance, changes in technology (discussed further in chapter 6) increase the demand for skilled relative to unskilled labor. But the form these changes take, in part, is the result of managerial decisions—how to spend scarce research dollars—and those with market power, the managers, have decided to do so in ways which reduce the bargaining power of workers, and especially unskilled workers.

8. I hasten to add that this is not the only source of inequality, as the discussion below will make abundantly clear. And it is not just market power of the corporation in its dealing with consumers; it is also its market power in dealing with workers.

9. Firms can also pry wealth from others by taking advantage of their weaknesses—for instance, enticing them to gamble away their wealth or persuading them to borrow at usurious interest rates. Even to make money by taking advantage of weaknesses, such as gambling or alcohol, requires market power, because in our amoral society, there is an ample supply of those able and willing to do so, and in the absence of market power, profits even for nefarious activities would be driven down to zero.

10. While traditionally, corruption focuses on instances such as these, in fact there is widespread corruption in the private sector, as when an employee (even a CEO) takes advantage of his position to enrich himself, or when a company behaves dishonestly, to enrich itself at the expense of others.

11. Adam Smith, *An Inquiry into the Causes of the Wealth of Nations*, 1776.

12. Actually, the passage was in response not just to the *potential* for monopolization, but the pervasive presence of market power that had emerged at the end of the nineteenth century, including in oil, railroads, meatpacking, and tobacco.

13. There are, of course, fluctuations in the risk premium that the market requires, depending on judgment about risk in the economy.

14. For a close look at the corporate sector, see Simcha Barkai, "Declining Labor and Capital Shares" (working paper, 2017). Barkai has done an excellent job at parsing out the capital share and showing that the decrease in capital share cannot be accounted for by intangible capital. For a study using firm-level data, see Jan De Loecker and Jan Eeckhout, "The Rise of Market Power and Macroeconomic Implications" (NBER Working Paper No. 23687, 2017).

15. See, for instance, Jacob A. Robbins, "Capital Gains and the Distribution of Income in the United States," Brown University, Dec. 2018.

16. See Joseph E. Stiglitz, "New Theoretical Perspectives on the Distribution of Income and Wealth among Individuals." For a discussion of the role of housing, see Matthew Rognlie, "Deciphering the Fall and Rise in the Net Capital Share: Accumulation or Scarcity?," *Brookings Papers on Economic Activity* 46, no. 1 (Spring 2015): 1–69. See also Thomas Piketty, *Capital in the Twenty-First Century.*

17. The right to obtain a certain rent stream, year after year, has a market value, and this is called the capitalized value of the rents. Thus, owning a monopoly will give the owner profits each year. The owner could sell that stream of profits. The value today of that stream is called the capitalized rents.

18. See Mordecai Kurz, "On the Formation of Capital and Wealth: IT, Monopoly Power and Rising Inequality" (Stanford Institute for Economic Policy Research Working Paper 17-016, 2017).

19. In mid-twentieth-century capitalism, corporations with market power shared their monopoly rents with their unionized workers. In twenty-first-century capitalism, not only may there may be more market power on average, but there is also less sharing of the rents. Firms' shareholders, and especially managers, have appropriated the returns for themselves, leading to increased inequality. But these changes also have productivity effects, as shortsighted managers, unconstrained by unions, invest less in their workers, or even in the future of the enterprise. (When those at the top are grabbing for themselves more rents, there may be morale effects down below. To avoid this, firms may "vertically disintegrate," outsourc-

ing, for instance, janitorial or other low-paid services. High-wage workers are increasingly likely to work in high-wage firms and with other high-wage workers, and conversely for low-wage workers. See Song et al., "Firming Up Inequality," Card et al., "Firms and Labor Market Inequality," and Furman and Orszag, "A Firm-Level Perspective on the Role of Rents in the Rise in Inequality.")

20. See "Benefits of Competition and Indicators of Market Power" (Council of Economic Advisers Issue Brief, Apr. 2016). The report states, "Several indicators suggest that competition may be decreasing in many economic sectors, including the decades-long decline in new business formation and increases in industry-specific measures of concentration. Recent data also show that returns may have risen for the most profitable firms. To the extent that profit rates exceed firms' cost of capital they may reflect economic rents, which are returns to the factors of production in excess of what would be necessary to keep them in operation. Such rents may divert resources from consumers, distort investment and employment decisions, and encourage firms to engage in wasteful rent-seeking activities."

Even the normally conservative magazine *The Economist* has rung the alarm bell, noting that "between 1997 and 2012 the weighted average share of the top four firms in each sector has risen from 26 percent to 32 percent." It notes that revenues in sectors that are not concentrated are falling, while those in which it is are rising. See "Too Much of a Good Thing: Profits Are Too High. America Needs a Giant Dose of Competition," Mar. 26, 2016.

A series of papers have pointed out the consequences of lack of competition among employers in labor markets: See José Azar, Ioana Marinescu, and Marshall Steinbaum, "Labor Market Concentration," (NBER Working Paper No. 24147, Dec. 2017); José Azar, Ioana Marinescu, Marshall Steinbaum, and Bledi Taska, "Concentration in US Labor Markets: Evidence from Online Vacancy Data," (IZA DP No. 11379, Mar. 2018); Arindrajit Dube, Jeff Jacobs, Suresh Naidu, Siddharth Suri, "Monopsony in Online Labor Markets," (NBER Working Paper No. 24416, Mar. 2018); and Efraim Benmelech, Nittai Bergman, and Hyunseob Kim, "Strong Employers and Weak Employees: How Does Employer Concentration Affect Wages?" (NBER Working Paper No. 24307, Feb. 2018).

21. Gustavo Grullon, Yelena Larkin, and Roni Michaely, "Are US Industries Becoming More Concentrated?," 2016, available at http://finance.eller.arizona.edu/sites/finance/files/grullon_11.4.16 .pdf. According to Furman and Orszag, between 1997 and 2012,

market concentration increased in 12 out of 13 major industries for which data is available. They cite a range of micro-level studies of sectors, including air travel, telecommunications, banking and food processing, that have all shown evidence of greater concentration. See Furman and Orszag, "A Firm-Level Perspective on the Role of Rents in the Rise in Inequality" and Card et al., "Firms and Labor Market Inequality."

22. Not surprisingly, large firms with more market power have higher returns. Furman and Orszag suggest that increased concentration may play a role in the large and growing disparity in returns across major corporations, with that of the most profitable firms (those in the 90th percentile) now six times larger than those at the median, more than twice the difference in 1990. See Furman and Orszag, "A Firm-Level Perspective on the Role of Rents in the Rise in Inequality"; and Furman and Orszag, "Slower Productivity and Higher Inequality: Are they Related?" (Peterson Institute for International Economics, Working Paper 18-4, June 2018). It should be noted not all economists agree with the existence of a strong link between concentration and profitability; indeed, some research purports to show that there is not a strong correlation between profits and concentration, and even that average concentration has not gone up (in spite of the evidence presented, for instance, in the Council of Economic Advisers report "Benefits of Competition and Indicators of Market Power"). Still, there is a very strong presumption that the weaker the competition, the greater markups (described below) and the larger profits (both as a share of GDP and in terms of returns to equity). Later, we'll explain why in a few critical sectors, margins have decreased even as concentration has increased, but these are exceptions.

23. De Loecker and Eeckhout, "The Rise of Market Power and Macroeconomic Implications." Market concentration has also been linked to reduced investment in the economy. See Germán Gutiérrez and Thomas Philippon, "Declining Competition and Investment in the U.S." (NBER Working Paper No. 23583, 2017). This can also be linked to the phenomenon of the long-term interest rate falling because of a fall in demand for capital. See Ricardo J. Caballero, Emmanuel Farhi and Pierre-Olivier Gourinchas, "Rents, Technical Change, and Risk Premia Accounting for Secular Trends in Interest Rates, Returns on Capital, Earning Yields, and Factor Shares," *American Economic Review* 107, no. 5 (2017): 614–20.

24. This is the return to capital, excluding good will. See Tim Koller, Marc Goedhart, and David Wessels, *Valuation: Measuring and Managing the Value of Companies/McKinsey & Company* (Hoboken, NJ: Wiley, 2015). As we note below, the return to capital is increasing even as the return on government bonds is decreasing and as risk management techniques improve, provides strong support for the hypothesis of increasing rents. (The recorded "return to capital," as we have noted, includes monopoly/oligopoly rents. In economics jargon, it should not be thought of as the value of the marginal product of capital.) What is particularly striking is the level of returns at the top, with the average returns to the top 10 percent of firms exceeding 80 percent, to the top 25 percent, 40 percent. See Furman and Orszag, "A firm-Level Perspective on the Role of Rents in the Rise in Inequality."

25. Matt Kranz, "6 percent of Companies Make 50 percent of U.S. profit," *USA Today*, Mar. 2, 2016.

26. *America's Concentration Crisis: An Open Markets Institute Report*, Open Markets Institute, Nov. 29, 2018. Available at https://concentrationcrisis.openmarketsinstitute.org.

27. See the Mar. 26, 2016, issue of *The Economist*.

28. Formally, what matters is the marginal cost.

29. While there is some presumption that this is the case, it is not necessarily so. Competition from Amazon has forced consolidation of the retail sector, but even with this consolidation, profit margins in the bricks-and-mortar retail sector have been low, and bankruptcy is not uncommon.

    When there are only a few firms in a market, it is easy for them to collude, often tacitly. While proving such tacit collusion is difficult, the effects are often easy to ascertain in the form of higher prices.

30. There are, of course, some instances where the market power of a firm can be huge: the single owner of water on an oasis in the desert. Individuals cannot survive without water, and someone who controlled that could impose a high price. Those who controlled other near necessities, like salt, for preserving food in the era before refrigeration, could extract a high price too; the government, knowing this, often established a public monopoly. At least then, the money that is extracted went for public purposes or there is a cap on the price charged.

31. A 2015 *New York Times* series showed the extent to which mandatory arbitration panels have skewed justice in the US. See Jessica Silver-Greenberg and Robert Gebeloff, "Arbitration Everywhere,

Stacking the Deck of Justice," *New York Times*, Oct. 31, 2015. There have been terrible stories of those cheated by nursing homes finding it impossible to find redress for themselves or their parents because of these arbitration clauses. They have also seeped into almost all employment contracts.

32. In spite of this, the Supreme Court has ruled that by signing arbitration clauses, one has waived away one's right to trial in our public legal system. Epic Systems Corp v. Lewis No. 16–285, Decided May 21, 2018.

33. These techniques (like FUD) raise the rivals' cost of production without affecting the incumbent. It is the quintessential method of creating a moat around a product. The theory had been described earlier by Thomas G. Krattenmaker and Steven C. Salop, "Competition and Cooperation in the Market for Exclusionary Rights," *American Economic Review* 76, no. 2 (1986): 109–13; Steven C. Salop and David T. Scheffman, "Raising Rivals' Costs," *American Economic Review* 73, no. 2 (1983): 267–71.

34. Even established firms sometimes have trouble, and even when the patent is not held by a large company but by what are called "patent trolls," firms whose main business model is not innovation— bringing their patent to market—but suing for patent infringement. This happened to Blackberry, at one time one of the leading mobile phone companies, which, after extensive litigation, had to pay $612 million just to continue offering its services, whether the patents which it allegedly infringed were eventually held to be valid or not.

   For start-ups, such suits are even more daunting. For example, Vlingo was a start-up that worked on speech recognition technologies. However, it was hit by a series of lawsuits by a much larger firm called Nuance. Ultimately Vlingo agreed to be acquired by Nuance, but that was after $3 million legal expenses, despite winning the first lawsuit (there were six filed in total). See Charles Duhigg and Steve Lohr, "The Patent, Used as a Sword," *New York Times*, Oct. 7, 2012. See also Colleen V. Chien, "Patent Assertion and Startup Innovation" (Santa Clara University of Law Legal Studies Research Paper Series 26-13, 2013).

35. Chicago economists defend these anti-competitive practices by saying that these restraints are just the natural way that efficient competition takes in two-sided markets. According to these economists, two-sided markets are just a "meeting place"—today, typically an electronic platform—for two sets of agents to interact

with each other. Credit cards bring together customers with stores. They argue that courts shouldn't interfere with the workings of markets. To say that these arguments ignore the actual workings of the marketplace is an understatement. Nevertheless, with these arguments, they succeeded in persuading some courts—including the US Supreme Court in another one of its five-to-four split decisions—to allow these abuses of market power to continue. For an excellent discussion, see Benjamin E. Hermalin and Michael L. Katz, "What's So Special About Two-Sided Markets?" in Martin Guzman, ed. *Toward a Just Society* (New York: Columbia University Press, 2018), 111-130.

36. The contract provisions are so strongly anticompetitive that even a firm with a small market share (like Discover Card) could and did charge exorbitant prices, far in excess of costs. Australia forbade these contracts, and the result was a much more competitive market, with lower fees charged to merchants—and lower profits for the credit card companies.

37. It also means that other consumers, such as those paying cash, are made worse off.

38. In a parallel case, employing much the same economic analysis, a dominant airline reservation system, Sabre, was found guilty of using analogous contractual provisions to restrain competition. In that case, airlines were charged fees far higher than the costs of the computer reservation system's delivery of the service. The contractual provisions stifled entry and innovation. They even inhibited airlines from trying to steer customers to their much cheaper online reservation system, prohibiting them as well from offering discounts to those who took advantage of that system, by-passing the large fees that Sabre imposed. See US Airways Inc. v. Sabre Holdings Corp et al., U.S. District Court, Southern District of New York, No. 11-cv-2725. As this book goes to press, the case is under appeal. (For full disclosure: I was an expert witness for the plaintiffs' claiming that the contract provisions were anticompetitive in this case as well as in several of the credit card cases.)

39. For example, King Drug Company v. Smithkline Beecham Corporation, United States Court of Appeals for the Third Circuit, No. 14-1243, November 19, 2014. The Supreme Court later declined to review the ruling. Also, see FTC v. Actavis, Inc., Supreme Court No. 12-416 (2013).

40. For instance, they wait until the expiration of a patent to introduce a time-release version of the drug. The time-release version should

not be able to be patented—one is supposed to be able to get a patent only on a nonobvious innovation, and at this point, a time-release version of an existing drug is obvious. India has recognized this, much to the chagrin of the US.

Often the government assists Big Pharma in keeping out generics, in provisions called "data exclusivity," limiting the use of data on the original drug to be used for assessing the safety and efficacy of the generic.

41. In chapter six, we provide several examples of such preemptive mergers.

42. There are other reasons that the evolution of the economy may be leading to more market concentration. Chapter 6 discusses how Big Data gives rise to a natural monopoly that may advantage firms like Google and Amazon over others. In these circumstances, it is hard to get competition to work. It just won't happen.

43. Thus, in mid-twentieth century United States, there were three dominant producers (GM, Chrysler, and Ford) and a couple of small firms (Studebaker, Nash-Rambler). Today, the three US automakers face stiff competition from multiple Japanese, Korean, German, and Italian producers.

44. Another way of seeing that standard competition in such markets is not viable is to observe that if price were equal to marginal cost (the extra cost of producing an extra unit), as suggested by standard competitive theory, these industries couldn't survive.

45. Ironically, a change in the rules of the game that has contributed both directly and indirectly to more market power, and a weaker economy with greater inequality, is lower tax rates at the top, as we noted earlier. Lower tax rates may encourage "rent-seeking behavior," where firms attempt to increase profits not by producing a better product, but by, for instance, getting favors from the government. See Piketty, Saez, and Stantcheva, "Optimal Taxation of Top Labor Incomes." The 2017 tax bill illustrates a related phenomenon: when corporate taxes are lowered to favor corporate donors to the party in power, there is the danger of riddling the tax law with provisions favoring one group relative to another, thereby distorting the economy and reducing overall efficiency.

46. The fact that market concentration has increased in the United States while it has not in Europe suggests that it is not technology but policy that is crucial. Germán Gutiérrez and Thomas Philippon attribute the difference to antitrust enforcement. See Gutiér-

rez and Philippon, "How EU Markets Became More Competitive than US Markets: A Study of Institutional Drift" (NBER Working Paper No. 24700, June, 2018).

47. That is, it leads to lower levels of national income (and more of national income going to the monopolist.) Further, this increase in market power also leads to lower growth, partly because the incentives to innovate may be lowered with the weakening of competition, partly because the entry barriers created by those with market power discourage entry of other innovators, partly because more of what is spent on research is devoted to sustaining and increasing market power and devising better ways of exploiting it.

    Price discrimination—where firms charge different prices to different customers, an increasing characteristic of the digital economy as firms use the data they have collected on each of us to determine how much we are willing to pay—introduces further distortions, as we discuss in chapter 6.

48. "Aggregate Productivity and the Rise of Mark-Ups," *Vox*, Dec. 4, 2017; and David R. Baqaee and Emmanuel Farhi, "Productivity and Misallocation in General Equilibrium" (NBER Working Paper 24007, 2018).

49. John Haltiwanger and his collaborators' detailed studies have forcefully documented this. See Ryan Decker, John Haltiwanger, Ron S. Jarmin, and Javier Miranda, "The Secular Decline in Business Dynamism in the US" (manuscript, 2014); John Haltiwanger, Ian Hathaway, and Javier Miranda, "Declining Business Dynamism in the U.S. High-Technology Sector" (Kauffman Foundation, 2014); Ryan Decker, John Haltiwanger, Ron S Jarmin, and Javier Miranda, "The Role of Entrepreneurship in US Job Creation and Economic Dynamism," *Journal of Economic Perspectives* 28, no. 3 (2014): 3–24. See also Ian Hathaway and Robert E. Litan, "Declining Business Dynamism in the United States: A Look at States and Metros" (Brookings Papers, 2014). It shows up too in OECD data, where the United States is not the worst performer, but, contrary to our image, it is far from the best. See Chiara Criscuolo, Peter N. Gal, and Carlo Menon, "The Dynamics of Employment Growth: New Evidence from 18 Countries" (OECD, Science, Technology and Industry Policy Papers no. 14, May 21, 2014).

    Furman and Orszag provide further evidence on the decline of dynamism in the US economy, which they link in part to a decrease in competition. See Furman and Orszag, "Slower Productivity and Higher Inequality: Are they Related?"; and Furman and Orszag, "A Firm-Level Perspective on the Role of Rents in the Rise in Inequality."

50. Furman and Orszag also make note of the fact that big businesses are investing less even as their returns seem so high, which they too attribute in part to a reduction in competition. See Furman and Orszag, "A Firm-Level Perspective on the Role of Rents in the Rise in Inequality"; and Furman and Orszag, "Slower Productivity and Higher Inequality: Are They Related?" Gutierrez and Philippon (2017) similarly find that investment in the US today is weak relative to measures of profitability and valuation, and find that lack of competition and short-termism, related to the corporate governance problems discussed briefly below, are the two key explanations. See Germán Gutiérrez and Thomas Philippon, "Investment-less Growth: An Empirical Investigation," Sept. 2017, New York University and Brookings, https://www.brookings.edu/wp-content/uploads/2017/09/2_gutierrezphilippon.pdf.

    The weakness in investment also, of course, has an adverse effect on aggregate demand, of critical importance in periods such as that after the 2008 financial crisis where lack of aggregate demand is the critical constraint in the economy. Data is from "Shares of Gross Domestic Product: Gross Private Domestic Investment," St. Louis FRED, accessed July 17, 2018, available at https://fred.stlouisfed.org/series/A006RE1Q156NBEA#0.

51. Princeton: Princeton University Press. Much as some of the bad actors on the internet are phishing for phools, looking for those whom they can entrap.

52. This issue received some attention from the Obama administration. See CEA Issue Brief, "Labor Market Monopsony: Trends, Consequences, and Policy Responses," Oct. 2016.

53. See, for example, Alan Manning, "Imperfect Competition in Labour Markets," in *Handbook of Labor Economics*, eds. Orley Ashenfelter and David Card, vol. 4 (Amsterdam: North-Holland, 2011); and John Schmitt, "Why Does the Minimum Wage Have No Discernible Effect on Employment?" (CEPR Publication, 2013).

54. In many instances, such as for fast food workers, there is no possible justification in terms of the loss of a trade secret or "inside information." Alan Krueger and Eric Posner find that a quarter of all American workers are exposed to noncompete or nonpoaching agreements at some time in their career. They are often used on workers who are most vulnerable. See "A Proposal for Protecting

Low-Income Workers from Monopsony and Collusion," *The Hamilton Project Policy Proposal* 5 (2018).

55. Smith, *An Inquiry into the Causes of the Wealth of Nations*.

56. A recent study showed that "Among employees paid by the hour who work over 40 hours in a week, 19 percent were paid less than the 'time-and-a-half' standard for overtime." Susann Rohwedder and Jeffrey B. Wenger, "The Fair Labor Standards Act: Worker Misclassification and the Hours and Earnings Effects of Expanded Coverage" (Rand work paper, Aug. 7, 2015).

57. One of the most telling pieces of evidence comes from a recent econometric study on online labor markets. One would have expected that monopsony power be very low, yet the evidence is to the contrary. See Dube, Jacobs, Naidu, and Suri, "Monopsony in Online Labor Markets" and Azar et al., "Concentration in US Labor Markets: Evidence from Online Vacancy Data."

  We see evidence of employer market power too in the racial, ethnic, and gender discrimination that abounds in the labor market. Competitive theory says that such discrimination can't exist; but anyone with eyes can see that it does, and its existence is evidence itself of the absence of power of these groups relative to that of employers.

58. A number of factors, in turn, have contributed to the weakening of unions, besides the changes in the rules of the game and changing market structure which have made unionization more difficult. Many of these changes have fed on each other. Globalization, in the manner in which it has been structured, has diminished the ability of unions to gain pay raises for their workers, and this reduction in their effectiveness has contributed to diminished membership. Union leaders sometimes do not adequately reflect the interests of their members, referred to as the principal agent problem—something that arises in all organizations in the presence of imperfect information/accountability.

59. Alexander Hertel-Fernandez has done interesting work on the links between the decline of unions, increasing inequality, and how these trends are related to politics. See his book *Politics at Work: How Companies Turn Their Workers into Lobbyists* (New York: Oxford University Press, 2018).

60. More generally, there are a whole set of rules that govern unions, which affect how easily they can get members and collect dues, how likely they can win an election to give them the right to

represent the workers in a plant, and how effectively they can bargain. Traditionally, employers not only fired workers who were caught organizing, but blacklisted them, so they couldn't get a job elsewhere. That's now illegal, but there are a variety of subtle and not so subtle, legal and illegal, ways that employers try to discourage unionization. The National Labor Relations Board oversees labor laws and regulations, interpreting and enforcing them. Mark Stelzner of the University of Connecticut has been able to show that a large fraction of the decline in workers' position is a result of changes in a few key rules and their interpretations that have worked to the disadvantage of unions. See Mark Stelzner, "The New American Way—How Changes in Labour Law Are Increasing Inequality," *Industrial Relations Journal* 48, no. 3 (2017): 231–55.

Unions have also played an important role in reducing wage inequalities, so the weakening of unions is naturally associated with an increase in inequality. See David Card, "The Effect of Unions on Wage Inequality in the U.S. Labor Market," *Industrial and Labor Relations Review* 54, no. 2 (2001): 296–315. One of the reasons that inequality is worse in the US is that unions are weaker. For a global perspective, see Era Dabla-Norris, Kalpana Kochhar, Nujin Suphaphiphat, Frantisek Ricka, and Evridiki Tsounta, "Causes and Consequences of Income Inequality: A Global Perspective," IMF Staff Discussion Note No. 15/13 (Washington, DC: International Monetary Fund, 2015); and Florence Jaumotte and Carolina Osorio Buitron, "Inequality and Labour Market Institutions," IMF Staff Discussion Note No. 15/14 (Washington, DC: International Monetary Fund, 2015).

In June 2018, the Supreme Court's decision in *Janus v. American Federation of State, County and Municipal Employees* took away the right of public sector unions to collect dues from non-union members. By forcing unions to devote more attention to fund raising and member retention, these measures also weaken their ability to engage in other activities, including political activities directed at enhancing workers' well-being. See James Feigenbaum, Alexander Hertel-Fernandez, and Vanessa Williamson, "From the Bargaining Table to the Ballot Box: Political Effects of Right to Work Laws" (NBER Working Paper 24259, 2017).

Space limitations make it impossible to spell out the whole agenda for restoring workers' market and political power—besides reversing the laws that have been designed to undermine it. Changes in the economy, the growth of the service sector, the diminution of manufacturing, the development of the gig economy, have all increased these challenges. See Brishen Rogers and Kate Andrias, *Rebuilding Worker Voice in Today's Economy* (Roosevelt Institute, 2018); and Kate Andrias, "The New Labor Law," *Yale Law Journal* 126, no. 1 (Oct. 2016).

61. For a discussion of the role of unions in wage determination, see Henry S. Farber, Daniel Herbst, Ilyana Kuziemko, and Suresh Naidu, "Unions and Inequality Over the Twentieth Century: New Evidence from Survey Data" (NBER Working Paper No. 24587, 2018).

62. See John Kenneth Galbraith, *American Capitalism: The Concept of Countervailing Power* (Boston: Houghton Mifflin, 1952). His idea was that then (as now) the economy was not well described by a competitive marketplace, but rather by pervasive market power, with large unions and large corporations keeping each other in check—the system worked because of these countervailing powers.

63. The subject of updating antitrust laws has attracted enormous interest from academics and policymakers in recent years. See, for instance, Tim Wu, "Antitrust in the New Gilded Age" (Columbia Business School Global Reports, 2018); a series of Roosevelt Institute blogs and papers, including the following: Marshall Steinbaum, "Crossed Lines: Why the AT&T–Time Warner Merger Demands a New Approach to Antitrust," Feb. 2, 2017; "Airline Consolidation, Merger Retrospectives, and Oil Price Pass-Through," Apr. 6, 2018; "It's Time for Antitrust to Take Monopsony Seriously," Oct. 17, 2017; "A Missing Link: The Role of Antitrust Law in Rectifying Employer Power in Our High-Profit, Low-Wage Economy," Apr. 16, 2018; Marshall Steinbaum, Eric Harris Bernstein, and John Sturm, "Powerless: How Lax Antitrust and Concentrated Market Power Rig the Economy Against American Workers, Consumers, and Communities," Mar. 27, 2018; and Adil Abdela, "Market Concentration and the Importance of Properly Defined Markets," Apr. 23, 2018. See also Joseph E. Stiglitz, "Towards a Broader View of Competition Policy," in *Competition Policy for the New Era: Insights from the BRICS Countries*, eds. Tembinkosi Bonakele, Eleanor Fox, and Liberty Mncube (Oxford: Oxford University Press, 2017); (lecture presented to the 4th BRICS International Competition Conference in Durban, November 2015); and Joseph E. Stiglitz, "America Has a Monopoly Problem—and It's Huge," *Nation*, Oct. 23, 2017. See also Barry Lynn's Open Markets Institute website, https://openmarketsinstitute.org/. Barry Lynn was a

scholar at the New America Foundation, but he and his team left, allegedly after pressure from Google, because of Lynn's praise for the antitrust ruling by the EU against Google. See Barry Lynn, "I Criticized Google. It Got Me Fired. That's How Corporate Power Works," *Washington Post*, Aug. 31, 2017.

64. Actually, these doctrines were strong at the University of Chicago even before Friedman arrived on the scene. But he did more than anybody else to popularize them, e.g., in his book *Free to Choose*, written with his wife, Rose Friedman (New York: Harcourt, 1980).

65. For instance, a third of a century ago, Partha Dasgupta and I showed that the Schumpeterian claim that monopolies were temporary was wrong: they had the power and incentives to ensure that their market power persisted. See Dasgupta and Stiglitz, "Uncertainty, Industrial Structure, and the Speed of R&D," *Bell Journal of Economics* 11, no. 1 (1980): 1–28. With other colleagues, we showed that the fight to be the monopolist didn't necessarily have the positive effect on innovation that Schumpeter has assumed, but, on the contrary, could dampen it. See, for instance, Kenneth J. Arrow, "Economic Welfare and the Allocation of Resources to Invention," and Drew Fudenberg, Richard Gilbert, Joseph E. Stiglitz, and Jean Tirole, "Preemption, Leapfrogging and Competition in Patent Races," *European Economic Review* 22 (June 1983): 3–32 (Jean Tirole received the Nobel Memorial Prize in Economics in 2014). These conclusions have been reinforced by more recent results of Greenwald and Stiglitz, *Creating a Learning Society*, especially chapters 5 and 6.

Arnold Harberger of the University of Chicago claimed that the loss in consumer welfare from monopoly power was of second-order importance (around 0.1 percent of GDP). See Arnold C. Harberger, "Monopoly and Resource Allocation," *American Economic Review* 44, no. 2 (1954): 77–87. More recent research has shown that Harberger underestimated the costs by some two orders of magnitude. See Baqaee and Farhi, "Productivity and Misallocation in General Equilibrium." Even if Harberger's conclusion were true in the 1950s, the subsequent increase in market power (and the associated increase in markups), described earlier in this chapter, imply that it is no longer true.

66. That is, in the enforcement of antitrust laws, there are two possible types of errors: finding a noncompetitive practice to be competitive, or finding a competitive practice to be noncompetitive. They focused their attention on the latter, in the belief that the likelihood that any noncompetitive practice could survive was, in any case, low.

67. The Supreme Court seemed to buy this argument in Brooke Group Ltd. v. Brown & Williamson Tobacco Corp., 509 U.S. 209 (1993). Even at the time that these arguments were first put forward by Chicago lawyers, for instance by Robert Bork, they were skewered by economists such as Nobel Prize winner Oliver Williamson in "Review of *The Antitrust Paradox: A Policy at War with Itself* by Robert H. Bork," *University of Chicago Law Review* 46, no. 2 (1979): 10. Developments of economic theory since then have reinforced these conclusions.

      It's ironic that at the same time the US has made it difficult to win a predatory pricing case *within* the country, it's easy to win the analogous case when charging foreign companies with unfair trade practices, charging prices below costs.

68. Currently, the burden falls on the plaintiff (the party claiming that the firm is acting in a noncompetitive way) to show that the anticompetitive effects outweigh the efficiency gains. This is based on the presumption that markets work well and are competitive, so something that is seemingly anticompetitive is actually likely to be procompetitive.

69. Thus when Google sells directly, it has a conflict of interest with advertisers who are using Google to market its products. Conflicts of interest are even more pervasive on Amazon. We'll discuss some other regulatory issues posed by the new platforms later in this book, but the challenges they pose for our economy, including for competition, go beyond what we can cover. See, for instance, Lina M. Khan, "Amazon's Antitrust Paradox," *The Yale Law Journal* 126, no. 3 (Jan. 2017).

70. There should also be changes to some of the conventional procedures for determining market power. Often, those claiming an antitrust violation are asked to show that the given firm has a large market share. Again, the presumption is that without a large market share, it simply couldn't engage in an anticompetitive practice. As a theoretical matter, that's just wrong. But as a practical mat-

ter, it's worse—establishing what is the relevant market is often hard. When there is *direct* evidence of market power (of the kind discussed above—high markups, price discrimination, excessive returns with no entry, forcing buyers to accept terms, like arbitration clauses, that should be unacceptable), that should be proof enough.

For further discussion of other procedural changes, see Wu, "Antitrust in the New Gilded Age."

71. "Costly Choices for Treating Wilson's Disease," *Hepatology* 61, no. 4 (2015): 1106–8. The editorial notes that Merck, which originated the drug, had for twenty years kept the costs at around ½ of 1 percent of that charged by Valeant.

72. After acquiring Daraprim, a sixty-two-year-old, out-of-patent drug in 2015, Turing Pharmaceuticals increased the price from $13.50 a tablet to $750. There are many, many other examples. See Andrew Pollack, "Drug Goes from $13.50 a Tablet to $750, Overnight," *New York Times*, Sept. 20, 2015.

73. Similarly, if share prices go up by more than the claimed savings, it suggests that an increase in market power may be an important driver of the merger or acquisition. There also needs to be close post-merger review, with a credible threat that if the merger does result in higher prices when what was promised was just the opposite, the merger may be undone.

74. Chapter 6 explains how regulations requiring net neutrality are required to avoid the abuse of market power arising from such conflicts of interest by the internet companies.

Traditionally, antitrust has focused on mergers within an industry, and presumed that vertical mergers are not anticompetitive. But with the recognition that in many markets competition is limited, vertical mergers are now understood to have "horizontal" effects and to reduce competition even further. The continuing influence of the Chicago School, which begins with the presumption that markets are basically competitive, can be seen in recent court decisions, e.g., in allowing the merger of AT&T and Time Warner (currently under appeal). See also "Brief for 27 Antitrust Scholars as Amici Curiae in Support of Neither Party," United States Of America, Plaintiff-Appellant, v. AT&T Inc.; Directv Group Holdings, LLC; And Time Warner Inc., Defendants-Appellees. On Appeal from the United States District Court for the District of Columbia, No. 1:17-cv-2511 (Hon. Richard J. Leon). United States Court of Appeals for the District of Columbia Circuit, Document: #1745344. Filed: August 13, 2018.

75. This is another instance where what may be good for the individual may not be good for the economy and society. Risk-averse owners of a start-up are content at getting a reasonable payout for their efforts today, rather than bear the uncertainty of a risky market tomorrow. But society has a fundamental interest in maintaining a competitive marketplace.

76. In particular, the noncompete and nonpoaching provisions.

77. Some of the more innovative ways are discussed in chapter 6.

78. In Europe, there is a great deal of concern about maintaining a level playing field across countries, so that state aid in any form is prohibited, including through the kinds of tax benefits that Amazon sought.

79. See Joseph E. Stiglitz, "Economic Foundations of Intellectual Property Rights," *Duke Law Journal* 57 (2008): 1693–1724; and Claude Henry and Stiglitz, "Intellectual Property, Dissemination of Innovation, and Sustainable Development," *Global Policy* 1, no. 1 (2010): 237–51.

80. The Copyright Term Extension Act of 1998 extended copyrights to life of the author plus 70 years and extends corporate works to 95 years from the year of first publication or 120 years from the year of creation, whichever expires first. Standard economic theory suggests that these provisions have little if any incentive effect for the creation of new intellectual property, but obviously, once one has created something as durable as Mickey Mouse, it greatly enhances the rents that can be appropriated.

81. This example is discussed further in chapter 6.

82. "Declaration of Joseph E. Stiglitz and Jason Furman," Before the United States Department of Justice, Civil Action No 98-1232 (CKK) and Civil Action No 98-1233 (CKK). Available at https://www.justice.gov/sites/default/files/atr/legacy/2002/06/05/mtc-00030610c.pdf.

83. See, for instance, Andrea Prat, "Media Power," *Journal of Political Economy* 126, no. 4 (2018): 1747–83; and Andrea Prat, 2015, "Media Capture and Media Power," in *Handbook of Media Economics*, eds. Simon Anderson, Joel Waldfogel, and David Stromberg, vol. 1b (Amsterdam: North-Holland, 2015). See also Timothy Besley and Andrea Prat, "Handcuffs for the Grabbing Hand? The Role of the Media in Political Accountability," *American Economic Review*, 96, no. 3 (2006): 720–36.

84. Economists say that information is a "public good" that will be undersupplied in a market economy without government support. Having an active media not only has benefits to advertisers and consumers, but also to society more generally, and not just through having a more informed citizenry. The media play an important role in government accountability and curbing corruption.

85. The case of Sinclair Broadcast Group, for example, and its acquisitions of television stations throughout the country has been followed by changes in programming to highly conservative content. See Sheelah Kolhatkar, "The Growth of Sinclair's Conservative Media Empire," *The New Yorker*, Oct. 22, 2018.

86. Another arena in which market power needs to be judged by a higher standard is finance. In all economies, large banks and other financial institutions can exert disproportionate power.

87. Vincent Larivière, Stefanie Haustein, and Philippe Mongeon, "The Oligopoly of Academic Publishers in the Digital Era," *PLoS ONE* 10, no. 6 (2015): e0127502, https://doi.org/10.1371/journal .pone.0127502.

88. Research over the past half century has identified a large number of "market failures," circumstances in which markets fail to produce efficient outcomes, including the absence of perfect risk and capital markets and imperfect and asymmetric information. This chapter (and more broadly this book) has focused on one market failure—lack of competition—because I believe it is central to the maladies facing the economy.

89. CEO compensation in the US has increased enormously over the past four decades, and is much larger than in other advanced countries. These levels of compensation cannot be justified in terms of productivity—it's not that our CEOs are that much more productive than CEOs elsewhere, or our CEOs are that much more productive relative to workers today than they were forty years ago. (The average CEO pay among the top 350 companies in 2017 was more than 300 times that of the average compensation of their workers, up from 20 times in 1965. See Lawrence Mishel and Jessica Schieder, "CEO Compensation Surged in 2017," Economic Policy Institute, Aug. 16, 2018, available at https://www.epi.org/ publication/ceo-compensation-surged-in-2017/.) In comparison, Norway's CEOs earn only 20 times the average worker's pay. The US outranks every other country in the world, beating our neighbor to the north, Canada, by a sizable margin. Anders Melin and Wei Lu, "CEOs in U.S., India Earn the Most Compared with

Average Workers," *Bloomberg*, Dec. 28, 2017, available at https://www.bloomberg.com/news/articles/2017-12-28/ceos-in-u-s-india-earn-the-most-compared-with-average-workers.

90. I elaborate on this in chapter 8.

91. A sense of powerlessness has, for instance, multiple effects on health, including a greater incidence of depression. That it also has significant political consequences has been recently documented by a Stanford University study: Jojanneke van der Toorn, Matthew Feinberg, John T. Jost, Aaron C. Kay, Tom R. Tyler, Robb Willer, and Caroline Wilmuth, "A Sense of Powerlessness Fosters System Justification: Implications for the Legitimation of Authority, Hierarchy, and Government," *Political Psychology* 36, no. 1 (Feb. 2015).

92. Suits brought representing a large group of individuals (say, buyers of Microsoft programs) that are hurt by exploitive and illegal business practices. No single individual could or would bring a suit—the "injury" to each may be only a few hundred or thousand dollars, not enough to pay the legal bills that can go into the millions. But collectively, the damages can be enormous. The business community has campaigned to make it more difficult to bring such suits, knowing that without class action suits, they are basically immune to legal action by those they injure.

93. Song et al. in "Firming Up Inequality" show that increases in differences of compensation within a firm play an important role in growing wage inequality, though not as much as the increases in differences between firms, which, as noted, are largely accounted for by changes in the skill composition of firms.

94. For instance, measures to curb the power of corporate leaders could include requiring the disclosure of the ratio of executive pay to that of the average worker and the disclosure of the value of executive stock options to shareholders or giving shareholders more say in determining the pay of their executives. Even these mild reforms have (not surprisingly) met with enormous resistance from corporate executives, who worry that the result would be downward pressure on exorbitant executive compensation.

Another proposal receiving some attention recently is to incentivize firms to pay CEOs and top management less exorbitantly either by providing lower corporate income taxes for those corporations that do so or taxing the compensation itself at higher rates. At the very least, the special tax provisions that have encouraged stock options should be eliminated.

For a more extensive discussion of the issue and what might be done about it, see Stiglitz, *The Price of Inequality*; and Stiglitz, *The Roaring 90s*. Investor Stephen M. Silberstein has pushed, so far unsuccessfully, for legislation in California that would have tied corporate tax rates to CEO compensation; see also Gary Cohn, "Overcompensation: Tying Corporate Taxes to CEO Pay," *Capital & Main*, Aug. 6, 2014. Over the past few years, there have been a rash of popular books addressing the country's system of incentive pay and more broadly, its system of corporate governance. See, for instance, Steven Bavaria, *Too Greedy for Adam Smith: CEO Pay and the Demise of Capitalism*, 2nd ed. (Chestnut Ridge: Hungry Hollow Books, 2015); Michael Dorff, *Indispensable and Other Myths: Why the CEO Pay Experiment Failed and How to Fix It* (Berkeley: University of California Press, 2014); Steve Clifford, *The CEO Pay Machine: How it Trashes America and How to Stop it* (New York: Blue Rider Press, 2017); and Lynn Stout, *The Shareholder Value Myth: How Putting Shareholders First Harms Investors, Corporations, and the Public* (San Francisco: Berrett-Koehler, 2012).

95. This book emphasizes the role of market power—the increase of that of large corporations and CEOs, the domination of that of workers and consumers, and how we need to rewrite the rules of the market economy that have resulted in more power to CEOs and corporations and less power to workers and consumers. But these are representative of a larger set of changes to the rules of the game that have to be made if we are to achieve a more dynamic and equitable economy. See Stiglitz et al., *Rewriting the Rules of the American Economy*.

CHAPTER 4: AMERICA AT WAR WITH ITSELF OVER GLOBALIZATION

1. Deals that Trump repeatedly called "the worst ever."
2. Leading, for instance, to NAFTA (North American Free Trade Agreement) in 1994 or to the creation of the World Trade Organization in 1995. There are a host of other bilateral trade agreements, for instance between the US and Chile and the US and Korea.
3. For a popular account, see Daron Acemoglu and James A. Robinson, *Why Nations Fail: The Origins of Power, Prosperity, and Poverty* (New York: Crown Business, 2013).
4. Modern economic science had long established that without active government intervention, trade between countries with large wage differences would result in the lowering of wages in the advanced country. It had provided ample warning of what in fact has hap-

pened. (The results were first established by Paul Samuelson and Wolfgang Stolper in 1941 ("Protection and Real Wages," *Review of Economic Studies* 9, no. 1 [1941]: 58–73). See also Samuelson, "International Trade and the Equalisation of Factor Prices," *Economic Journal* 58, no. 230 [1948]: 163–84.

Thus, trade between the US and China has fundamentally different consequences than trade between two regions with roughly equal wages, such as Europe and the US. For a more extensive discussion of these issues, see Stiglitz, *Globalization and its Discontents Revisited* and *Making Globalization Work.*

5. See David H. Autor, David Dorn, and Gordon H. Hanson, "The China Syndrome: Local Labor Market Effects of Import Competition in the United States," *American Economic Review* 103, no. 6 (2013): 2121–68.

6. The list of problems with globalization is not meant to be complete. For instance, globalization often increases risk, in particular, increasing risks against which firms and households can't insure. For a fuller discussion, see Stiglitz, *Globalization and its Discontents Revisited.*

7. The relevant provisions are contained in investment agreements embedded in trade agreements, for instance, Chapter 11 of NAFTA. These provisions are now a standard part of all of our trade agreements, though they really are about investment, not trade. Not surprisingly, they were put there at the behest of large corporations, who have expressed opposition to any trade agreement that does not include them.

8. Decreases in the value of investments that arise when a regulation is changed are called regulatory takings. Congress and courts have consistently found that corporations in the US are not entitled to compensation for regulatory takings, but our investment agreements have provided for such compensation. Corporations are allowed to sue governments directly, and disputes are resolved through systems of arbitration where the corporations appoint one of the three arbitrators. This system has been justly criticized. See, for instance, Joseph E. Stiglitz, "Regulating Multinational Corporations: Towards Principles of Cross-Border Legal Frameworks in a Globalized World Balancing Rights with Responsibilities," *American University International Law Review*, 23, no. 3 (2007): 451–558, Grotius Lecture presented at the 101st Annual Meeting of the American Society for International Law, Washington, DC, Mar. 28, 2007; and "Towards a Twenty-first Century Investment Agree-

ment," Preface in *Yearbook on International Investment Law and Policy 2015–2016*, eds. Lise Johnson and Lisa Sachs (New York: Oxford University Press), xiii–xxviii, available at http://ccsi.columbia.edu/files/2014/03/YB-2015-16-Front-matter.pdf.

9. There is other evidence that globalization was designed to advance corporate interests, at the expense of workers and society more generally. The Republican advocates of globalization typically strongly opposed trade adjustment assistance—the kind of help to those displaced by globalization which would have ensured that globalization had fewer large losers. Anyone wanting to ensure broad long-term support for globalization would, of course, have wanted to do everything they could to reduce the likely opposition from those suffering greatly from globalization. Our corporate leaders, however, were more focused on the short-term gain in lower wages and worsening of working conditions that resulted from their stronger bargaining position.

   So too, the design of intellectual property provisions, especially those related to pharmaceuticals, increased profits of the pharmaceutical companies, at the expense of consumers and government (which picks up much of the resulting higher costs of medicine.)

10. These are called "inversions." Often, little changes other than the *official* headquarters. Where business actually occurs remains unchanged. The fact that these firms are so willing to move shows their deep lack of loyalty—their only true loyalty is to money and profits. Yet, the US government fights for their interests in international forums and in trade negotiations, showing once again the power of campaign contributions. The drug companies illustrate best what is at issue: the drugs give rise to few jobs; often they are manufactured in China, not the US. They have arranged their affairs to pay little taxes—they shift their patents to a low tax jurisdiction as part of a strategy of tax avoidance. Yet, central provisions of recent trade agreements—and the most controversial—are designed to disadvantage generic medicines, resulting in higher profits for Big Pharma. Thus, American citizens are actually hurt as a result of the higher prices. Even Obama, who prided himself in his efforts to lower the cost of medicine, in the TPP (the Trans-Pacific Partnership Agreement) betrayed his principles.

11. The race to the bottom takes many other forms: banks, for instance, said that unless regulations were loosened, they would relocate their activities elsewhere. The result was a regulatory

race to the bottom. The 2008 global financial crisis was among its consequences.

12. Taxes are only one of many variables that affect where firms locate, as we have already noted. But even focusing just on taxes, lowering taxes will induce firms to relocate if the country from which we are trying to steal jobs doesn't respond. If they lower their taxes, we get no advantage. At the end, the only winners from this race to the bottom are the corporations who stirred up this race in the first place.

13. See chapters 1 and 9 for some of the evidence and the theoretical analyses that explain why these tax measures did not have the benefits claimed by their advocates.

14. In part, because of the large deficit that the tax cut will generate, in part because the bill favored real estate speculation and discouraged economic activity in the most dynamic parts of the economy, and especially their investments in infrastructure and education. Standard modeling suggests that the level of gross national income (taking into account that to finance the deficits, we will have to borrow abroad, and that the higher level of national debt will crowd out some private investment) in ten years, in 2027, will likely be at or below current levels. I am indebted to Jason Furman, chairman of President Obama's Council of Economic Advisers, for these calculations, based on joint work with Robert Barro of Harvard University (personal correspondence).

15. The effective corporate tax rate was 18.6 percent. "International Comparisons of Corporate Income Tax Rates," CBO, Mar. 8, 2017, available at https://www.cbo.gov/publication/52419.

16. When the EU got wind of Apple's secret deal with Ireland, it ordered Apple to pay 13 billion euro (a little more than 14.5 billion dollars).

17. The extent of the use of these secrecy havens for tax avoidance, money laundering, and other nefarious activities was exposed by the release of two treasure troves of documents by the Investigative Consortium of Investigative Journalists, one called the Panama Papers, which mostly had documents from law firm Mossack Fonseca, the other the Paradise papers, which had documents from law firm Appleby.

18. While it's clear that, accordingly, the banks and their corporate and ultra-rich clients will resist tamping down on these fiscal paradises, it's also clear that it can be done. After 9/11 the US became concerned about their use for terrorism, and successfully managed to

greatly narrow the use of the fiscal paradises for these purposes. In fact, there has been some progress both in curbing some of the worst extremes, with large fines imposed against some banks for egregious activities involved in tax evasion. These successes have shown, however, how much more could and should have been done.

19. Such changes in technology are referred to as "skilled-biased." While toward the end of the twentieth century, much of the increase in inequality was blamed on skill-biased technological change, there is a growing consensus that it can account for only a fraction of the increase in inequality over the past two decades. Even skilled workers are having a hard time. See, for example, the discussion of skill-biased technological change in Piketty, *Capital in the 21st Century*, and John Schmitt, Heidi Shierholz, and Lawrence Mishel, "Don't Blame the Robots: Assessing the Job Polarization Explanation of Growing Wage Inequality" (Economic Policy Institute, November 19, 2013).

There's a deeper question: with unemployment among the unskilled already so high and their wages so low, why has our market economy proceeded to innovate in ways that increase their unemployment and lower their wages? Something is wrong with an innovation system that rather than directing research at real societal needs—such as saving the planet from climate change—exacerbates existing social problems.

There is an old and distinguished literature, dating back to the 1960s, explaining the direction of technological change, whether it increases the productivity of skilled or unskilled labor, capital or natural resources. See Emmanuel M. Drandakis and Edmond S. Phelps, "A Model of Induced Invention, Growth, and Distribution," *Economic Journal* 76 (Dec. 1966): 832–40; William Fellner, "Two Propositions in the Theory of Induced Innovations, *The Economic Journal* 71, no. 282 (1961): 305–8; Charles Kennedy, "Induced Bias in Innovation and the Theory of Distribution," *Economic Journal* 74, no. 295 (1964): 541–7; and Paul A. Samuelson, "A Theory of Induced Innovation along Kennedy-Weisäcker Lines," *The Review of Economics and Statistics* 47, no. 4 (1965): 343–56. More recently, I have attempted to explain why market solutions are typically inefficient, putting too little emphasis on saving natural resources and too much emphasis on saving labor and especially unskilled labor. These problems have been exacerbated by monetary policies in the post-2008 crisis world, which have reduced the cost of capital, making it relatively more attractive to save labor.

20. This, of course, also contributed greatly to the increase in inequality. See David H. Autor, Alan Manning, and Christopher L. Smith, "The Contribution of the Minimum Wage to US Wage Inequality over Three Decades: A Reassessment," *American Economic Journal: Applied Economics* 8, no. 1 (2016): 58–99. The latter finds that about a third of the growth in US inequality between the median and the bottom 10 percent is due to the declining real value of the minimum wage.

21. Tariffs, by increasing the costs of imports, discourage trade. But there are a host of other provisions that make imports less competitive. Agriculture goods are often excluded because they don't meet our "phyto-sanitary conditions." Europe's regulations concerning genetic modified organisms (GMO), discussed below, similarly make it difficult for American wheat and corn farmers to export there. Many of these regulations are justified—they reflect genuine societal concerns about health and safety. However, some of these regulations are imposed mainly to discourage imports. Distinguishing the two situations is often difficult.

22. Though calling the agreement "partnerships" was itself somewhat misleading. It was a partnership where the US dictated almost all the terms. The name of trade agreements has long been famously misrepresentative. NAFTA, the North American *Free Trade* Agreement, was not a free trade agreement, which entails the elimination of all barriers to free trade, including subsidies. The US kept all of its massive agricultural subsidies. TPP was often referred to as a free trade agreement, but its 6000 pages with specific agreements affecting myriad sectors shows that this and other trade agreements more appropriately should be viewed as *managed* trade agreements.

23. See "Trans-Pacific Partnership Agreement: Likely Impact on the U.S. Economy and on Specific Industry Sectors" (United States Trade International Commission, Investigation No. TPA-105-001, USITC Publication 4607, 2016). Another study found negative effects for growth of the US economy. Jeronim Capaldo, Alex Izurieta, and Jomo Kwame Sundaram, "Trading Down: Unemployment, Inequality and Other Risks of the Trans-Pacific Partnership Agreement" (Global Development and Environment Institute working paper 16-01, Tufts University, 2016). The usual champions of trade liberalization found, perhaps not surprisingly, somewhat larger positive effects than the US government did, at least by 2030: Peter A. Petri and Michael G. Plummer (Peterson Institute for International Economics) and the World Bank both

estimated that the TPP would increase annual GDP by 0.5 by 2030. See World Bank Group, *Global Economic Prospects: Spillovers amid Weak Growth. A World Bank Group Flagship Report* (Washington, DC: World Bank, 2016), 219–34.

24. It is worth noting the use of language: by referring to intellectual property *rights*, it gave to these provisions a standing similar to that of human rights—even as the consequence of IPR, by raising prices of life-saving medicines to a level that made them unaffordable to many in the developing world and emerging markets, was to deny the most fundamental right, the right to live. By referring to them as *Trade Related* Intellectual Property Rights, it seemed to give legitimacy to including them in a trade agreement, even though the provisions affected intellectual property of goods whether traded or not, and even though there was an already existing international body that was supposed to be setting international standards for intellectual property, WIPO (the World Intellectual Property Organization) in Geneva.

    While the pharmaceutical industry has provided the major impetus for the IPR provisions in trade agreements, it is not alone. Entertainment (films) played a particularly important role in shaping provisions related to copyright. See the earlier discussion of "Mickey Mouse."

25. Interestingly, when the US dropped out of TPP, the remaining countries proceeded with a trade agreement, now called the Comprehensive and Progressive Agreement for Trans-Pacific Partnership, and they dropped the most noxious health provisions that the US had insisted upon.

26. The intellectual property regime has resulted in a drain of money out of developing countries and emerging markets to pay for the use of intellectual property. The US received more than $17 billion in royalties and licensing fees from developing countries in 2016 (author's calculation based on data from the United States International Trade Commission).

27. Traditional knowledge includes that related to foods (a US company was granted a patent on India's traditional food, basmati rice) and medicines (US patents were granted for medicinal uses of turmeric and neem oil, well known in traditional Indian medicine).

    TRIPS and similar provisions in subsequent trade agreements also adversely affected developing countries in other ways, including in provisions related to agriculture (seeds). See, for instance, Mario Cimoli, Giovanni Dosi, Keith E. Maskus, Ruth L. Okediji,

Jerome H. Reichman, and Joseph E. Stiglitz (eds.), *Intellectual Property Rights: Legal and Economic Challenges for Development* (Oxford: Oxford University Press, 2014).

28. When Trump finally figured that out, he ordered his Secretary of Treasury to reverse long-standing policies that the US believed in a "strong" dollar. As he tried haltingly to enunciate this new policy, havoc broke out in the exchange rate market, but only for a short while. The words of the secretary of the treasury, or even the president (even a president who is taken seriously) typically affect markets only for a short while, before underlying economic forces restore their dominance.

29. Thus, in March 2018, Trump announced 25 percent tariffs against foreign steel from certain countries: this increases the price Americans who want to buy steel from these countries have to pay by 25 percent. China's sales were essentially cut off.

30. The fiscal and trade deficits typically move so closely together that they are often referred to as the twin deficits. There are a few instances where this does not happen because of other ongoing changes in the economy. When the US lowered its fiscal deficit in the 1990s, the trade deficit did not come down in tandem because of the boom in investment that was occurring simultaneously.

31. With or without new trade agreements, in a limited number of niche markets, there will be some return of manufacturing (sometimes called onshoring), as new technologies, such as 3-D printing, allow some production to occur closer to the point of consumption.

32. As we have noted, Trump's policies, taken as a whole, are likely to increase the trade deficit (from what it otherwise would be). Not surprisingly, then, in spite of Trump's promise to reduce the trade deficit, in his first year in office it increased by more than 10 percent, from $502 billion in 2016 to $552 billion in 2017. There are, of course, many other factors that impinge on both the exchange rate and the trade deficit. If, for instance, there is pessimism about the future of the country, those in the country may try to get their money out of the country, and this will drive down the exchange rate. Thus, investors worried about the implications of a large fiscal deficit for the future of the economy may try to take their money out of the country, and thus the short-run impact of the passage of legislation creating a larger fiscal deficit may be to depress the exchange rate. Over the medium term, however, the forces we have just described tend to dominate.

33. Professor Lawrence J. Lau, in *The China–U.S. Trade War and Future*

Economic Relations (Hong Kong: Chinese University Press, 2018), has shown that focusing on value added reduces the magnitude of the apparent bilateral trade deficit by 40 percent. (By the same token, with a low fraction of value added in China, a 25 percent tariff will induce many companies to relocate at least the final stages of production.) He estimates that the impact on the Chinese economy of the US trade war will be at most to reduce GDP by just over 1 percentage point, easily absorbed in an economy growing at more than 6 percent a year.

34. The *Washington Post* conducted a poll with George Mason University that showed 56 percent of US voters thought the trade war was bad for US jobs. See Aaron Blake, "How Trump's Trade War with China Could Go Sideways on Him," *Washington Post*, July 7, 2018.

35. There have been two other complaints concerning China's stance on intellectual property. One is that it refuses to enforce conventional IPR. While these charges were common a decade or so ago, they are heard less often today, perhaps because Chinese firms themselves are getting an increasing number of patents, and want strong enforcement. The second is cybertheft. While under the Obama administration, there was an agreement to curtail this, it appears not currently being enforced. Because it is done secretly, it is hard to know the magnitude on either side, but it appears to be significant and growing. US complaints about intellectual property rights conflates these three different issues, and would be more effective if attention were directed particularly at cybertheft.

36. The irony is that it might have been possible to reach an international investment agreement that addressed such issues but American negotiators, representing interests of their business community, "overreached," demanding not just protection against discrimination, but also compensation for changes in, say, regulations.

37. Chinese firms receive about ten times as many US patents as they did ten years ago. See Susan Decker, "China Becomes One of the Top 5 U.S. Patent Recipients for the First Time," *Bloomberg*, Jan. 9, 2018.

38. Critics of the US position also noted that it is hypocritical: the US stole or took advantage of others' intellectual property (sometimes unintentionally) in the nineteenth and early twentieth centuries, e.g., the Bessemer process for making steel (See Philip W. Bishop, *The Beginnings of Cheap Steel* [Project Guttenberg, http://www .gutenberg.org/files/29633/29633-h/29633-h.htm]). The critical innovation in flight was by a Brazilian, done years earlier, not

the Wright Brothers. So too for many of the important advances that led to the automobile. Now that the US has climbed up the ladder, it wants to make it more difficult for others to follow, the central message in Ha-Joon Chang's forceful book, *Kicking Away the Ladder: Development Strategy in Historical Perspective* (New York: Anthem, 2002).

39. Of course, there are always concerns about "unfair" trade practices, and the WTO rules were designed to provide a basic set of rules to prevent such practices. When a country violates these rules, it can be brought to "court," to a WTO tribunal, and if it is found guilty, either it stops the practices or the trade partner is allowed to impose commensurate tariffs and other trade restrictions. Sometimes, there are mutual accusations: the US believes that Europe unfairly subsidizes Airbus, and Europe believes that US unfairly subsidizes Boeing. The problem is that the two countries have taken quite different approaches to subsidies. Many regulations that are imposed because they reflect domestic concerns are viewed by others as an unfair trade barrier, as we noted in our discussion of GMOs.

40. There are many other provisions of these investment agreements that need to change, including the system of dispute resolution. There should be a requirement that domestic courts be used before turning to the special provisions of the investment agreement. This is especially important in investment agreements with other advanced countries, where there is a presumption that they have good judicial systems. If there is a problem, it should be addressed symmetrically, for both domestic and foreign investors. There also needs to be a change in the magnitude of compensation in the event of a violation—now it is based on the amorphous idea of what profits would otherwise have been, rather than simply compensation for lost investment. See Stiglitz, "Towards a Twenty-First-Century Investment Agreement."

41. I experienced an extreme example of the closed-mindedness of the USTR during the negotiations of the Trans-Pacific Partnership. I was concerned about the adverse effects of the provisions on the availability of generic medicines. I succeeded in arranging a meeting with all of the negotiators in this area—except with those from the United States.

42. There are hardened individuals who suggest that we shouldn't help these individuals. Some hundred years ago, there was a notion called "Social Darwinism," which held that society was better off

if we just let those who couldn't fend for themselves suffer. The motto was "survival of the fittest." Not only were these doctrines inhumane, but also the analyses that suggested that such policies would be beneficial were based on a totally incorrect interpretation of Darwin's evolutionary theories.

43. Sometimes, industrial policies are viewed as protectionist—when their intent is to protect old, dying industries, as Trump is trying to do. The kinds of industrial policies I am advocating are just the opposite—trying to help the economy move into new sectors, to adapt to changing markets and technology. There needs to be strong oversight to ensure that industrial policies are not abused to protect incumbent firms against competition, another form of rent-seeking.

CHAPTER 5: FINANCE AND THE AMERICAN CRISIS

1. Later in the chapter, I describe one of the early attempts to undo key parts of Dodd-Frank. In 2018, banks with less than $250 billion in assets were removed from the tighter oversight provided by Dodd-Frank.

   Every step along the way, the banks put up resistance. As one regulator put it to me: if there is any space between the wall and the wallpaper, the banks will take advantage of it. And they work hard to make sure that there is plenty of space between the two.

2. Since the crisis, two of the major participants in the rescue— Geithner and Federal Reserve Chair Ben Bernanke (both Republicans, appointed by Obama)—have written their memoirs. (Ben Bernanke, *The Courage to Act* [New York: W. W. Norton, 2015]; Timothy F. Geithner, *Stress Test: Reflections on Financial Crises* [New York: Broadway Books, 2014].) Their weak defenses of what they did—widely noted in the reviews of the two books (see, e.g., "Does He Pass the Test?" by Paul Krugman, *New York Review of Books*, July 10, 2014; "More Talk, More Action," *The Economist*, Oct. 17, 2015)—reinforces the view that it was a rescue in which the financial sector's interests were placed at the top, and the rest of the country's interests below.

3. Many of the ideas in this section are elaborated in my book *Freefall*.

4. I should note, our bankers were not alone: Trump demonstrated even worse behavior in his business dealings and in Trump University. Nor were the problems limited to the US. Some of the worst banking practices were found abroad.

The extensive cheating by car companies as they pretended that their products were more environmentally sound than they were shows that moral turpitude was not limited to finance. Still, in the sheer dollar value of the fraudulent and dishonest activities, the financial sector wins out. The Bernie Madoff pyramid scheme alone represented some $65 billion missing from individuals' accounts. And because the financial sector touches virtually every other sector of the economy, the financial sector spread the virus through much of the economy.

5. Thus, as the complex securities such as residential backed mortgage securities (RMBS) developed, for these securities containing thousands of mortgages to work, the originators and investments had to issue what could be viewed as equivalent to a money-back guarantee: banks had agreed to buy back any mortgages that were not as represented to those who had invested in or insured the securities. It was virtually the only way that the insurers and investors had any confidence in what they were insuring or buying. When it turned out that many mortgages were not as represented (for instance, a mortgage for a property that was described as owner-occupied was in fact for one that was a rental), the banks often refused to do as they had promised. It made a difference because the default rates on owner-occupied properties are much lower. Eventually, at least in several instances, after years and years, the banks paid what was due. (For full disclosure: I was an expert witness in some of the resulting lawsuits. More than a decade after the events, the litigation goes on.)

6. At a congressional hearing, Senator Carl Levin told Goldman's CEO and Chairman Lloyd Blankfein that he "wouldn't trust" Goldman, as he repeatedly asked whether the bank would disclose its position "when they're buying something you solicit them to buy, and then you're taking a position against them?" "I don't believe there is any obligation" to tell investors, Mr. Blankfein responded. See James Quinn, "Goldman Boss Lloyd Blankfein Denies Moral Obligation towards Clients," *Telegraph*, Apr. 28, 2010. The full exchange can be viewed on C-Span. Blankfein's prepared comments and a video of the hearing can also be found on the website of the Homeland Security and Governmental Affairs Permanent Subcommittee on Investigations, accessed July 23, 2018, https://www.hsgac.senate .gov/subcommittees/investigations/hearings/-wall-street-and-the -financial-crisis-the-role-of-investment-banks.

7. Taking that position may indeed be part of Goldman Sachs's short-

sightedness: they saw the possibility of making the money on the trade today. They discounted the future loss of profits from the loss of reputation.

8. *Financing SMEs and Entrepreneurs 2018*, OECD. The figures on US loans to SMEs refer to the stock of outstanding business loans. Strikingly, the proportion of loans going to small businesses has also dramatically declined, from 30.1 percent in 2007 to 18.5 percent in 2016.

9. It was founded by five leading emerging markets, Brazil, Russia, India, China, and South Africa, a grouping called (after their initials) the BRICS.

10. Back in 1996, effective reform of the welfare system was stymied because of the lack of just $5 billion per year for training and childcare of those who were being pushed off of welfare. Two decades later, in fiscal year 2015, spending under the US program for needy families (called TANF, Temporary Assistance for Families in Need), was just $16.5 billion.

11. They succeeded in getting this provision passed by a sophisticated legislative maneuver, attaching it to a bill that had to be passed to keep the government open. See Erika Eichelberger, "Citigroup Wrote the Wall Street Giveaway the House Just Approved," *Mother Jones*, Dec. 10, 2014.

12. Several banks have been fined heavily for stepping over the line. Credit Suisse, for instance, paid a $2.6 billion fine. Foreign banks rightly complain that the US government has been more assiduous at going after them rather than American banks for wrongdoing.

13. These advantages occur because most of the money received is taxed as capital gains rather than as dividends.

14. The wealthy recipients of this money will consume a little; they may spend some on real estate—inflating real estate prices; they may diversify their portfolio, investing abroad. They may take some of this and gamble, buying derivatives and CDSs (credit default swaps). Or they may channel some of this money into new productive investments elsewhere in the economy. The worry is that a much smaller fraction of corporate profits gets redeployed in real economic investment in the US, one of the reasons for the fall in the nation's investment rate.

15. The total flow of funds out of firms (dividends plus share buybacks) doubled from less than 3 percent of GDP in the '60s to around 6 percent in more recent years. Since 2005, share buybacks by non-financial corporations have exceeded net capital formation. See

Lester Gunnion, "Behind the Numbers," *Deloitte Insights*, Nov. 2017, based on data from the Bureau of Economic Analysis. The fact that there has been an overall trend of increasing share buybacks and decreasing corporate investment doesn't, on its own, imply that one caused the other. Indeed, both can be thought of as manifestations of the increased market power discussed in chapter 3, which simultaneously increased profits and reduced, at the margin, incentives to invest.

16. As of December 6, 2018, US companies had announced $969 billion in share buybacks, which was expected to cross $1 trillion by end of the year. See Michael Schoonover, "Will the Record-Setting Buyback Trend Continue in 2019?," *Catalyst Fund Buyback Blog*, Dec. 7, 2018. Given that so much of the benefit of the tax cut went to share buybacks and dividends, it was no surprise that investment didn't increase much and workers' compensation, hardly at all. The Economic Policy Institute estimated that workers' bonuses resulting from the tax cut gave workers 2 cents more per hour during 2018. In the 145 companies in the Russell 1000 that had announced how they were spending their tax savings by December 10, 2018, just 6 percent went to workers. (https://justcapital.com/tax-reform -weekly-updates/). Remarkably, a year after the passage of the tax bill, and the enormous giveaway to corporations, not even the stock market was higher, and the CBO was estimating that growth will be slowing to 1.6 percent from 2020 through 2022. See *Vox*, "Republican Tax Cut Bill One Year Later: What It Did—and Didn't—Do," https://www.vox.com/policy-and . . . /tax-cuts-and-jobs-act-stock-market-economy.

17. In the modern literature, these are referred to as the adverse incentive and adverse selection effects of increasing interest rates. See, e.g., Joseph E. Stiglitz and Andrew Weiss, "Credit Rationing in Markets with Imperfect Information," *American Economic Review* 71, no. 3 (1981): 393–410.

18. Though it had its origins back in the early 1990s. See Vitaly M. Bord and Joao A. C. Santos, "The Rise of the Originate-to-Distribute Model and the Role of Banks In Financial Intermediation," *Federal Reserve Bank of New York Policy Review*, July 2012, 21–34, available at https://www.newyorkfed.org/medialibrary/media/research/epr/12v18n2/1207bord.pdf.

19. The role of reserves can be seen quite simply. Assume the bank has deposits of $1000 and lends $1000, but a net worth of $100 held in

reserves; if more than 10 percent of the loans go bad, it gets back less than $900, which with the $100 in reserves, is insufficient to repay the depositors. There will have to be a government bailout. If the bank had taken in $10,000 in deposits and lent out the same amount, a mere 1 percent failure of loans to be repaid would result in the bank being in trouble of not paying back depositors. Before the crisis, reserve requirements were so low that a small level of nonrepayment could present a problem.

20. His remark became the title of the popular 2011 movie "The Flaw" on the financial crisis, directed by David Singington.

21. This is only one of the areas of misalignment of incentives. Bankers and others in the financial sector make more money the more transactions that occur. They like "transaction costs" and fees, for it is out of these that much of their profits are derived. Of course, the higher the fees, the worse off the banks' customers. In a competitive market with fully informed rational customers, bankers couldn't get away with overcharging, but financial markets are far from this ideal.

When bankers get hold of an account to manage on someone else's behalf, they like to churn the account, buying and selling, claiming that they are always trying to put money where it will get the highest return. The evidence is to the contrary: a monkey throwing darts could pick stocks as well as most investment managers. But the monkey is at least honest. In the case of asset managers, there are conflicts of interest. They make more money putting the money into one mutual fund than another because they get a bigger commission, and they certainly make more money the more the money is churned. When the Obama administration proposed that certain asset managers be subject to a fiduciary standard—where they would have to act in the best interests of their clients—there was a hue and cry from the bankers and wealth managers, who claimed that they simply couldn't survive with this fiduciary standard, that is, if they couldn't from time to time take advantage of their customers. They were shameless in admitting that they couldn't commit to serve the best interests of their clients. The bankers saw nothing wrong with having conflicts of interest, as they enriched themselves—by an estimated $17 billion per year—at the expense of retirees. Like Goldman Sachs's Blankfein's admission earlier, this represents the new immorality of the financial sector, and a disregard for reputation.

22. Milton Friedman, the high priest of the Chicago School to whom

we referred earlier, was asserting these positions, even as advances in economics were explaining why shareholder value maximization does not, in general, lead to societal well-being. See, for instance, Sanford Grossman and Joseph E. Stiglitz, "On Value Maximization and Alternative Objectives of the Firm," *Journal of Finance* 32, no. 2 (1977): 389–402; and "Stockholder Unanimity in the Making of Production and Financial Decisions," *Quarterly Journal of Economics* 94, no. 3 (1980): 543–66.

23. See Tooze, *Crashed*.

24. The Republican tax bill has pushed profits even higher. For example, Bank of America's quarterly earnings in the first three months of 2018 were nearly $7 billion, the highest ever. Even as profits surged, Bank of America's tax bill decreased some 26 percent because of the new law. See Matt Egan, "Big Banks Are Minting Money Right Now," *CNN Money*, Apr. 18, 2018.

25. In the 2016 Democratic primary, there was a foolish debate about whether the crucial issue was the too-big-to-fail banks and restoring some version of Glass–Steagall, which had separated commercial banking from investment banking, or the shadow banking system. The correct answer is that we needed reforms in *both*. See, e.g., Stiglitz, *Freefall*; Commission of Experts on Reforms of the International Monetary and Financial System appointed by the President of the United Nations General Assembly, *The Stiglitz Report: Reforming the International Monetary and Financial Systems in the Wake of the Global Crisis* (New York: The New Press, 2010); Simon Johnson and James Kwak, *13 Bankers: The Wall Street Takeover and the Next Financial Meltdown* (New York: Random House, 2010); and Rana Foroohar, *Makers and Takers: How Wall Street Destroyed Main Street* (New York: Crown, 2016).

CHAPTER 6: THE CHALLENGE OF NEW TECHNOLOGIES

1. Google's Go-playing computer program AlphaGo, developed by the tech giant's AI company, DeepMind, beat Go world champion Lee Se-dol in March 2016. See Choe Sang-Hun, "Google's Computer Program Beats Lee Se-dol in Go Tournament," *New York Times*, Mar. 15, 2016. A year and a half later, Google announced the release of a program with even larger AI capabilities. See Sarah Knapton, "AlphaGo Zero: Google DeepMind Supercomputer Learns 3,000 Years of Human Knowledge in 40 Days," *Telegraph*, Oct. 18, 2017.

2. Robert J. Gordon, *The Rise and Fall of American Growth: The US Standard of Living since the Civil War* (Princeton: Princeton University Press, 2016). I should hasten to add that not all scholars agree with Gordon. Joel Mokyr, a distinguished economic historian, like Gordon at Northwestern University, takes a much more optimistic view. See, for instance, Joel Mokyr, "The Next Age of Invention: Technology's Future Is Brighter than Pessimists Allow," *City Journal* (Winter 2014): 12–20. Some suggest that there are significant measurement errors in GDP, so that it underestimates the true rate of growth, but in my judgment, while there are significant measurement problems, they do not change the overall picture, in particular, the pace of increase in GDP today is lower than it was in earlier periods. Of course, by its very nature, we cannot be sure about the future pace of innovation.

3. Referred to as the "singularity." See also Stanislaw Ulam, "Tribute to John von Neumann," *Bulletin of the American Mathematical Society* 64, no. 3, part 2 (1958): 5. See also Anton Korinek and Joseph E. Stiglitz, "Artificial Intelligence and Its Implications for Income Distribution and Unemployment," in *Economics of Artificial Intelligence* (Chicago: University of Chicago Press, forthcoming).

4. Rapid advances in artificial intelligence in the last five years has led to extensive speculation about when AI will exceed human performance in a range of jobs. A survey of AI experts predicts that by 2024, AI will be better than humans at translating languages, and by 2027 at driving a truck. These experts believe there is a 50 percent chance of AI outperforming humans in all tasks in 45 years. See Katja Grace, John Salvatier, Allan Dafoe, Baobao Zhang, and Owain Evans, *Journal of Artificial Intelligence Research* (2018), arXiv:1705.08807.

5. See Carl B. Frey and Michael A. Osborne, "The Future of Employment: How Susceptible Are Jobs to Computerisation?," *Technological Forecasting and Social Change* 114 (2017): 254–80. Also see the book by Erik Brynjolfsson and Andrew McAfee, *Race against the Machine* (Lexington: Digital Frontier Press, 2011).

6. For one version of this story, see "Difference Engine: Luddite Legacy," *The Economist*, Nov. 4, 2011.

7. See Stiglitz, *The Great Divide*, 393–403, based on earlier research by Domenico Delli Gatti, Mauro Gallegati, Bruce Greenwald, Alberto Russo, and me, "Mobility Constraints, Productivity Trends, and Extended Crises," *Journal of Economic Behavior & Organization* 83, no. 3 (2012): 375–93; and "Sectoral Imbalances and

Long Run Crises," in *The Global Macro Economy and Finance*, eds. Franklin Allen, Masahiko Aoki, Jean-Paul Fitoussi, Nobuhiro Kiyotaki, Roger Gordon, and Joseph E. Stiglitz, International Economic Association World Conference vol. 150-III (Houndmills, UK and New York: Palgrave, 2012), 61–97.

8. As an example of declining agricultural prices during this period, consider wheat, whose price declined some 60 percent in the early 1920s; the early 1930s saw another decrease of some 70 percent. "The Wheat Situation," Bureau of Agricultural Economics, US Department of Agriculture, WS-61, Nov. 1941.

9. See Delli Gatti et al., "Mobility Constraints, Productivity Trends, and Extended Crises." Other studies have found decreases in income of a similarly impressive scale. See "Wages and Income of Farm Workers, 1909 to 1938," *Monthly Labor Review* 49, no. 1 (1939): 59–71; this paper suggests a fall in income of over 50 percent.

10. For a discussion of the declining land values during the period, see "Publications: Trends in U.S. Agriculture: Land Values," United States Bureau of Agriculture, National Agricultural Statistics Service, accessed July 2, 2018, available at https://www.nass.usda.gov/Publications/Trends_in_U.S._Agriculture/Land_Values/index.php.

11. There can be a mismatch between the skills needed and the skills workers currently have. If so, retraining programs can help provide workers with the requisite skills. But this mismatch hasn't been the key feature in recent years; if it were, wages of skilled workers would be rising much more rapidly than they have been.

12. I say nasty politics, because when the Republicans saw the opportunity to help their own party and those rich corporations and billionaires who supported them, they threw aside all ideological commitments to balanced budgets, commitments that had seemingly prevented them from supporting the fiscal policies that would have allowed us to more quickly emerge from the Great Recession.

13. There was a trade-off: a short-term increase in the demand for labor as a result of the increased investment, and a longer-term decrease as machines replaced workers. The lower interest rates also reduced consumption of those elderly dependent on interest from government bonds.

14. By the same token, changes in the structure of the labor market— the gig economy—may result in jobs that are insecure and without good benefits.

15. In many of these sectors, wages are low because the jobs were traditionally gendered, and there was systematic wage discrimination against women.

16. The defenders of Big Tech's use of Big Data also argue that it allows them to steer individuals to products that better meet their needs. Putting aside the Big Brother aspects of this "steering," it should be clear that the motive is not to make individuals happier but to increase Big Tech's profits and that of the companies that advertise on their sites. Unfortunately, as the discussion below will illustrate, there are many uses of Big Data that disadvantage consumers as a whole, and especially informationally disadvantaged consumers. Some have referred to the market economy that is evolving using Big Data as *surveillance capitalism*. See, for instance, John Bellamy Foster and Robert W. McChesney, "Surveillance Capitalism," *Monthly Review*, July 1, 2014; Shoshana Zuboff, "Big Other: Surveillance Capitalism and the Prospects of an Information Civilization," *Journal of Information Technology 30*, no. 1 (2015): 75–89; and Shoshana Zuboff, *The Age of Surveillance Capitalism* (New York: Public Affairs, 2019).

17. "Perfect" price discrimination is the practice of trying to charge each consumer the maximum he is willing to pay for a good or service. In each market for a good or service, there are potential buyers—consumers—who would be willing to pay a range of prices for the same item, depending on their preferences and means. Take a pair of fashionable shoes that costs $100 to produce. There are consumers who are only willing to pay $1 for the shoes, others who would pay $500, and many in between. A firm can maximize its profits by selling shoes to all consumers who are willing to pay more than $100, *at the maximum price that each consumer is willing to pay*. Some pay $101, others $200, and a handful will pay $500. Firms use different methods to discriminate among the consumers willing to buy their products: branding, sales, and discounts for certain groups are examples. Such discrimination adds nothing to society—it is just a way to extract as much money from consumers as possible. Economists technically refer to this as "extracting consumer surplus," that is, grabbing for the corporation as much of the total value of the good to the individual as possible. Charging different prices for different individuals unrelated to costs was made illegal under the Robinson-Patman Act of 1936, but the act has rarely been enforced. For a discussion of price discrimination in the context of Big Data, see Silvia Merler, "Big Data

and First-Degree Price Discrimination," *Bruegel*, Feb. 20, 2017, available at http://bruegel.org/2017/02/big-data-and-first-degree -price-discrimination/.

18. The standard argument for efficiency of markets is based on the notion that individuals' *marginal* valuation of a good are the same and the same as the marginal cost, and this is true because they all face the same prices. While there can still be market efficiency if there is *perfect* price discrimination, the real world of imperfect price discrimination is marked by pervasive inefficiencies and distortions. See, e.g., Stiglitz, "Monopoly, Non-Linear Pricing and Imperfect Information: The Insurance Market," *Review of Economic Studies* 44, no. 3 (1977): 407–30. Reprinted in *Selected Works of Joseph E. Stiglitz, Volume I: Information and Economic Analysis* (Oxford: Oxford University Press, 2009), 168–92.

   AI also results in information asymmetries. Some firms know more than others, and the Big Tech firms know more than consumers. Markets are only efficient in the absence of distortionary asymmetries in information, whether those were natural or created by the market. Big Data is increasing these asymmetries, and thereby potentially making resource allocations less efficient.

19. Jennifer Valentino-DeVries, Jeremy Singer-Vine, and Ashkan Soltani, "Websites Vary Prices, Deals Based on Users' Information," *Wall Street Journal*, Dec. 24, 2012.

20. To use the colorful language of Nobel Prize winners George Akerlof and Robert Shiller, to "phish for phools." See Akerlof and Shiller, *Phishing for Phools*.

21. See Tüfekçi's TED talk, "We're Building a Dystopia Just to Make People Click on Ads," Oct. 27, 2017.

22. Others joined in the suit against Myriad, including the University of Pennsylvania and researchers at Columbia, NYU, Emory, and Yale. The American Civil Liberties Union and the Public Patent Foundation provided legal representation for the plaintiffs. I wrote an expert report for the plaintiffs on the economics of the case, arguing that the removal of the patent would stimulate innovation. What happened subsequently was consistent with my analysis.

23. The government has the power to get access to data that is in private hands when it wants to; in the US, it's harder than in some other countries, like China, but we shouldn't pretend that there's an iron wall between the two. And, equally worrying, in the absence of constraints, the private sector has a greater incentive to use and abuse the data for commercial reasons.

24. George Orwell, *1984* (New York: Harcourt, Brace, 1949); Dave Eggers, *The Circle* (New York: Alfred A. Knopf, 2015).

25. See Greenwald and Stiglitz, *Creating a Learning Society*, and the works cited there.

26. Many in the tech sector say simply: "Leave it to us. We're smart. We created the problem. We'll solve it. All that is required is a little self-regulation. We can police ourselves." We heard this before. The banks said exactly the same thing, and we know where that got us. It should be obvious that one can't just leave it to the private sector. Their incentives are not well aligned with the rest of society. Their interest is in profits, not societal well-being.

27. In its GDPR (General Data Protection Regulation). While it is an important first step, it is far from sufficient to address the issues we've discussed.

28. For instance, the Trump administration has accused Europe of using its privacy policies to create a trade barrier.

29. Equifax provided information to others about an individual's credit standing. There is no regulatory structure to ensure that a firm like Equifax has adequate security. Firms are shortsighted—focusing on profits today. Spending money increasing security lowers profits today, so there is a strong incentive to underspend on security, in the absence of adequate regulatory oversight. Moreover, the benefits of greater security largely accrue to others—those whose data they have assembled—and they evidently care little about them.

30. There are many complexities in the design of each of the regulatory proposals. For instance, if an individual has a repeat grocery order, that kind of information could be stored—but not used for other purposes.

31. Anonymizing data may not suffice. Since the Big Data companies can figure out who the individual is, if they are given enough data about the individual, some of the information in the data set itself will have to be stripped away.

32. Platforms were granted immunity under section 230 of the Communications Decency Act. Liability associated with the posting of defamatory articles could easily bankrupt the platforms, so it might be necessary to impose some limitations on their liability—enough to provide them some incentive to exercise care over what is posted, but not so much as to make it impossible for them to operate.

   Publishers also have to honor copyrights, but the platforms have been granted immunity, under Section 512 of the Digital Millennium Copyright Act. This too needs to change. But it will be necessary to fine-tune the regulations. The viability of search engines might be impaired if they had to pay for each snippet of information displayed.

33. Some of the tech giants have taken an inconsistent view, claiming to be publishers when it works to their advantage and not to be when it does not.

34. Jason Horowitz, "In Italian Schools, Reading, Writing, and Recognizing Fake News," *New York Times*, Oct. 18, 2017, https://www.nytimes.com/2017/10/18/world/europe/italy-fake-news.html. Unfortunately, historical experiences with consumer education suggest that it has only limited efficacy.

35. After stripping out Instagram and WhatsApp.

36. Some aspects of that oversight that are especially relevant to our political processes are discussed in greater length later in the book.

It may be desirable for the government to create a *public option*, an alternative platform to compete with the private platform. (Public options are discussed more generally in chapter 10). The public option would be free of the adverse incentives posed by private ownership—to monetize data, in ways which can be exploitive, or to encourage addiction, in ways which may be destructive.

37. The measurement of the social value of social media is in fact complex and difficult. Because it is provided seemingly for free (ignoring the value of the data), our national income statistics don't capture the value generated to its users. On the other hand, the profits of the social media firms are counted as part of national income, but an increase in profits does not necessarily mean an increase in societal welfare. As we have already noted, if the increased profit is a result of a better use of the data to exploit consumers (to "monetize" an individual's consumer surplus), the increase in profits comes at the expense of the well-being of individuals. Moreover, some of its profits are at the expense of the "legacy" publishers, such as newspapers, and these too provided services of enormous value to consumers, such as investigative reporting, the social value of which was also not included in national income.

38. For instance in health, where Big Data and AI are important—and where issues of privacy are even more sensitive.

39. The term "splinternet" was popularized by Scott Malcomson in his book *Splinternet: How Geopolitics and Commerce Are Fragmenting the World Wide Web* (New York: OR Books, 2016). Former Google executive chairman Eric Schmidt, along with coauthor Jared

Cohen, explored the idea that the internet is becoming balkanized in *The New Digital Age: Reshaping the Future of People, Nations and Businesses* (New York: Alfred A. Knopf, 2013).

40. In particular, the GDPR regulations referred to in note 27.

41. There are those who claim that since markets are essentially local, the value of global information will be limited. The marginal value of having information from multiple markets (from, say, China plus the United States plus Europe) would, in this view, be sufficiently small that we could ignore the "unfair" advantage deriving from different regulatory regimes.

42. Online disinformation presents a particular challenge, especially in a world in which the "truth-telling institutions" are under attack (see chapter 1). Discussing the appropriate policy response would, however, take us beyond this short book.

CHAPTER 7: WHY GOVERNMENT?

1. Sir Isaac Newton in 1675 said: "If I have seen further it is by standing on the shoulders of Giants."

2. I first articulated some of these ideas in a little book, *The Economic Role of the State* (Oxford: Basil Blackwell, 1989).

3. Or "Samuelsonian pure public goods," after Paul A. Samuelson, who first articulated clearly the differences between such goods and ordinary "private" goods, in "The Pure Theory of Public Expenditure," *The Review of Economics and Statistics* 36 (1954): 387–9. Since then, a large literature has developed describing different kinds of publicly provided goods, e.g., publicly provided private goods, and goods which are "impure" public goods. See, e.g., Anthony B. Atkinson and Joseph E. Stiglitz, *Lectures on Public Economics* (New York: McGraw-Hill, 1980; reprinted in 2015, with a new introduction, Princeton: Princeton University Press).

4. This can be put another way: everyone wants to be a free-rider on the efforts of others. They can enjoy the benefits of the public goods provided by others without bearing the cost. (Not surprisingly, this is called the free-rider problem in the provision of public goods.)

5. Elsewhere I have referred to this as society's soft infrastructure. Many of the difficulties confronting the countries making the transition from Communism to a market economy were the result of the absence of this soft infrastructure. See Joseph E. Stiglitz, *Whither Socialism?* (Cambridge, MA: MIT Press, 1994).

6. Modern economic theory has explained many of the market failures. Those in insurance markets are often related to asymmetries of information, problems of adverse selection (where there are important differences among individuals that firms, whether as employer, lender, or insurer, cannot easily ascertain), and moral hazard (where, for instance, the provision of insurance leads individuals to act in ways that expose the insurance company to more risk, but which the insurance firm cannot monitor and therefore cannot control). The government can avoid, for instance, some of the adverse selection problems because through Social Security it is insuring the entire population.

7. Private programs providing essentially the same services as Medicare have cost as much as 20 percent more. Administrative costs in the private sector in managing annuities are often ten times or more than in the public sector. There is good reason for lower government costs and better outcomes: it doesn't have to spend on advertising or on exerting market power. The private sector is always engaged in cream-skimming, trying to find the best risks. The private sector is always trying to exploit what market power it has.

8. Private prisons have been even more problematic. The prisons are interested in maximizing their profits, which may entail curtailing expenditures on training or even food, and being little concerned with rehabilitation. Their profits in fact increase when more of those who get released return to prison. The public interest is to have them rejoin society as quickly as possible. It is hard to align public and private interests. See Seth Freed Wessler, "The Justice Department Will End All Federal Private Prisons, Following a 'Nation' Investigation," *The Nation*, Aug. 18, 2016. The general theory explaining the failure of private contracting is set forth in David Sappington and Joseph E. Stiglitz, "Privatization, Information and Incentives," *Journal of Policy Analysis and Management* 6, no. 4 (1987): 567–82.

9. There are multiple other examples demonstrating these points. New York State public mortgage programs performed far better than did the private programs in the 2008 crisis. By most accounts, the privatizations of UK railroads, US production of enriched uranium, or Chile's or Mexico's roads have not gone well, and in some cases, there has had to be a renationalization. In developing countries where privatization improved performance, it was sometimes due to the removal of artificial constraints on access to finance that had

been imposed by the IMF. See Anzhela Knyazeva, Diana Knyazeva, and Joseph E. Stiglitz, "Ownership Changes and Access to External Financing," *Journal of Banking and Finance* 33, no. 10 (Oct. 2009): 1804–16; and "Ownership Change, Institutional Development and Performance," *Journal of Banking and Finance* 37 (2013): 2605–27.

10. See Elizabeth Warren's powerful speech on regulation, delivered at Georgetown Law on June 5, 2018, available at https://www.warren.senate.gov/newsroom/press-releases/senator-warren-delivers-speech-on-dangers-of-deregulation.

11. Economists refer to these effects as externalities.

12. The EU has an alternative way of issuing and enforcing certain types of regulations, which in many ways is less subject to politicization than in the United States.

13. Thus, in discussions leading up to the 1995 telecommunications bill, there was a heated debate about whether technology would evolve in ways that would ensure competition without government intervention, or whether it might evolve in ways that would lead to even more concentration of market power. I was strongly on the latter side, but argued further that prudence required that even if there were a probability that that was right, we should have in place institutional arrangements to check the growth and abuse of market power. As it turned out, unfortunately, my guess turned out to be correct. See Stiglitz, *The Roaring Nineties*.

14. Trump has undermined confidence in the regulatory system that is essential for protection of our health, safety, the environment, even the economy, basing it on a false and deceitful characterization of the regulatory system. He tried to characterize regulations as set by faceless unaccountable bureaucrats. Just as, as a school boy, Trump seemed to have missed the elementary classes on the separation of powers and the importance of checks and balances, he seems to have missed the more advanced classes on our system of regulations, and apparently has done nothing to try to remedy these and other deficiencies in his education.

15. Even worse, these institutions and their financial backers not only resisted regulation, but they also succeeded in inserting provisions in America's bankruptcy law that made it virtually impossible to discharge these debts.

Trump University became emblematic of these exploitive institutions.

16. Moreover, in most localities, choice is even more restricted—there are only one or two providers.

17. The Trump administration, not noted for intellectual coherence, has taken a contradictory stance on competition in the communications sector. It tried to stop the merger of Time Warner (CNN's parent company) and AT&T, on the grounds that that would hurt competition. I think they are right, though the District Court ruled otherwise. This is a vertical merger, that is, Time Warner and AT&T are not in the same industry. One provides services to the other. Traditionally, competition authorities have looked only at competition within a market, not so much at how markets interact. But we know that is wrong. Microsoft's control of the PC operating system was leveraged into its market dominance in a whole range of applications. In this case, the possible adverse consequences of the merger have been amplified by the repeal of net neutrality.

18. Which means, of course, no choice. See Jon Brodkin, "50 Million US Homes Have Only One 25 Mbps Internet Provider or None at All," *Ars Technica*, June 30, 2017.

19. This example also illustrates the complex nature and consequences of monopoly power. The internet providers can be thought of as selling their services (transmission between the content providers and customers) to content providers, like Netflix. By exercising their market power, internet providers affect the market for content providers, and thus indirectly, but importantly, consumers. Alternatively, they can be thought of as selling programming to consumers, buying content (such as movies, provided by Netflix) from others. Here, they have monopsony power, since there are only one or two firms that "buy" content to deliver to internet consumers. They use their market power over the internet to advantage their own content-providing services over those of rivals. From either perspective, though, ultimately consumers suffer, from higher prices and/or less innovation and poorer products.

20. In *The Economic Role of the State*, I explain why we can't just rely on voluntary collective action. For instance, because of the "free-rider" problem in the provision of public goods, everybody would like to enjoy the benefits without contributing to the costs.

21. See, e.g., Joseph E. Stiglitz, "Some Lessons from the East Asian Miracle," *World Bank Research Observer* 11, no. 2 (Aug. 1996): 151–77; and *The East Asian Miracle: Economic Growth and Public Policy*, a World Bank policy research report (New York: Oxford University Press, 1993). So central was the role of government that scholars referred to these countries as having a development state. See,

for instance, Atul Kohli, *State-Directed Development: Political Power and Industrialization in the Global Periphery* (Cambridge: Cambridge University Press, 2004).

22. See, for instance, Mariana Mazzucato, *The Entrepreneurial State: Debunking Public vs. Private Sector Myths* (London: Anthem Press, 2013) and Chang, *Kicking Away the Ladder.*

23. Some argue that this is not an accident. Both parties are a coalition of different groups. The Republican Party is a coalition of evangelicals, big business, the ultra-rich, and libertarians, and part of the strategy of those advocating the corporatist/elite economic agenda is to fuel the culture wars, hoping that in the distraction many of the evangelicals will not notice that the economic policies they are pushing run counter to their economic interests. See Thomas Frank, *What's the Matter with Kansas: How Conservatives Won the Heart of America* (New York: Henry Holt, 2004). He argues further that the New Democrats under Bill Clinton and the Democratic Leadership Council played into this, as they forged an economic agenda to attract finance and other business elites, ignoring blue-collar workers, their traditional base.

24. It is hard to come by a precise number for those who lost their homes—it was somewhere between three and ten million, depending on what time period is defined and how home loss is counted. At the peak of the recession, fifteen million Americans were unemployed (Bureau of Labor Statistics data).

25. See Jesse Eisinger, *The Chickenshit Club: Why the Justice Department Fails to Prosecute Executives* (New York: Simon and Schuster, 2017); Rana Faroorhar, *Makers and Takers: The Rise of Finance and the Fall of American Business* (New York: Crown Business, 2016); and Danny Schechter, *The Crime of Our Time: Why Wall Street Is Not Too Big to Jail* (San Francisco: Red Wheel Weiser, 2010). More than a thousand bankers were jailed in the much smaller savings and loan crisis twenty years earlier. Yet in this crisis few were charged, and still fewer convicted. William D. Cohan, "How Wall Street's Bankers Stayed Out of Jail," *Atlantic*, Sept. 2015. Schechter suggests that after the savings and loan crisis, bankers invested massively in lobbying to ensure that the laws were such that they wouldn't go to jail for their misdeeds.

26. Mostly Republicans, but there were also many on the more conservative side of the Democratic Party who were cheerleaders for both. More typically, the Democrats at least argued for programs to protect those who might be hurt by these policies. In particular,

in the case of globalization, the Democrats argued for trade adjustment assistance, but when, given Republican opposition, adequate assistance failed to be provided, many continued their support nonetheless, seemingly in the belief that somehow trickle-down economics would, after all, work.

27. In such systems, it may even be difficult to ascertain systemic stability. See Stefano Battiston, Guido Caldarelli, Robert M. May, Tarik Roukny, and Joseph E. Stiglitz, "The Price of Complexity in Financial Networks," *PNAS (Proceedings of the National Academy of Sciences of the United States of America)* 113, no. 36 (2016): 10,031–6; and Tarik Roukny, Stefano Battiston, and Joseph E. Stiglitz, "Interconnectedness as a Source of Uncertainty in Systemic Risk," *Journal of Financial Stability* 35: 93–106.

28. See note 92 in chapter 3 for a further discussion of class action suits.

CHAPTER 8: RESTORING DEMOCRACY

1. Harry Enten, "The GOP Tax Cuts Are Even More Unpopular than Past Tax Hikes," *FiveThirtyEight*, Nov. 29, 2017, https://fivethirtyeight.com/features/the-gop-tax-cuts-are-even-more-unpopular-than-past-tax-hikes/.

2. In her book *Democracy in Chains.* See also Steven Levitsky and Daniel Ziblatt, *How Democracies Die* (New York: Crown, 2018).

3. It actually begins before that, with immigration: trying to restrict entry into the country of those who are more likely to vote Democratic. The conflict over immigration policy is, in part at least, a conflict over future voters.

4. So too, remarkably, in many states prisoners and convicted felons are deprived of the right to vote, though they are counted for purposes of representation. Some states have located prisons in particular locations as an additional instrument in facilitating gerrymandering.

5. See Michelle Alexander, *The New Jim Crow: Mass Incarceration in the Age of Colorblindness* (New York: The New Press, 2010).

6. This compares with 1.8 percent of non-African American adults. A disproportionate number of disenfranchised African Americans are men. See "6 Million Lost Voters: State-Level Estimates of Felony Disenfranchisement, 2016," Sentencing Project, Oct. 2016.

    One of the big successes of the 2018 mid-term election was the referendum in Florida restoring voting rights to 1.5 million in that state, roughly a third of whom were African American.

7. In 2018, five states (Indiana, Kentucky, New Hampshire, Ohio, and Oklahoma) either tried to or succeeded in enacting a restrictive voting law. "Voting Laws Roundup 2018," Brennan Center for Justice, Apr. 2, 2018, https://www.brennancenter.org/analysis/voting-laws-roundup-2018.

8. There is a rich and distinguished literature on disenfranchisement in the US, aimed not only at workers, but also at women (who were more likely to be antiwar) and recent immigrants. See Alexander Keyssar, *The Right to Vote: The Contested History of Democracy in the United States* (New York: Basic Books, 2000). My Columbia University colleague Suresh Naidu showed that in the postbellum South, these efforts at voter suppression were successful, reducing the overall electoral turnout by 1 percent to 7 percent and increasing the Democratic vote share in national elections by 5 percent to 10 percent. He also shows that these, in turn, had large effects on expenditures in black schools, with huge distributive effects: "black labor bore a collective loss from disenfranchisement equivalent to at least 15% of annual income, with landowners experiencing a 12% gain." ("Suffrage, School, and Sorting in the Post-Bellum U.S. South," NBER Working Paper no 18129, June 2012). More recent attempts at disenfranchisement focus on Hispanics.

9. See "State Poll Opening and Closing Times (2018)," Ballotpedia, available at https://ballotpedia.org/State_Poll_Opening_and_Closing_Times_(2018).

10. Advances in technology have increased the power of gerrymandering, making it ever more difficult to get fair representation.

11. This is especially true when one considers not just the turnout of registered voters but also the percentage of the voting-age population that casts ballots. In the 2016 national election, this latter figure was under 56 percent. (With Trump getting just 46 percent of those who voted, this means that he got a small minority, just 26 percent of the voting-age population.) For comparison, in recent national elections the participation of the voting-age population in Belgium was 87 percent; in Sweden it was 83 percent. See Drew DeSilver, "U.S. Trails Most Developed Countries in Voter Turnout," Pew Research Center, May 15, 2017. This is to say nothing of state and local elections, which tend to have much lower turnout still. In California in 2018, for example, the turnout for the March primary election was just 36 percent of registered voters—in a state that is touted as being politically fired up in resistance to the Trump administration.

12. In addition to the suppression of voting among those who are entitled to vote, and to legal migrant laborors who pay taxes but are not allowed to vote, something like 2.5 million undocumented immigrants—one in ten Californian workers—reside in California alone. See "Just the Facts: Undocumented Immigrants in California," Public Policy Institute of California, accessed Mar. 11, 2018, available at http://www.ppic.org/publication/undocumented -immigrants-in-california/.

13. The system was designed to prevent a mad ruler like King George III with authoritarian tendencies from engaging in abuses of power. A major lesson of Trump's presidency is just how important this system of checks and balances is.

14. The importance of such a bureaucracy was emphasized by the great sociologist and economist Max Weber (*Economy and Society* [Berkeley: University of California Press, 1922]). It is ironic that while the Republicans have often criticized our faceless bureaucracy, Americans look very favorably at the performance of many, if not most, of the branches of the bureaucracy, such as the National Park System and our Social Security and Medicare systems.

    Every schoolchild knows that one of the key criticisms of Andrew Jackson was his introduction of the "spoils system."

15. It is worth noting that most conservatives support an independent monetary authority, worrying about the economic dangers of politicization of the determination of the money supply. For an excellent account of the principles and controversies surrounding central bank independence, see Paul Tucker, *Unelected Power: The Quest for Legitimacy in Central Banking and the Regulatory State* (Princeton: Princeton University Press, 2018).

16. Two tweets after the terrorist attacks in New York City reflect Trump's low regard of the judiciary: "We need quick justice and we need strong justice—much quicker and much stronger than we have right now. Because what we have right now is a joke and it's a laughingstock. And no wonder so much of this stuff takes place," and ". . . The courts are slow and political!" See also, for example, Kristine Phillips, "All the Times Trump Personally Attacked Judges—and Why His Tirades Are 'Worse than Wrong,'" *Washington Post*, Apr. 26, 2017.

17. Of course, before President Johnson, the Democrats were also a peculiar coalition of Northern liberals and Dixiecrats.

18. There was, as to be expected, some elegant sophistry, explaining how it was that this time they came out against states' rights; but it was the outcome that clearly mattered.

19. Of course, the decisions of any political group, representing compromises between different interests and perspectives, may seem
unprincipled, in that they lack consistency. (This is the central
insight of Kenneth J. Arrow's famous impossibility theorem;
Arrow, *Social Choice and Individual Values* (New York: Wiley, 1951).
But the greater the divergence in beliefs, interests, and preferences,
the more likely is it that large inconsistencies appear.

20. With decisions undermining, for instances, key provisions of the
Voting Rights Act and the Affordable Care Act. The latter, *National
Federation of Independent Business v. Sebelius*, is mostly remembered
for upholding most provisions of Obamacare in 2012. However,
the decision also allowed states to opt out of the Medicaid expansion that the Affordable Care Act originally mandated. Nineteen
states did that, resulting in some 2.2 million people winding up
without health insurance, disproportionately African Americans. In the 2018 election, voters in Idaho, Nebraska, and Utah
reversed those decisions. See, for example, Scott Lemieux, "How
the Supreme Court Screwed Obamacare," *The New Republic*, June
26, 2017.

   In June 2013, the Supreme Court (in a five-to-four decision) ruled that a central piece of the 1965 Voting Rights Act
was unconstitutional—a provision which had played a key role
in restoring voting rights to African Americans; the decision was
reminiscent of the 1883 decision of the Supreme Court that struck
down the Civil Rights Act of 1875. See Lawrence Goldstone,
*Inherently Unequal: The Betrayal of Equal Rights by the Supreme Court,
1865–1903* (New York: Walker, 2011).

21. See, for example, Lee Drutman, "The Case for Supreme Court
Term Limits Has Never Been Stronger," *Vox*, Jan. 31, 2017. See
also the writing of Norm Ornstein, including "Why the Supreme
Court Needs Term Limits," *Atlantic*, May 22, 2014.

22. Under the above proposal, with deaths or resignations, this would
enable the Court to remain at nine. If there were no resignations
or deaths, and the number on the Court was already nine, the
president might still be allowed to make an additional appointment
on a regular basis, but the appointee would not take his seat until
there was a vacancy. If the number of sitting judges were an odd
number, then the appointee would similarly not take his seat until
there were two appointments in waiting.

23. The refusal to ratify a candidate would not increase the number of
positions available for appointment by the next president.

24. See, for example, Stefano DellaVigna and Ethan Kaplan, "The Fox News Effect: Media Bias and Voting," *The Quarterly Journal of Economics,* 122, no. 3 (2007): 1187–234.

25. For example, the Congressional Budget Office (CBO) has estimated that if the government were allowed to compel name-brand drug manufacturers to pay a minimum rebate on certain drugs covered under Medicare, taxpayers could save an average of $11 billion a year. See "Options for Reducing the Deficit: 2015–24" (CBO, Nov. 2014), 51. It is not surprising that, given this largesse, the drug industry has spent enormously to maintain it. "Since January 2003, drug manufacturers and wholesalers have given $147.5 million in federal political contributions to presidential and congressional candidates, party committees, leadership PACs and other political advocacy groups." Most went to Republicans. From Stuart Silverstein, "This Is Why Your Drug Prescriptions Cost So Damn Much: It's Exhibit A in How Crony Capitalism Works," *Mother Jones,* Oct. 21, 2016.

26. These include Sheldon Adelson, who, with his wife and the companies they control, spent more than $82 million in support of Republicans and conservative outside groups in the 2016 election cycle alone; and Steve Wynn, who served as the Finance Chairman of the Republican National Committee until he was brought down by allegations of extreme sexual misconduct. See "Top Individual Contributors: All Federal Contributions," OpenSecrets.org, https://www.opensecrets.org/overview/topindivs.php. These are just one group of the many "rent-seekers" who feature so prominently in the Republican Party. (Recall that "rent-seekers" are those who get their riches not by enlarging the size of the national pie, for example, by producing more goods that people want or need, but by getting a larger slice of a pie.)

27. The tax benefits for real estate trusts are even greater than those for small businesses, because there are limits to the extent that individuals can take advantage of the latter that don't apply to the former.

28. The Obama administration in its final years enacted a little change in regulations, making it easier to detect money laundering, but applicable only to New York and a few other locations. It has reportedly had a major impact on real estate prices in the multi-million-dollar range, confirming the role that money laundering plays in this market.

29. *Citizens United v. Federal Election Commission,* 2010. The *Citizens*

United decision gave rise to the secretive Super PACs through which so much of the political money flows. In *SpeechNow.org v. FEC*, a lower court ruled that *Citizens United* implied that limitations on any group making independent political expenditures are unconstitutional.

30. In some cases, the CEO might defend his political support of a party or candidate by saying it will lead to an increase in the profits of the corporation, and his primary responsibility is increasing profits. But in a well-functioning economy and society, corporations need to take a broader view. It is obviously wrong for the corporation to enhance its profits by cheating—but it should be equally obvious that it is wrong for a firm to enhance profits by campaigning to ensure that the government allows it to "cheat." Regulations can create a playing field in which those who do not want to "cheat" are not forced to do so lest their competitors who are engaging in nefarious activities get the upper hand.

31. Professor John Attanasio (formerly dean of SMU Dedman School of Law), in his book *Politics and Capital* (Toronto: Oxford University Press, 2018) provides data showing the links between *Citizens United* and increased campaign spending by the very rich, with contributions from the top 0.01 percent increasing 65 per cent in just the eleven months after the decision. After *Citizens United* contributions to the secretive 501(c) (4) organizations, which can avoid disclosing contributors, almost tripled.

    There is a large body of political science literature showing that donations lead to increased access and that access leads to increased influence, with legislative consequences. Attanasio emphasizes the importance of an earlier Supreme Court decision, *Buckley v. Valeo*, 424 U.S. 1 (1976), striking down campaign contribution limits. The Court, while recognizing the importance of money in the dissemination of ideas, gave no weight to concerns about equalizing access to the political arena. (See also the discussion in note 35 below. With the country's high level of inequality, the Supreme Court seemed to approve of a system which ensured that there would be "government of the 1 percent, for the 1 percent, and by the one percent."

    More broadly, Benjamin I. Page and Martin Gilens, in their book *Democracy in America?: What Has Gone Wrong and What We can Do About It* (Chicago: University of Chicago Press, 2017), show that the opinions of the broad middle- and lower-income classes have almost no influence on policy, not only because of money, but also because of a variety of antidemocratic measures, like gerrymandering, the excessive influence of small states, with their two senators having the same vote as New York, California, and Texas, and the Hastert Rule, introduced by the Republican Speaker of the House Dennis Hastert (1999–2007), whereby only bills supported by a majority of Republicans would be voted upon.

32. Economists often use more colorful language to describe this process: they speak of "capture." The term seems to have originated at the World Bank around the end of my term as chief economist, and was a natural extension of the term "regulatory capture" used by Nobel-Prize-winning Chicago economist George Stigler ("The Theory of Economic Regulation," *The Bell Journal of Economics and Management Science* [Spring 1971]: 3–21).

33. Money interests, especially from the financial sector, have, of course, played a large role in the Democratic Party as well. Still, many leading Democrats have come out strongly for these reforms. It is noteworthy that the usual 5-to-4 split on the unbridled use of money in politics followed along party lines.

34. The law was slightly more complicated than just depicted. The candidate opting into public funding could not use any money from private donations, personal money, PACs, etc., and there was an upper limit of $75,000 for candidates opting into this program, so an individual running against a candidate who has not opted for public funding would have match funding only up to $75,000. If the rival could raise more than $75,000, that would not be matched.

35. The state's law was the result of a referendum initiated by citizens. Supreme Court Justice Elena Kagan, arguing on behalf of the four dissenters, said: "The First Amendment's core purpose is to foster a healthy, vibrant political system full of robust discussion and debate. Nothing in Arizona's anti-corruption statute, the Arizona Citizens Clean Elections Act, violates this constitutional protection." She went on to argue that states have an interest in combating "the stranglehold of special interests on elected officials." The law "fostered both the vigorous competition of ideas and its ultimate object—a government responsive to the will of the people." Critics of the court decision, like Monica Youn, formerly of New York University's Brennan Center for Justice, rightly pointed out that the Court had created a new right, the "right to preserve monetary advantage." The majority of the Court brushed aside these concerns, as it had done before, arguing in effect that leveling

the playing field was taking away an individual's right to use his money for his own advantage. See, e.g., Robert Barnes, "Supreme Court Strikes Arizona's 'Matching Funds' for Publicly Financed Candidates," *Washington Post*, June 27, 2011. The case was formally known as *McComish v. Bennett*, and was decided in 2011.

36. While there have been changes in Court membership since *Citizens United*, one can anticipate that were a similar case to come before the Court again, it would again be a 5-to-4 decision. A single change in vote—or increasing the size of the Supreme Court by two—would reverse this unfortunate decision.

37. The list of mechanisms by which money exerts influence discussed in this chapter is not meant to be complete. Lobbying, for instance, plays an important role. Efforts to curb the influence of lobbying have been partially successful, but there is room for improvement. Again, better disclosure, including making available lists of those who meet with government officials, might help. The Trump administration has taken the opacity of outside influences to new extremes by refusing to publish the White House visitor logs. See Julie Hirschfeld Davis, "White House to Keep Its Visitor Logs Secret," *New York Times*, Apr. 14, 2017.

38. Donald Trump was doubly a minority candidate: even if he had more support than any of the other sixteen candidates, it was clear that he had the support of less than half the party. But the electoral system allowed him to manage a takeover of the Republican Party, and then to become president with far fewer votes than his opponent received. Some say this is a process that has also been going on in the Democratic Party, but there are fundamental differences. The extremists in the Republican Party have managed a takeover of the party. In the House, the Tea Party has been sufficiently strong to block legislation that it opposed. Even Bernie Sanders and Elizabeth Warren are mainstream "social democrats," little different (and in many cases slightly to the right) of European social democrats.

39. As political scientist Russell J. Dalton and his coauthors have pointed out, there is a long history of disenchantment with the party system, but the reality is that it is essential to the functioning of American democracy. See Russell J. Dalton, David M. Farrell, and Ian McAllister, *Political Parties and Democratic Linkage: How Parties Organize Democracy* (New York: Oxford University Press, 2011) and Sean Wilentz, *The Politicians and the Egalitarians* (New York: W. W. Norton, 2016).

40. Obviously, weaknesses in our education system make our electorate more vulnerable to the distortions and lies of Trump and Fox News. But the public education system will never excel if those who are wealthy can opt out or design enclaves for themselves.

41. Chapter 6 showed how new technologies may have even given them more power to do this.

CHAPTER 9: RESTORING A DYNAMIC ECONOMY WITH JOBS AND OPPORTUNITY FOR ALL

1. It is perhaps ironic that the Democrats, who have been viewed as the critics of markets, have had to take up the role of making markets work, while the Republicans have given into special corporate interests who want the distorted rent-seeking economy that we've become.

2. In fact not even GDP per capita provides a good measure of living standards, as we observed in chapter 2: in the standard measures of living standards, the US performs far more poorly than several countries with higher GDP per capita. For a broader discussion of why GDP is not a good measure, see Joseph E. Stiglitz, Jean-Paul Fitoussi, and Amartya Sen, *Mismeasuring Our Lives: Why GDP Doesn't Add Up* (New York: The New Press, 2010), the report of an international commission I chaired on the measurement of economic performance and social progress.

3. We could do something about birthrates, but it isn't clear that we would want to, given the challenges we face, especially those presented by climate change.

4. See the discussion of Case and Deaton, "Rising Morbidity and Mortality in Midlife among White Non-Hispanic Americans in the 21st Century."

5. The advocates of the tax bill claimed that it would lead to more private investment. As we already noted, the additional money that went into corporate coffers was spent overwhelmingly on dividends and share buybacks.

6. I was at a discussion in Davos in January 2018, just weeks after the tax bill was passed, as Trump's secretary of transportation, Elaine L. Chao, reiterated her commitment to infrastructure, but then went on to point out that there was one problem—a lack of money. Implicitly, the administration had articulated its priorities: Even a poorly designed tax cut for the rich was more important than infrastructure.

7. Through provisions limiting tax deductibility of state income and property taxes.

8. He said it would be so large that tax revenue would increase. Needless to say, the deficit increased enormously.

9. The personal savings rate fell to 2.2 percent, and remained low until the financial crisis. The failures of the Bush tax cuts to promote savings, investment, and growth are discussed further in note 44 in chapter 1.

10. There is, of course, much more to be said on how to create a society that facilitates innovation. See, for instance, Stiglitz and Greenwald, *Creating a Learning Society.*

11. The name "industrial policies" is misleading: they do not necessarily promote industry. They simply promote one sector of the economy or one technology or encourage businesses to locate in particular places.

12. Thus, active labor market policies have sometimes been criticized: while they have worked in some countries, like those of Scandinavia, they have met with mixed success elsewhere. There's a reason, and important lessons to be learned from these failures: if individuals are trained for jobs that don't exist—either because macroeconomic policy has failed to create jobs or because training policies have failed to link education programs with the jobs that do exist—it is obvious that they will fail.

    Industrial policies were also criticized by neoliberal orthodoxy. Government shouldn't pick winners, it was said. But the reality is that every successful country has had an industrial policy; much of the US's policy was embedded in the Defense Department. We wouldn't be the leader in the internet if it weren't for government research programs. In any case, all governments have to make long-term decisions about designing education systems and infrastructure, and these have to be based on a vision of where the country is going. For a more extensive discussion, see Stiglitz and Greenwald, *Creating a Learning Society,* and Mazzucato, *The Entrepreneurial State.*

13. Economists and sociologists similarly refer to organizational and social capital that resides within the community. This capital gets destroyed when communities get destroyed. See, for example, Robert J. Putnam, *Bowling Alone* (New York: Simon and Schuster, 2000); and Robert J. Sampson, *Great American City: Chicago and the Enduring Neighborhood Effect* (Chicago: University of Chicago Press, 2011).

14. More generally, the spatial allocation of economic activity is not efficient because of strong congestion and other location-specific externalities (externalities, recall, arise whenever the full consequences of an individual's decisions are not reflected in the costs he has to bear; and whenever there are externalities, markets are not efficient.)

15. The role played was partially inadvertent, a by-product of World War II, as government helped move people from the rural to the urban sector for war production and as it helped ensure that those returning from the war had the skills necessary for success in the new industrial economy, through the GI Bill. For a greater elaboration of this point, see the studies cited in chapter 6, note 7.

16. Modern economic theory (based on asymmetric information) has explained why this is so, and why the problems are inherent.

17. This idea has been elaborated in Joseph E. Stiglitz and Jungyoll Yun, "Integration of Unemployment Insurance with Retirement Insurance," *Journal of Public Economics*, 89, no. 11–12 (2005): 2037–67; and "Optimal Provision of Loans and Insurance Against Unemployment From A Lifetime Perspective" (NBER Working Paper No. 19064, 2013).

18. I am indebted to Alan Krueger for discussions on these issues. The government might, for instance, pay part of the difference between the wage at the old job and that at the new, at least for a while; the individual could continue to search for the better job. Eventually, he either will find that job or have his expectations revised downward. But at least under this program he will have a job.

19. Thus, automatic stabilizers inject money into the economic system even before standard indicators (like the growth in GDP or the level of unemployment) may indicate that there is a problem. Especially in the US, with its gridlocked political system, even recognizing that there is a problem doesn't suffice, as we saw in the response to the Great Recession. There can be long, costly delays before Congress votes for the needed injection of funds into the economy.

20. There has been a plethora of books advocating a UBI, including the following: Guy Standing, *Basic Income: A Guide for the Open-Minded* (New Haven: Yale University Press, 2017); Annie Lowrey, *Give People Money: How a Universal Basic Income Would End Poverty, Revolutionize Work, and Remake the World* (New York: Crown, 2018); and Philippe Van Parijs and Yannick Vanderborght, *Basic Income: A Radical Proposal for a Free Society and a Sane Economy* (Cambridge,

MA: Harvard University Press, 2017). The titles suggest the trans-formative role that the authors believe a UBI would have for our society.

21. Some have suggested that there are also political advantages—universal programs, like Social Security, receive more support, simply because they are universal. There is an old adage that means-tested programs (where eligibility depends on, say, income, i.e., "means") are *mean*, in the old English use of the term, meaning stingy.

22. Maintaining ultra-low interest rates can distort the economy and especially the financial sector, encouraging excessive investments in capital-intensive technologies and leading to too-low risk premia. Relying on monetary policy also puts an undue burden on interest-sensitive sectors.

23. OECD data.

24. See Peter Wagner and Wendy Sawyer, "Mass Incarceration: The Whole Pie 2018," Prison Policy Initiative, Mar. 14, 2018.

25. "Employed Full Time: Median Usual Weekly Real Earnings: Wage and Salary Workers: 16 Years and Over," St. Louis FRED Economic Data, accessed July 14, 2018, available at https://fred .stlouisfed.org/series/LES1252881600Q. Some have suggested that the reason for the low labor force participation is that those not in the labor force don't have the skills required by the jobs that are being created. Such skills mismatch does not explain fully the current labor market because were that the case, one would have expected to see increases in wages for those skills in short supply, while downward-rigidities of wages in other areas would have led to limited decreases there; accordingly, we should have seen much more rapid increases in average wages than we have seen.

26. As the US did during the Iraq and Afghanistan War. See Stiglitz and Linda Bilmes, *The Three Trillion Dollar War: The True Cost of the War in Iraq* (New York: W. W. Norton, 2008).

27. Not paying for a true social cost (such as the value of the environmental damage) is, in effect, a subsidy. When there are no carbon taxes, firms do not bear any of the costs of the environmental damage they cause. By not forcing polluting firms to pay for the damage they impose on society, we are effectively subsidizing them.

28. Even as conventionally measured, not taking into account the benefits of the better environment. Some of the revenue of such a tax could, in turn, be used to invest in a "green" economy, for instance, which would retrofit our public infrastructure. All of this

(including the private and public job creation that would result) is part of what is coming to be called the Green New Deal.

Some have advocated a carbon tax, along the lines of the recommendation by the High-Level Commission on Carbon Prices, which I cochaired with leading British economist Lord Nicholas Stern, but suggested that the revenues be returned to taxpayers. The advocates of such a policy ignore our important warning about the scope of new investment, including public sector investment, that greening the economy requires. (We had been tasked by a global business-government consortium headed by, at the time, France's environmental minister Ségolène Royal and a leading Dutch businessman, to ascertain the carbon tax that would be required to achieve the goal of limiting global warming to the 1.5°C to 2°C increase set in the international agreements of Paris and Copenhagen. See "Report on the High-Level Commission on Carbon Prices," also known as "The Stern-Stiglitz Report," Carbon Pricing Leadership Coalition, accessed July 4, 2018, available at https://www.carbonpricingleadership.org/report-of-the-highlevel-commission-on-carbon-prices/.)

A carbon tax would have the further advantage of encouraging research to focus on reducing carbon emissions—on saving the planet. In our current system, where firms bear no cost of carbon emissions, they have little incentive to innovate to reduce emissions.

29. The argument is simple: the expansionary effect of the government spending outweighs the contractionary effect of the tax. The contractionary effect will be particularly small when the taxes are imposed on the super-rich; and the expansionary effects may be particularly large for certain types of investments, such as those associated with education and technology and many investments in the environment.

30. See Mazzucato, *The Entrepreneurial State.*

31. "Some Dates and Figures," European Investment Bank, accessed July 4, 2018, available at http://www.eib.org/about/key_figures/index.htm.

32. Early on in the Trump administration, there were proposals to enlist hedge funds to provide infrastructure finance through providing them large tax benefits. Tax benefits are, of course, not free; they deprive the government of money that it could have spent elsewhere. The cost to the public of funds raised through a national infrastructure bank would be far smaller than the cost of

enticing hedge funds, which, in any case, would be more interested in funding airports and other things from which they could get a direct revenue stream than rural roads and other more neglected aspects of our infrastructure.

33. Evidence elsewhere shows the impact of such efforts not only on the quality of life but even in encouraging learning and discouraging crime.

   There is other work that needs to be done in assisting in hospitals, schools, and retirement homes. Shortening lines for those waiting for public services has a value that is not well captured in our national income statistics.

34. For a description of the successes of the Indian program, see Jayati Ghosh, "Can Employment Schemes Work? The Case of the Rural Employment Guarantee in India," in *Contributions to Economic Theory, Policy, Development, and Finance: Essays in Honor of Jan A. Kregel*, ed. Dmitri Papadimitriou (London: Palgrave Macmillan, 2014), 145–71. Of course, the structure of the Indian labor market is markedly different from that in the United States, necessitating that the program would have to be designed differently. Still, the point remains: a much poorer country, with a much smaller fraction of workers in formal employment, could afford a guaranteed employment program and succeed in getting it to work. The US should be able to do so too.

   There are many technical details that will have to be resolved in implementing such a program. On the one hand, it would be wrong to pay these workers below a decent wage. On the other hand, one wouldn't want to discourage private sector employment.

   This measure should be thought of as a last resort: the hope is that with appropriate monetary and fiscal policy, full employment *for all groups* is achievable. The evidence, however, is that this may not be the case. Unemployment rates are often twice as high for African Americans as for the rest of the population, partly because of discrimination; and this means that unless the government succeeds in getting the overall unemployment down very low, there will be unacceptable levels of unemployment among this and other groups.

   Guaranteed employment schemes are, of course, similar to workfare, which has had a mixed history. Often the tasks that were assigned did not represent meaningful work, individuals may not have been appropriately trained for the tasks, and there was little effort to contribute to skill formation that might enable individuals to be reintegrated into the market labor force. Insights from these failures could help inform a well-designed employment guarantee scheme.

Even an imperfectly designed program might be desirable, once we recognize the very high social costs of extended periods of unemployment, particularly when such unemployment is concentrated in certain places or among certain subgroups of the population.

35. Some on the Right claim that everything should be left to the market. If the net benefits of working, including paying for child care, are insufficient, the individual shouldn't work; child care subsidies, in this perspective, distort the labor market. This ignores the multiple distortions already present in the labor market and elsewhere in society, including rampant gender discrimination; and it ignores the social value that society may attach to the dignity of work and the increase in human capital that results from work.

36. It goes without saying that this entails providing workers with skills that are better matched to the needs of the labor market.

37. On pre-distribution, see Jacob S. Hacker and Paul Pierson, *Winner-Take-All Politics: How Washington Made the Rich Richer—And Turned Its Back on the Middle Class* (New York: Simon & Schuster, 2010); and Stiglitz, *The Price of Inequality*.

38. For a fuller discussion of the determinants of wage inequality, see the discussion in chapter 2, including note 23.

39. So too, the repeal of the Glass-Steagall Act, the law that separated commercial and investment banks, has been followed by an enormous increase in concentration in the banking sector, giving them still more market power. The assets of the five largest banks as a share of total commercial banking assets increased from 29 percent in 1998 (the year before the repeal of Glass-Steagall) to 46 percent in 2015. "5-Bank Asset Concentration for United States," St. Louis FRED Economic Data, accessed July 14, 2018, available at https://fred.stlouisfed.org/series/DDOI06USA156NWDB.

40. There is a heated dispute about the relative merits of increasing the minimum wage vs. increasing a wage subsidy. I believe that the US needs both.

41. Miles Corak has empirically documented the relationship between equality of incomes and equalities of opportunity, a relationship which Alan Krueger, chairman of the Council of Economic Advisers under President Obama, referred to as the Great Gatsby Curve. See Corak, "Income Inequality, Equality of Opportunity, and

Intergenerational Mobility," *Journal of Economic Perspectives* 27, no. 3 (2013): 79–102; and Krueger, "The Rise and Consequences of Inequality in the United States," speech at the Center for American Progress, Jan. 12, 2012.

42. The richest 25 percent of school districts spend 15.6 percent more funds than the poorest 25 percent, according to the Department of Education. Data from the Education Finance Statistics Center, accessed July 4, 2018, available at http://nces.ed.gov/edfin/xls/A -1_FY2012.xls. A study by C. Kirabo Jackson, Rucker C. Johnson, and Claudia Persico finds that every 10 percent increase in per pupil spending on their 12 years of education leads to 7 percent higher wages, and a 3.2 percent decrease in annual incidence of poverty. See Jackson, Johnson, and Persico, "The Effects of School Spending on Educational and Economic Outcomes: Evidence from School Finance Reforms," *Quarterly Journal of Economics* 131, no. 1 (2016): 157–218.

These results are consistent with those noted earlier (chapter 2), that those growing up in certain locations are less likely to succeed.

43. Not surprisingly, given the importance of education, there have been innumerable reform efforts and books proposing alternative approaches. A few paragraphs can't do justice to this rich literature. I've discussed one of the reform efforts, incentive pay. Another focuses on charter schools—allowing new schools to be created. On average, these schools do not perform better than public schools (Philip Gleason, Melissa Clark, Christina Clark Tuttle, and Emily Dwoyer, "The Evaluation of Charter School Impacts: Final Report (NCEE 2010-4029)" [Washington, DC: National Center for Education Evaluation and Regional Assistance, Institute of Education Sciences, U.S. Department of Education, 2010]) but there are a few that have had some notable successes. They should be viewed as "laboratories of educational innovation," with successful projects brought into the public schools. They should not be viewed as an alternative to public schools. That almost inevitably will lead to a more economically and socially, and probably racially, segregated school system. A third pillar of reform has centered around union bashing—curious because among the best-performing public school systems are those that are highly unionized. The anti-worker anti-union attitudes common within the corporate sector have, not surprisingly, found their way into the educational reform debate.

44. In *Shelby County v. Holder*, declaring a key provision of the Act

unconstitutional. The Act had placed those parts of the country with a historical legacy of voter discrimination under federal supervision. Released from these constraints, many of these places have undertaken actions (like closing and changing voting locations) in a way to discourage voting by African Americans. Lack of voting power has consequences for the allocation of public resources. For a fuller discussion of these issues, including the Supreme Court decision, see chapter 8.

45. Source: World Prison Population List, International Center for Prison Studies.

46. This system of mass incarceration came to be called the "new Jim Crow." As we noted in chapter 8, however, it serves a political purpose—facilitating disenfranchisement of large numbers of African Americans. See Alexander, *The New Jim Crow*.

It is also exploitive. As we have noted, almost 5 percent of all industrial labor in the US today is provided by convict labor, typically at wages far below the minimum wage.

47. The financial crisis showed America's economic and judicial system at its worst. Banks like Wells Fargo targeted African Americans for their predatory lending. Almost none of the rich bankers who were responsible for the crisis (or for this discrimination) were held accountable—even for the crime of throwing people out of their homes *who didn't owe any money*, including many homeowners for whom the bankers could not find appropriate documents. See "Justice for Some," in Stiglitz, *The Great Divide*, 70–73.

48. See Andrea Flynn, Dorian T. Warren, Susan Holmberg, and Felicia Wong, "Rewrite the Racial Rules: Building an Inclusive American Economy," Roosevelt Institute, June 2016.

49. One of the repeated themes in interviews with Trump supporters was that they felt others were being given a "go" card to pass them on the ladder of life. In golf, we understand a level playing field entails providing a handicap. So too, we need to recognize that in life, there are some who begin with disadvantages, and need help to ensure that there is a truly level playing field.

50. These arguments are part of a suit being brought on behalf of twenty-one young children against the Trump administration for its climate policies. The case, called *Juliana v. US*, is currently on hold, awaiting trial in Eugene, Oregon, after the Supreme Court (in a 7–2 decision) upheld the right of the children to sue. I serve as an expert witness in the case.

51. See Stiglitz, "Reforming Taxation to Promote Growth and

Equity," Roosevelt Institute White Paper, May 28, 2014. Key
reforms include full taxation of dividends, capital gains, interest
on local bonds, and the elimination of a host of loopholes, including the provision providing for a step-up in basis for capital gains
taxation when assets are inherited, so that taxes are only paid on
the difference between the price at which the asset is sold and the
price at the time of inheritance—the entire capital gain during the
previous generation goes untaxed.

52. Among these is the "carried interest" provision (in the Internal
    Revenue Code of 1986) noted earlier: those in private equity (buy-
    ing firms, restructuring them, and then selling them) typically pay
    the low capital gains tax rate on their income, rather than the far
    higher rate that those working in other sectors have to pay.

53. Though the evidence, in each of these cases, is that the responses
    are normally small, or as economists say, the tax elasticities are low.

54. See Henry George, *Progress and Poverty: An Inquiry into the Cause
    of Industrial Depressions and of Increase of Want with Increase of Wealth*
    (San Francisco: W. M. Hinton & Company, printers, 1879), 38.

55. This can be looked at another way: the value of land will decrease,
    and so if individuals want to hold a certain amount of wealth for,
    say, their retirement, more of that wealth will have to be held in
    productive capital.

56. See "The Stern-Stiglitz Report" discussed in note 28 above.

57. Of course, it makes sense too to cut off our large subsidies to fossil
    fuels (estimated to be $20.5 billion annually in corporate welfare,
    much of it through the tax system, and that would generate even
    more money to be spent elsewhere). David Roberts, "Friendly Pol-
    icies Keep US Oil and Coal Afloat Far More than We Thought,"
    Vox, Oct. 7, 2017, based on data from Oil Change International.
    This data omits many categories of subsidies, such as those that go
    directly to consumers. The IMF estimates energy subsidies (most
    of which go to fossil fuels) at $5.3 trillion in 2015, or 6.5 percent
    of global GDP. David Coady, Ian Parry, Louis Sears, and Baoping
    Shang, "How Large Are Global Energy Subsidies?," *International
    Monetary Fund*, 2015. They estimate US subsidies at $600 billion
    annually.

58. Total global losses from natural disasters totaled $335 billion. The
    United States experienced 88 percent of the global economic losses.
    Natural Disasters 2017, www.emdat.be/publications (accessed Jan.
    28, 2019). See also Pascaline Wallemacq and Rowena House, "Eco-
    nomic Losses, Poverty and Disasters 1998–2017" (United Nations

Office for Disaster Risk Reduction and Centre for Research on the Epidemiology of Disasters, 2018), accessed January 24, 2019, available at https://www.unisdr.org/we/inform/publications/61119.

59. Indeed, it actually interferes with the efficiency of financial markets. As Michael Lewis, in his 2014 book *Flash Boys: A Wall Street Revolt* (New York: W. W. Norton) points out, much of high-frequency trading amounts to nothing more than a technologically advanced way of "front running," which in less sophisticated forms is illegal. The money going to these traders is money that otherwise would have gone to those investing in *real* information that might enhance the overall efficiency of the economy. See Joseph E. Stiglitz, "Tapping the Brakes: Are Less Active Markets Safer and Better for the Economy?," presented at the Federal Reserve Bank of Atlanta 2014 Financial Markets Conference: Tuning Financial Regulation for Stability and Efficiency, Apr. 15, 2014, available at http://www.frbatlanta.org/documents/news/conferences/14fmc/Stiglitz.pdf.

CHAPTER 10: A DECENT LIFE FOR ALL

1. Even Costa Rica, with a quarter of US per capita income, has a longer life expectancy, in part because it provides high-quality medical care to all.

2. U.S. Bureau of Economic Analysis data. Gross debt peaked at 119 percent of GDP after World War II. "Gross Federal Debt as Percent of Gross Domestic Product," St. Louis FRED, accessed July 15, 2018, available at https://fred.stlouisfed.org/series/GFDGDPA188S.

3. The returns on the investments in education were enormous—by one Congressional account, $7 for every dollar spent. There were large differences across races in take-up of educational benefits: Only 12 percent of African Americans went on to higher education, as opposed to 28 percent of whites. Edward Humes explains the mechanism by which such discrimination occurred in "How the GI Bill Shunted Blacks into Vocational Training," *The Journal of Blacks in Higher Education*, no. 53 (Autumn 2006): 92–104. It is noteworthy that while the GI bill did have an effect on educational attainment in the North, it was not so in the South. See Sarah Turner and John Bound, "Closing the Gap or Widening the Divide: The Effects of the GI Bill and World War II on the Educational Outcomes of Black Americans," *The Journal of Economic*

History 63, no. 1 (2003), 145–77. The GI Bill also provided housing benefits, but again red-lining in lending meant that African Americans were not able to fully take advantage of these benefits. See Edward Humes, *Over Here: How the G.I. Bill Transformed the American Dream* (New York: Diversion Books, 2006).

4. While the discussion of this chapter emphasizes the role of government programs (including new public options) in ensuring a decent life for all Americans, it is important to recognize that the regulatory frameworks discussed in the previous chapter are equally important. One can't have a decent life if employees can be easily exploited by their employers (for instance, through split shifts and zero-hour jobs) or the environment is spoiled or if one is constantly exploited by the firms one has to deal with—whether it's the internet provider, one's cellphone company, or airlines.

5. The public option thus may be preferable to having *just* the government provide the given service.

6. Ironically, Congress did create a limited private option to Medicare—but it had to provide substantial subsidies to the private providers to enable them to compete.

7. Even before Trump tried to undermine the Affordable Care Act, some 12 percent of US adults were uninsured, or about 30 million people. See Zac Auter, "U.S. Uninsured Rate Steady at 12.2% in Fourth Quarter of 2017" (Gallup, Jan. 16, 2018); and Edward R. Berchick, Emily Hood, and Jessica C. Barnett, "Current Population Reports, P60-264, Health Insurance Coverage in the United States: 2017" (US Government Printing Office, Washington, DC, 2018). The Congressional Budget Office (CBO) estimated in November 2017 that as a result of the 2017 tax bill, an additional 13 million will join the uninsured by 2027. See "Repealing the Individual Health Insurance Mandate: An Updated Estimate" (CBO, Nov. 8, 2017).

8. This option basically means that what were subsidies provided by the healthy to the unhealthy through the private insurance system are instead achieved through the tax system.

9. See Peter R. Orszag and Joseph E. Stiglitz, "Rethinking Pension Reform: Ten Myths about Social Security Systems," in *New Ideas about Old Age Security*, eds. Robert Holman and Joseph E. Stiglitz (Washington, DC: World Bank, 2001), 17–56. Most individuals don't know the fees charged by alternative plans, and thus don't realize the impact of fees on their retirement income. In the US, transaction costs on IRA accounts are estimated to reduce retirement benefits by some 30 percent. See Robert Hiltonsmith,

"The Retirement Savings Drain: The Hidden and Excessive Costs of 401(k)s," New York: Demos.org, 2012, accessed Jan. 24, 2019, available at https://www.demos.org/publication/retirement -savings-drain-hidden-excessive-costs-401ks.

10. See the discussion in note 21, chapter 5. The Trump administration, siding with the bankers and their desire to enrich themselves at the expense of retirees by continuing to exploit conflicts of interest, delayed the implementation of the fiduciary standard—of the kind that other advanced countries have. Then, the Fifth Circuit Court, covering Texas, Louisiana, and Mississippi, overturned the rule. All of this makes the provision of the *public option* more important. For further discussion, see, for example, Alessandra Malito, "The Fiduciary Rule Is Officially Dead. What Its Fate Means to You," *Market Watch*, June 25, 2018, https://www.marketwatch.com/story/is-the-fiduciary -rule-dead-or-alive-what-its-fate-means-to-you-2018-03-16.

11. The originate-to-distribute system, where mortgage brokers helped banks sell mortgages, which they then sold on to investment banks to be packaged as securities, to be sold on to pension funds and others seeking a diversified portfolio, described in chapter 5.

12. See Laurie Goodman, Alanna McCargo, Edward Golding, Jim Parrott, Sheryl Pardo, Todd M. Hill-Jones, Karan Kaul, Bing Bai, Sarah Strochak, Andrea Reyes, and John Walsh, "Housing Finance at a Glance: A Monthly Chartbook," Urban Institute, Dec. 2018, available at https://www.urban.org/research/publication/housing-finance -glance-monthly-chartbook-december-2018/view/full_report.

13. The economic modeling is called "hedonic pricing," ascertaining the value that markets associate with various attributes of a house, including location and various amenities.

14. For instance, the mortgage companies and investment banks often represented rental properties as owner-occupied. This is important, because the risk of default is much higher for the former than the latter.

15. Economists refer to these as "economies of scope." For most individuals, payments could be directly linked to payrolls, with effectively zero marginal cost. There is a series of practical questions and issues that need to be addressed with this proposal. While these critical details require attention, our point here is only that there is ample scope for creating a public lending authority that would be markedly more efficient than existing arrangements—which in any case leave the government with assuming risks and engaging in underwriting, whether implicitly or explicitly.

16. The thirty-year-mortgage product defaulted far less than the prod-
    ucts that private markets gravitated toward in the years before the
    crisis, such as those with variable interest rates and balloon pay-
    ments; but even this product is not as efficient in risk-sharing and
    stabilizing the economy as many others that have been proposed
    (such as that just described in the text), and in some cases, offered
    in other countries (including the famous Danish mortgage bonds).

17. See, for example, Deirdre Bloome, Shauna Dyer, and Xiang Zhou,
    "Educational Inequality, Educational Expansion, and Intergenera-
    tional Income Persistence in the United States," *American Sociologi-
    cal Review* 83, no. 6 (2018): 1215–53.

18. See James J. Heckman, "Invest in early childhood development:
    Reduce deficits, strengthen the economy," https://heckmanequation
    .org/www/assets/2013/07/F_HeckmanDeficitPieceCUSTOM
    -Generic_052714-3-1.pdf and Ajay Chaudry, Taryn Morrissey,
    Christina Weiland, and Hirokazu Yoshikawa, *Cradle to Kindergar-
    ten: A New Plan to Combat Inequality* (New York: Russell Sage
    Foundation, 2017).

19. The alternatives differ most importantly in the consequences for
    the intergenerational distribution of income, which is affected too
    by other policies, such as the design of Social Security (pensions).
    Income-contingent loans put the burden of paying for education
    on the generation receiving the education, while free tuition puts
    the burden on the current working population.

20. Individuals should be able to borrow from the government to pay
    back the private loan; any prepayment penalties should be outlawed.

21. For a discussion of the correlation between inequality and eco-
    nomic segregation, see Sean F. Reardon and Kendra Bischoff,
    "Income Inequality and Income Segregation," *American Journal of
    Sociology* 116, no. 4 (2011): 1092–1153.

CHAPTER 11: RECLAIMING AMERICA

1. Of course, the two are not fully distinct, as we saw so clearly in
   chapter 5: moral turpitude on the part of bankers has played an
   important role in the dysfunction of our financial system.

2. In the nineteenth century, this archetype was captured in a series
   of books by Horatio Alger, describing impoverished boys who rose
   to prosperity through determination and hard work.

3. Most of our nation's most selective schools have needs-blind admis-
   sions, accepting students regardless of their parents' financial cir-

cumstances, providing funding to ensure that all can enroll. Yet a remarkably small fraction (under 10 percent) comes from the bottom half of the income distribution. In the Ivy Plus (Ivy League plus MIT, Stanford University, Duke University, and University of Chicago), 14.5 percent of students come from the top 1 percent vs. 13.5 percent from the bottom 50 percent. Anthony P. Carnevale and Stephen J. Rose, "Socioeconomic Status, Race/Ethnicity, and Selective College Admission," in *America's Untapped Resource: Low-Income Students in Higher Education*, ed. Richard D. Kahlenberg (New York: Century Foundation, 2004); and Raj Chetty, John N. Friedman, Emmanuel Saez, Nicholas Turner, and Danny Yagan, "Mobility Report Cards: The Role of Colleges in Intergenerational Mobility," NBER Working Paper No. w23618, July 2017, https://www.nber.org/papers/w23618.pdf.

4. Modern behavioral economics has gone some ways in rectifying these problems. But much of current economic policy in the US and other advanced countries is based not on the insights of behavioral economics but on the prescriptions of standard economics based on unrealistic conceptions of individuals as fully rational, informed, and selfish.

5. The former attitude is reflected in the accolades given to political leaders advocating "reform," even when the reform simply means changing the rules of the game to favor one group at the expense of another or even of the whole economy. Reagan's reforms led to slower growth and more inequality; the only winners were those at the top.

 The latter attitude is reflected in those on the Supreme Court who seem to believe that the Founding Fathers should be our lodestar, even as we face quandaries that they could not possibly have conceived of.

6. In fact, as we noted earlier, Smith's first book was called *The Theory of Moral Sentiments*, originally published in 1759.

7. The list is not meant to be comprehensive, but to focus more on the key issues I have raised in this book; and I do not want to suggest that there would be unanimous support of any particular articulation of these values. Yet, it is hard for me to see many openly coming out against, say, a rule of law and a system of widespread tolerance. To be sure, there are those who would wish to articulate them in ways that make them more consistent with the advancement of their own self-interest.

8. The country got a taste of how important the government is to the functioning of our economy and our society when Trump shut down just a part of the government in late 2018 and early 2019.

9. In 2017 the federal government employed (not including the US Postal Service) 2.19 million people; in 1967 there were approximately 2.13 million employees (U.S. Bureau of Labor Statistics, All Employees: Government: Federal, Except U.S. Postal Service [CES9091100001], retrieved from FRED, Federal Reserve Bank of St. Louis; https://fred.stlouisfed.org/series/CES9091100001. Accessed Jan. 24, 2019).

10. This was the case before auto safety legislation, as documented by Ralph Nader in his classic book, *Unsafe at Any Speed: The Designed-In Dangers of the American Automobile* (New York: Pocket Books, 1965).

11. A president who claims an unfettered right to pardon himself and those who serve him is a president who claims unbridled authoritarian power, to be reined in by the single ultimate check provided by the Constitution, impeachment; and with such solid support among his own party (removing a president from office requires a two-thirds vote of the Senate), and with such overbearing confidence that he could claim that he could "shoot somebody" on Fifth Avenue and still not lose his loyal voters, he seems to have little to fear from that quarter.

12. Many important ones have received little notice: a simple change that removes the deference previously given to one's own physician in disability proceedings may result in large numbers being denied disability payments.

13. According to OECD data, in 2017, US real GDP per capita grew somewhat slower than the average of the OECD, but in 2018 it was somewhat greater.

14. In *Rewriting the Rules of the American Economy*, my coauthors and I describe globalization and technology as the large underlying global forces that then get translated through the rules that structure our economy into our daily experiences, including those that lead to inequality and exclusion. But the story is more complex: to a large extent even the large global forces of technology and globalization originate from and are shaped by policy. Technology is driven by basic research and even in the private sector, its direction is affected by policy. Stronger climate policies would have induced more investment in research to reduce climate emissions. Low interest rates have reduced the cost of capital relative

to labor, thus encouraging research and other investments to save labor. Globalization is largely driven by policies that affect cross-border movements of goods, services, capital, and people.

15. That's not quite accurate: as we noted in note 11, chapter 8, given the low voter turnout, Trump got the votes of "just 26 percent of the voting-age population."

16. I said as much in my books *The Price of Inequality* and *The Great Divide*. But I was not alone. See, for instance, Piketty, *Capital in the 21st Century*; and Angus Deaton, *The Great Escape: Health, Wealth, and the Origins of Inequality* (Princeton: Princeton University Press, 2013).

17. With respect to *Worcester v. Georgia*, 31 U.S. (6 Pet.) 515 (1832). Andrew Jackson's actual words to Brigadier General John Coffee were: "The decision of the Supreme Court has fell still born, and they find that it cannot coerce Georgia to yield to its mandate."

18. The South developed an economic system that maintained the dominance of the old slaveholding class through sharecropping. The South lagged in education, incomes, health—in every indicator of social and economic well-being—especially but not only for African Americans. Throughout, southern political leaders exploited racism to turn the anger of poor whites against their black neighbors.

   Eventually, the statistics in the South improved, helped along by the passage of a national minimum wage under President Franklin Delano Roosevelt in 1938, the massive migration of large numbers of African Americans from the South to the North, and the relocation of industry to the South in the search for low labor costs. It was hoped that the civil rights legislation of the 1960s, itself the result of a mass movement against these long-standing economic and racial injustices, would turn the tide, and at least for a while it seemed that that might happen. However, a quarter century later, recidivist forces, especially in the courts, halted progress if not turning the clock back: economic segregation, the racial economic divide, and political disempowerment then increased apace.

19. Trump's attempt to use racism for his political advantage has, of course, long historical antecedents. In the aftermath of President Lyndon B. Johnson's civil rights legislation, Republicans in the South took advantage of pervasive racism to encourage a major realignment of party affiliation.

20. Some have emphasized the equalizing role that wars have sometimes played. World War II created a solidarity that allowed highly

progressive taxation and set the stage for a postwar era of unusually low levels of inequality. But wars are neither necessary nor sufficient to bring about equalitarian societies—and a costly and inefficient way of doing so.

21. Consistent with the view that we (through the State) today hold our natural resources in trusteeship for future generations. This is sometimes called the Public Interest Doctrine and dates back to the Justinian Code, incorporated into US law in the late nineteenth century, and one of the bases of the suit by twenty-one children against the Trump administration for failing to take appropriate action on climate change to protect their interests that I discussed in note 50, chapter 9.

22. According to data from the Federal Deposit Insurance Corporation and the National Credit Union Administration (the regulator for credit unions), while before the crisis, credit unions failed at about the same rate as for-profit banks, in the crisis their failure rate was markedly lower. Moreover, while bank lending to small businesses contracted by almost $100 billion from 2008 to 2016, credit union lending more than doubled, from $30 billion to $60 billion. See the 2017 NAFCU 2017 report on credit unions available at https://www.nafcu.org/sites/default/files/data-research/economic-credit-union-industry-trends/industry-trends/Annual%20Report%20on%20Credit%20Unions/NAFCU%20Report%20on%20Credit%20Unions%20-%202017.pdf; and Rebel A. Cole, "How Did Bank Lending to Small Business in the United States Fare After the Financial Crisis?" (Small Business Administration, Jan. 2018).

23. For instance, Land O'Lakes, the largest butter producer in the country. Begun as the Minnesota Cooperative Creameries Association, it now has 10,000 employees working in fifty states and more than fifty countries, with $14 billion in net sales. Excluding cooperative housing, there are more than 64,000 cooperatives, including utilities and agriculture. Other familiar cooperatives are Sunkist and Ocean Spray (cranberries).

24. The most forceful denial of the role of collective action and societal well-being was given by former UK Prime Minister Margaret Thatcher in 1987: "There is no such thing as society."

25. See, for instance, Paxton, *The Anatomy of Fascism*.

INDEX